Historiography of India's Partition

An Analysis of Imperialist Writings

Bishwa Mohan Pandey

ATLANTIC

PUBLISHERS & DISTRIBUTORS (P) LTD

ATLANTIC
PUBLISHERS & DISTRIBUTORS (P) LTD

7/22, Ansari Road, Darya Ganj, New Delhi
Tel.: +91-11-4077 5252, 2327 3880
E-mail: orders@atlanticbooks.com
Web: www.atlanticbooks.com

Reprint 2025, 2018

Published by Atlantic Publishers & Distributors (P) Ltd.

Printed & bound in India by Atlantic Print Services

Dedicated to

Maa and Babuji

PREFACE

The impact of Partition on the people and the collective psyche of the two newly created nations is too deep-rooted to be treated lightly. As a metaphor, an event and memory, it has to be explained and interpreted afresh so as to remove misconceptions which are widely held.

The reading and writing of history provide an opportunity to look back on the past from the present context in order to avoid the path which might be disastrous for the human civilization in general and for the concerned society in particular. Hence, the interpretations of past keep on changing. This applies, without exception, to the modern Indian history as well. It may be noted that the colonial masters of India depended heavily on the imperial ideologues in the process of creating and maintaining the colonial structure. The imperial reconstruction of India's past in the 'judgmental framework' has given birth to an unending dissent and debate. This debate and the subsequent writings of different schools have been influencing the imperial assumptions and deductions in more than one ways. However, some of the imperial hypotheses and constructs, which are controversial and derogatory as well, are still being emphasized and used by different schools especially by the Oxbridge scholars. This becomes crystal clear in the following pages where an attempt has been made to deconstruct some of the prejudiced and biased constructs prevalent in the British writings on India's Partition.

An effort has been made to analyze the imperialist writings related to the partition of Indian subcontinent into two sovereign states of India and Pakistan. It may be noted here that the imperialist school is a heterogeneous group mainly consisting of the scholars affiliated to the Oxbridge ideology and administrator-turned historians of different generations. The literature produced by this group is vast and varied and covers a period of over fifty years. In view of the vastness and variety of the writings, it is not possible to analyze all the writings in one single book. Therefore, an attempt has been made to analyze the ideal representative works of all the sub-groups and generations. At the same time, the gradual changes in the British historiography of India's Partition have been traced. It has been observed that the changing contours of international relations and the post-colonial discourse have been the deciding factors in shaping the imperialist interpretations of the events preceding the Partition and of parties and personalities involved in it. Hence, we notice startling differences of opinion along with age-old cherished commonality of purpose.

I have accumulated uncountable debts for the last many years, especially over the last one decade since I started this study. I consider myself fortunate to have been a student of the Post-graduate Department of History, Patna University which can boast of some of the leading personalities as faculty members and even as students. The department instilled a self-confident, and independent and scientific tradition of reading and writing history.

I am heavily indebted to my teacher, Professor Nihar Nandan Singh, who helped me in writing this book and very kindly supervised it till its completion. His expertise and experience especially in historiography helped me in more than one ways. I am grateful to Professor Vijay Kumar Thakur who has been a constant source of inspiration. His personality and writings have played a decisive role in shaping my ideas. Whenever I faced ideological crisis and was in confusion, he spared time from his busy schedule and took pains in refining my vague and sometimes unintelligible raw ideas. I would like to offer my special thanks to Professor V.N. Datta, Professor Bipan Chandra, Professor Mushirul Hasan, Dr. Shekhar Pathak, Dr. J.P. Mishra and Professor Prabhakar Singh who have helped me on several occasions in different ways.

I am thankful to directors, librarians and staff of the Nehru Memorial Library, New Delhi, Indian Council of Historical Research Library, New Delhi, Indian Archives, New Delhi, Bihar State Archives, Patna, British Library, Patna, K.P. Jaiswal Research Society, Patna, A.N. Sinha Institute Library, Patna and above all the Library of the Department of History, Patna University, Patna.

I owe inexpressible debts to my family members, friends and colleagues. In spite of several constraints, my mother has always been an unending source of inspiration and strength for me. My father, who has been my ideal in various arenas, has extended constant ideological and material support in the whole effort. I do not have appropriate words to express my thanks to Smt. Brinda Singh and Sri R.N.P. Singh, Patna for their constant encouragement and support on all occasions in every possible way.

I consider myself fortunate enough to have a considerable number of friends who have extended their support as and when required. Mention may be made of Rajesh Kumar, Arvind Kumar, Sunil Kumar, Pankaj Kumar Jha, K.K. Mandal, Anil Kumar, Ashok Kumar, Anjan Jha and Abinash. Among the colleagues, I am thankful to Sri P.B. Pande, Sri Adheer Kumar and Sri Anil K. Joshi for the fruitful discussions that we had on several occasions.

I could remain indifferent to the household affairs and devote sufficient time and energy to the study only because of my wife, Aman. It would have been very difficult to complete this book without her assistance.

Finally, I am grateful to M/s Atlantic Publishers and Distributors, New Delhi for publishing this book. Although I have tried my best to minimize the mistakes, the responsibility for errors of facts and interpretations, if any, remains mine alone.

BISHWA MOHAN PANDEY

Contents

1

Introduction

PROBLEMS AND PERSPECTIVES OF THE STUDY OF PARTITION OF INDIA

The vivisection of the Indian subcontinent has been an issue of lively debate since 15 August 1947, when it was thrust upon 'the people' by the elites — alien and indigenous. What is noteworthy, is that this debate — academic and non-academic — is still inconclusive and seems to remain so in the near future.[1] Enormously rich literature — historical[2] and semi-historical[3] has been produced around the theme of partition. These works provide vivid picture of the upheaval preceding and succeeding the division and are reflective of multiple mindsets about the events, personalities, organisations and processes that contributed to it. At the same time, these works show use of a wide range of methodologies. In spite of the fact that a huge corpus of literature has been produced there is hardly any consensus over any of the issues, of the partition controversy. All attempts at interpreting the theme have rather produced greater disagreement and dissent. Consequently, the debate has been intensified gradually and the controversy deepened. Therefore, it is imperative to find out gaps in existing writings especially those by the imperial ideologues.

In the second half of the nineteenth century, when the British hegemony had been firmly established throughout the Indian subcontinent, some novel trends were in the making. As in the case of many other countries, colonialism[4] in India became the harbinger of some such processes which unfolded in the emergence of nationalism[5] and communalism.[6] Colonialism here, remained the main driving force throughout the period of its existence and played important but dubious role. The colonial regime throughout worked on an agenda which included both these forces and their strategy for promoting and opposing them, was determined by the main driving concern of protection of the colonial interest. Thus, the colonial regime was instrumental in the efforesence of both nationalism and communalism.

However, the colonial regime perceived immediately the inherent danger in the emerging secular nationalism. Therefore, it began to protect and promote the communalism among the Muslims and the Hindus. In this way, the nationalism had to struggle against the colonialism and communalism as well. This is the reason that the colonial policy-makers promoted and protected the communalism while imperial ideologues provided ideological support and justification to it. In this struggle the Indian National Congress,[7] the chief proponent of secular nationalism, made a mistake by concentrating itself on colonial front and ignoring the communal one.

However, the point to note here is that both the nationalism and communalism remained mainly the concern of the elites. Since elites donot believe in physical assault, the conflict remained confined to the theoretical and ideological level. In this conflict, the politics of history writing played important and at times decisive role. In this arena the imperial ideologues played the leading role. The writings of James Mill,[8] H.M. Elliot,[9] Edward Thornton[10] and others, had firmly laid down the tradition of communalising the Indian history. Elliot, the Secretary to the Government of India, while writing on medieval India opines that the Muslim rulers prohibited Hindu processions, worships etc., mutilated idols, razed temples, forcibly converted people and committed murders, massacres, confiscations, etc. Secondly, the legal entry of Christian missionaries since 1813, helped institutionalise the colonial interpretations of Indian history through writing and teaching of this form of history. Thus, the colonial regime succeeded in injecting communalism into the new middle class intelligentsia, who in turn communalised the masses.[11] The nationalists failed to counter this process while the communalists succeeded in their mission.

The partition, which may be taken as a symbol of the failure of the nationalists and success of the communalists of course, with colonial consent, had been attracting the attention of intellectuals on global basis. However, the scholars of the nations which effected and are effected by the partition have been continuously and keenly engaged in delineating its theme. These scholars have approached this issue mainly out of national affiliations.[12] That is why, we have the literature produced mainly by Indian nationalists,[13] Pakistanese[14] and British scholars. Besides it, we also come across the literature produced on the partition by the scholars of the Marxist[15] and subaltern[16] orientations.

The British historians mainly from Oxford and Cambridge have produced and have been producing variety of literature on India's partition theme. These imperial ideologues have been busy in interpreting different issues related to the partition since they started injecting the communal virus in the history writing. It could be traced back to the second half of the nineteenth century in explicit way.[17] They have touched upon countless issues in pre- and post-partition period possibly due to two reasons mainly. First, the English tradition of history writing has attracted the attention of the scholars toward this highly important and relevant topic. Secondly, the 'guilt consciousness' has also compelled them to interpret the theme of partition. Undoubtedly, the colonial regime played most important role in the partition of India. The imperial ideologues have been conscious of the blunders committed by the British-policy makers. Therefore, they have been busy in the 'face-saving and white washing' exercise. No wonder then, these scholars have shown keen interest in reconstructing India's distant and recent past in order to absolve the colonial regime and British policy-makers of all the responsibilities in the events like partition. With few 'exceptions,'[18] these committed ideologues support the colonial policies blindly and at times ahistorically and illogically. The entire intellectual effort has been sharply pointed at defending the rise and fulfilment of the British rule.[19]

In this way, the scholars of this imperial or Oxbridge school have approached the issues of communalism and the partition with a preoccupied and predetermined narrow mindset. Hence, there is a broader uniformity in the writings of the historians committed to this ideology crossing over the generations. However, we find some differences in these writings pertaining to comparative importance of controversial issues. Therefore, it is all the more necessary to analyse the partition historiography of British scholars to highlight the differences and similarities as well as to focus on the gap between their professed objectivity and actual work.

The vivisection of Indian subcontinent found its earliest echoes in the writings of the historians having imperial affiliations. Generally speaking, they have been presenting the theme in a way that could justify deliberate and/or unconscious fallacies of the colonial regime. They have exploited the complex Indian socio-cultural history to reinforce the theory of a permanent and unbridgeable communal divide. Thus, they traced origin and growth of communalism in the pre-colonial Indian milieu. It was the communalism, it has been argued, which culminated into the partition of India. Therefore, the partition was logical in the Indian situation.

Broadly speaking, the chief ideologues of this school have highlighted the plurality and diversity of the Indian society.[20] They opine unanimously that the Indian society has been a fragmented and divided society. The mechanisms of division are manifold, the chief and most fatal being the Hindu-Muslim divide.[21] Contrary to the nationalist contention, the Oxbridge group argues proudly that the Britishers tried their best to ensure unity and in this effort they succeeded up to an extent. However, due to socio-cultural divisions, the partition was logical and inevitable.[22]

Moreover, in British historiography of India's partition, the Indian National Congress has been held responsible for the partition on several counts. Almost all historians of this school regard it a Hindu body and equate it with the Hindu nationalism.[23] Among the Indian nationalist leaders, Mahatma Gandhi and Jawaharlal Nehru have been criticised in almost abusive language.[24] Some of the high profile scholars of this group regard the partition a by-product of Britain's gradual devolution of power to the Indians.[25] Some of scholars of this school have raised Jinnah to a very high pedestal. So much so, that they assigned higher place to him than Gandhi in the liberation movement.[26] To top it all, the historians of this school defend the Muslim League in different ways.

The imperialist scholars have been trying to negate the due role of the Indian liberation movement in order to undermine the importance of nationalist heroes.[27] This is being done to show the validity of 'Civilising Mission' and 'White Man's burden' theories. This has been attempted to emphasize the point that the English liberated India because Indians had been trained in the art of governance. In the post-War period, it was the Britain's internal compulsion[28] with the declining economic importance of India for Britain[29] which compelled the English to quit India. Last but not least it has been argued that the Britishers tried their best to preserve the unity that they had achieved but decided to partition because Indians themselves demanded it.[30]

In this way, the Oxbridge intellectuals have approached to Indian history in general and to partition issues in particular for the fulfilment of a particular aim. Their aim is to blame Indians and Indian objective-subjective conditions for all the ills and to credit the colonial regime for the good if it really took place. No doubt, the communalism and its fulfilment into the partition was one of the worst legacies of the colonial regime. Therefore, the sole aim of the imperial ideologues is to absolve the Britishers from any responsibility in the division of India. Naturally, therefore, the history that they have constructed is biased and prejudiced and devoid of the professed objectivity. They have over-emphasized the inter-community differences and over-looked the intra-community differences and inter-community similarities, which are at times more important to understand the complex socio-cultural mosaic of India.

Thus, we have enormously rich literature on partition theme produced by the scholars with imperial mindset. Almost all possible features and standard classical formulations of imperialist and neo-imperialist groups may be located in the writings of Percival Spear,[31] Allen Campbell Johnson,[32] H.V. Hodson,[33] Penderal Moon,[34] P.N.S. Mansergh,[35] and R.J. Moore.[36]

These writings have over-emphasized the element of inevitability and are full of ahistorical generalisations. These imperial ideologues start the discussion on partition even from early eighth century when the Arabs invaded India.[37] But the emphasis is on the developments of late nineteenth and early twentieth centuries. However, their focal point is the last decades of the Raj. They have tried to impress that towards the end, the communal and constitutional deadlock made the partition inevitable. They blame the Indians for it on the hypothesis that the Indians themselves demanded it[38] and both the major parties accepted it.[39] These writings do not explain as to how and why the Congress accepted it. In fact, the Congress opposed the partition up to 1945 but had to accept it as a remedial measure.[40]

Up to the mid-1946, communalism and the Muslim, League's demand of Pakistan had been regarded as 'unreal' by the Indian National Congress and its leaders like Jawaharlal Nehru. But when the League rejected long term provisions of the Cabinet Mission Plan and started 'Direct Action' from 16 August 1946, the Congress leaders were compelled to reconsider their approach towards the League and its demand. The League members and its National Guard started killing Hindus and Sikhs and the latter also retaliated.[41] Thus, almost a civil war situation prevailed in north, north-west and north-east India.[42] At this critical juncture, the colonial regime and the Congress made further mistake by inducting the League members into the Interim Government.[43] Henceforth, the League adopted two-pronged strategy — violent and constitutional. The League members in the government made its working impossible[44] while its National Guard continued the direct action.[45]

In this way, it is clear that by the early 1947, the situation in India was very grim. It seems that the Congress leaders had been fed up with the communal violence and the British policy of inactivity. The only way out of this communal and constitutional deadlock was the acceptance of the League's demand in some form or the other. That is to say, that the partition had become inevitable. Side by side, the pressure from below in India was nearing its climax.[46] At this juncture, the British government decided to quit in a way that could ensure the safety of their interests in the post-colonial South Asia. At the same time, they did not want to break their past record through betraying the League which had been nurtured by them. Therefore, the best option for them was granting independence but only after the division. However, this point has been bypassed or omitted by almost all the imperial ideologues. The prevalent communalism of varied denominations and the struggle for power among indigenous elites provided ready-made excuse. Thus, they gave an impression that they were implementing Indians' will.

The communalism — Muslim, Hindu and Sikh, has been said to have played a decisive role in the partition of India. Hence, a fresh and pointed discussion on communalism is required in order to solve this burning problem of South Asia. The emergence, growth and manifestations of communalism have been lively issues of academic and political debate, since the last quarter of the nineteenth century. Scholars with different mindsets have been busy in describing it in colonial and post-colonial context.[47] Among the present literature 'except few'[48] almost all writings are highly biased and tell us only one side of the issue. They are based on unscientifically reconstructed India's distant and recent past. The nationalist historians blame the colonial policy of divide and rule for it, while the imperial ideologues blame that Indian socio-cultural milieu itself was fertile for it. Thus, in this blame and counter-blame, the real issues have been missed. Both sides have misused the history in this politics of history writing. The imperial scholars including administrator-turned historians have provided the raw material for subsequent authors of different schools.

In the process of communalising Indian history, writings of James Mill,[49] V.A. Smith,[50] William Ward,[51] J.C. Marshman,[52] John Stuart Mill,[53] W.W. Hunter,[54] Valentine Chirol,[55] and other British scholars played a decisive role. It should be noted here that the divisive policy played decisive role in the conquest and consolidation of British Indian empire. But the imperial ideologues deny outrightly that the British created any divide.[56] They argue unanimously that the Muslims in India were foreigners and they had maintained their separate and distinct identity from that of the Hindus. Indian scholars with communal bent of mind were easily traped in this colonial game. This biased and falsified interpretation was readily accepted by the Muslim[57] and Hindu[58] communalists alike. Thenceforth, they have been misusing this myth to justify their own mutually antagonistic stands.

The Muslim communal ideologues maintained that since they were a distinct community, their interests were different from that of the Hindus. And since their interests differ, they required separate treatment and special safeguards, and this provided justification for the formation of the All India Muslim League (1906),[59] demand for separate electorate,[60] two-nation theory[61] and the partition of India.[62] On the other hand, the Hindu communal ideologues like their imperial counterparts[63] treated the India's medieval period as Muslim period only because most of the rulers and ruling aristocracy belonged to Islam. Thus, the religion of the ruler decided the nature of state and gave nomenclature to the period itself. They further maintained that Muslims were alien elements in the Indian society. Thus in a way, the Hindu communal-minded scholars, too, provided justification for the two-nation theory later propounded by the Muslim communalists and protagonists of Pakistan.[64] The Muslims in general were blamed for the decay of Hinduism. Thus, through generalisation, the Muslims were blamed for the mistakes committed by some of the co-religious rulers. Above all, those Hindu rulers who fought against the Muslim rulers have been made national heroes. Thus, started the process of claim and counter-claim which communalised the history and became one important factor for the emergence and intensification of communalism. In this game, the colonial regime acted as a supersensitive catalyst and remained the sole beneficiary of it.

In this way, the politics of history writing in combination with the adverse impact of colonial regime on Indian economy gave birth to communalism. Since this way of history writing and teaching suited the imperialists and the communalists, it was institutionalised and propagated through all possible means, audio-visual, written and oral. The educational institutions especially the denominational such as the Muhammadan Anglo Oriental School and College, Islamic schools, Dayanand Anglo Vedic schools and colleges, Sanatan Dharam and Sikh schools and colleges propagated the communal view of the Indian history. However, the schools and colleges started by the British especially the Christian missionaries acted as primary and main villain. The few who were educated in this system communalised the innocent masses, in due course, for their vested interest. So much so, that the secular nationalism came under heavy pressure and had to compromise with the communalism by accepting the partition as a final settlement.

It should be noted here that this trend of history writing is still prevalent in India.[65] It has been one of the important factors responsible for the resurgence and intensification of communalism in post-colonial India, especially, since the last decade of the twentieth century. However, there is a silverlining in the recent historigraphical developments. Scholars with secular mindset using scientific methodology, are trying to check this communalisation of history.[66] Therefore, it is not surprising that the imperial ideologues are still approaching the Indian history in general and the partition in particular in order to justify the acts and the writings of their predecessors.[67] Thus, fresh scholarly exercise is required to analyse the communal issues and the partition, so that its present manifestation could be solved or at least checked.

Initially, the imperialist ideologues used to trace the origin of the partition as far back as eighth century A.D. It was argued that in India Islam remained unabsorbed. Thus, Hinduism and Islam existed as separate religions having no meeting points. Therefore, its followers, irrespective of differences in language and other cultural elements were bracketed wrongly into one homogeneous group.[68] In other words, India was said to possess at least two nations. Hence, the partition is regarded logical and inevitable. But after the publication of archival materials by the British Government,[69] the emphasis has been confined to the last decades of the Raj.[70] However, it would not be historical to conclude on an issue like the partition on the basis of events just preceding it. Therefore, we have immense scope of explaining the partition. It should be explained as a process, which was entrenched in the logic of colonialism.

Moreover, historians were handicapped due to paucity of official primary sources pertaining to the last decades of the Raj. But with the publication of official documents and records, the scope of partition historiography has considerably been widened. A number of books have been published interpreting the partition from different angles. However, these studies have failed to solve most of the controversies, in stead it has been complicated beyond the reasoning of common man.

In recent decades research methodology in social science in general and history in particular has witnessed a great advance. Use of oral sources and multidisciplinary approach have enabled the historian to explain his/her concerned area more objectively. The oral sources based studies on the partition will reflect the real aspirations, expectations and frustrations of the masses. These sources should be exploited to tell the objective story. Though some historians have adopted psycho-analytical method to assess the role of individuals in the partition but they have failed to solve the inconclusive issues.[71] Therefore, there are better perspectives of study on partition.

In view of the vast primary sources that have been made public by the British Government, the scope to interpret the partition has considerably widened. Secondly, due to difference of opinion, it is imperative to have an objective interpretation of events and processes leading to the partition. Thirdly, the role and responsibility of three main parties — the metropolis, the Congress and the Muslim League — have been explained variously. These writings are almost officially sponsored, therefore, an analysis of the existing writings on historiographical line is the need of the hour. Last but not least, the partition of India was said to have been devised by the colonial regime and had been accepted by the indigenous elites and masses, in order to solve the communal problem and ensure social peace and harmony. But even after the passage of over half a century, the communal problems have not subsided, rather the partition has created more problems than it solved. The two sovereign States that emerged due to partition have been continuously engaged in armed and ideological war. Therefore, it is highly relevant to study partition and its historiography in a more meaningful and objective manner, so that the legacies of partition could be solved.

Pakistan which was based on religious nationalism comprised the units separated from each other by over a thousand miles of Indian territory.[72] These two units were different from each other in all aspects but religion. However, the independence of Eastern Pakistan (now Bangladesh) has falsified the theory that the religious uniformity is sufficient for nation building. Secondly, the position of migrant Muslims (*Muhajirs*) and regionalism in Pakistan are negation of the long cherished two-nation theory. And finally, the imperial hypothesis that the Muslim masses supported the League's demand for Pakistan, should be reviewed.

Therefore, in the light of vast sources that have been made publicly available as well as the new methodologies and new requirements, the task of deconstruction of imperialist historiography of Indian's partition has been undertaken here so that it could be reconstructed in the present context.

The literature produced by the historians with imperial affiliations is so vast and varied that it is not possible to analyse all the available writings in one volume. Therefore, the present work is aimed at analysing the works of some of the prominent historians of the Oxbridge group.[73]

NOTES AND REFERENCES

1. Since partition historiography comprises different schools and different generations within one school, the difference of opinion is obvious. Secondly, in spite of the fact that the British Government has published official documents and records under the title *Constitutional Relation between Great Britain and India, The Transfer of Power*, 1942-47, (eds.) P.N.S. Mansergh, E.W.R. Lumhy and Penderal Moon, London, 1970-83, some vital evidences and records have either been deleted or as V.N. Datta in his General President's address to the Fifty-seventh Session of Indian History Congress, has shown have been destroyed deliberately. Therefore, consensus is not likely.
2. Serious works around the theme of partition have been produced on global basis in general and in Britain, India and Pakistan in particular.
3. Larry Collins and Doninique Lapierre, *Freedom at Midnight*; Khushwant Singh, *Train to Pakistan;* Kuldip Nayar, *Distant Neighbours;* Salman Rushdie, *Midnight's Children,* etc.
4. The English motivated by mercantile and imperial interests captured Indian subcontinent by defeating other European powers and indigenous ruling houses. Thus, India became a colony of Britain. The colonialism was a complex system devised by the metropolis for the maximum exploitation of the colony. In the colonial set-up some new modes of production were introduced while most of the traditional modes were retained. Consequently, some new relations of production were produced. Therefore, the microanalysis of

colonialism would help us in understanding the class structure, class alignments, class contradictions and class struggle. Vast literature on this theme has been produced by sociologists, political scientists, economists and above all by historians. See Marx and Engels, *On Colonialism,* Moscow, 1959, (edn.) Bill Warren, *Imperialism : Pioneer of Capitalism,* London, 1980; Hamza Alvi *et al., Capitalism and Colonial Production,* London, 1982; K.S. Chalam (ed.), *Reading in Political Economy,* New Delhi, 1999; Bipan Chandra, *Essays on Colonialism,* New Delhi, 1999, etc.

5. The nationalism in India, too, emerged as an opposite ideology and got momentum from colonial exploitation and half-hearted modernisation of India. Therefore, the Indian nationalism had to fight the British colonialism and indigenous divisive forces — natural and artificial. For theoretical and factual detail, see, A.R. Desai, *Recent Trends in Indian Nationalism,* Mumbai, 1960.

6. The communalism in its modern connotation was a direct product of British rule over India. It has been defined variously like "above all an ideology," "a false consciousness," "a struggle for scarce resources," "a competition for jobs" and "an instrument of ruling class politics." However, it should be regarded as a social phenomenon with its root in contemporary politico-economic set up. It is a continuously changing entity. For detail see, K.N. Panikkar (ed.), *Selected Writings on Communalism.* New Delhi, 1994; Mehadi Arslan and Janaki Rajan (eds.), *Communalism in India : Challenge and Response,* New Delhi, 1994; and P.C. Joshi, 'The Economic Background of Communalism in India — A Model of Analysis' in B.R. Nanda (ed.) *Essays on Modern Indian History,* Oxford, 1980.

7. The Indian nationalism began to take definite shape in the second half of the nineteenth century. It manifested variously at different, levels. Its one manifestation and chief propagator was the Indian National Congress, which came into existence in 1885. The Congress professed to practise and disseminate secular nationalism. This is the reason that the colonial regime and communal forces began to oppose it unitedly. See A.M. Zaidi (ed.), *Encyclopedia of the Indian National Congress,* XIII Vols., New Delhi, 1981 and Pattabhi Sitaramayya, *History of the Indian National Congress,* 2 Vols., Bombay, 1947.

8. James Mill, *The History of British India,* 9 Vols., London, 1840-48.

9. He wrote the preface to Vol. I of his Bibliographical Index to the *Historians of Muhammedan India,* Calcutta, 1849 and later on along with Dawson wrote the eight-volume, *History of India as Told by its Historians.*

10. *The History of British Empire in India,* London, 1841-45.

11. See R.S. Sharma, *Communal History and Rama's Ayodhya*, New Delhi, 1992 (edn.), pp. 10-11.
12. Ravinder Kumar, 'Partition Historiography,' in Ramakant and Rajan Mahan (eds.), *India's Partition, Prelude and Legacies*, Jaipur, 1998, p. 34.
13. The nationalist historiography in India started in course of the liberation movement against the colonial regime. The British had captured India physically and resorted to indoctrination to consolidate its hold over 'this brightest jewel' in the British imperial crown. Therefore, the early nationalists had to face the material and ideological hegemonization of the metropolis. Thus started the nationalist historiography with the onset of the Indian National Movement. The standard Indian classical nationalist formulation which has been very popular among the historians and politicians, regards that the partition of India was the culmination of the colonial policy of *divide et empera*. Contrary to the imperial ideologues, the nationalist historians argue emphatically that in pre-colonial India, there was no inter-communitry rivalry and antagonism on religious line. The two major religious communities the Hindus and the Muslims — had intermingled inextricably and at times beyond recognition. In other words, the pre-colonial Indian society, in spite of being a plural society, exhibited a great cohesive force. They further argue that the colonial regime, in order to expand and consolidate its hold, adopted the divide and rule policy and gave different dimensions to it.

    In the aftermath of the 1857 rebellion, it has been argued, the British Indian Governemnt started encouraging the Muslim communalism. Since it was destined to weaken the emerging national movement, it became their main policy. It is said that this changed the nature and scope of the British historiography. Thus, started the process of communalisation of Indian history and politics. Henceforth, the communalism taking different forms at different junctures, culminated into the partition of India.

    In this way, the classical nationalist historians have formulated this 'Conspiracy theory' to explain the partition of India. They regard the partition a calamity or tragedy and blame the British divide and rule policy and Muslim communalism equally for it. See Dadabhai Nawroji, *Poverty and Un-British Rule in India*, Delhi, 1901; and *Speeches and Writings*, Madras, 1910; G.K. Gokhale, *Speeches*, Madras, 1920; R.C. Dutta, *The Economic History of India*, 2 Vols. London, 1901 and 1903; Tarachand, *History of Freedom Movement in India*, Vol. IV, New Delhi, 1967; B.N. Pandey, *The Break-up of British India*, London, 1969; Pattabhi Sitaramayya, *The History of the Indian National Congress*, Vol. II, Bombay, 1946; S.R. Mehrotra, *India and the Commonwealth 1885-1929,* Oxford, 1965; Ram Gopal, *How India Struggled for Freedom,* Bombay, 1961.

The subaltern studies like imperialist school, condemn the Indian national movement and blame the mainline leadership. These studies differ from the Oxbridge group only in terminology. It denounces the nationalism as 'elite affair' and highlights the subaltern resistance, culture and gender. It rejects all existing history as elitist, statist and unworthy. Almost in the same way, the orthodox Marxists term the national movement a bourgeois affair, struggling for safeguarding their class interests. Many complain the ignorance of communal violence in the history of partition.

In this way, the nationalist historiography of the national movement in general and of partition in particular has been attacked. In fact, the most serious mistake that the nationalist historiography made was the ignorance of the challenge of the imperial and communal ideologues. It failed to refute the charges labelled on it and made the unreal issue a real and unavoidable issue. In pre-Independent India it hoped that once freedom was achieved, the communal and other problems would be solved. But the post-colonial situation has falsified this nationalist hypothesis.

14. The communalism gave birth to Muslim separatism which achieved its climax when India was partitioned. Since the communalism was planted and promoted by the colonial regime, the communal and imperial approaches to history are almost same. This is the reason that Pakistan historiography of India's partition is quite different from the Indian nationalist historiography. In the Pakistanese literature on partition, the 'two-nation theory' is almost universal. This theory was propounded by the protogonists of Pakistan during their separatist movements in the 1930s. Since then, this theory has been the core of Pakistani historiography.

The foundation of the Pakistanese historiography was laid down in pre-partition period which has witnessed different changes. However, the fundamental has remained by and large unchanged. In the pre-partition period, its aim was to highlight the necessity of partition while in post-partition period the aim is to defend its leaders and provide justification for the two-nation theory. In this tradition Muhammed Ali Jinnah has been the only person credited for the creation of Pakistan.

Broadly speaking, in Pakistanese historiographical tradition, the creation of Pakistan has been interpreted as a result of the Muslim national movement. It is based on the assumption that Muslims in India remained a distinct and separate community, who were never fully assimilated into their Indian environment. Hence, it has been argued that India had perennially contained the seeds of two nations. Therefore, the creation of Pakistan in 1947 was natural. However, we witness certain shifts in this historiography since 1970s. The independence of East Pakistan (now Bangladesh) has compelled the scholars of this school to reconsider the two-nation theory. However, this two-nation theory got and is still getting support from the Oxbridge and the communal scholars — Hindus and Muslims.

The growth of Pakistanese historiography can be traced from Syed Ahmad Khan's books *The Causes of Indian* Revolt and *The Life* of *Mohomed.* Some important pre-partition literature includes — Chaudhary Rahmat Ali, *Now or Never,* 1933; *The Pirpur Report, The Shareef Report* and *The Fazlul Haque Report* of *1938-39, Qaid-I-Azam Paper and Muslim League Document.* Also see *A History of Freedom Movement* 1707-1947, in 3 Vols. each in two parts; K.B. Sayeed, *Pakistan : The Formative Phase 1857-1948,* London, 1968; Chaudhary Muhammad Ali, *The Emergence of Pakistan,* Lahore, 1973; Chaudhary Khaliquzzaman, *Pathway to Pakistan,* Lahore, 1961; L.A. Sherwani, *Partition Scheme,* Lahore, 1990; Z.H. Zaidi 'Aspect of the Development of Muslim League Policy. 1937-47' in C.H. Philips and M.D. Wainwright (eds.), The *Partition of India : Policies and Perspectives, 1935-47,* London, 1970, pp. 245-75; and Waheed Ahmad, 'Historiography of Partition,' in Ramakant and Rajan Mahan (eds.), *op. cit.*, pp. 84-94.

15. See Sumit Sarkar, *Modern India,* 1885-1947, New Delhi, 1983; P.C. Joshi, *For the Final Bid of Power,* Bombay, 1947; Sucheta Mahajan, *Independence and Partition,* New Delhi, 2000; Mushirul Hasan, (ed.), *India's Partition : Process, Strategy and Mobilisation,* Delhi, 1993 and (ed.) *India Partitioned* : *The Other Face of Freedom,* 2 Vols., New Delhi, 1995; G. Adhikari, *Communist Party and India, Path to National Regeneration and Socialism,* New Delhi, 1964; A.R. Desai (ed.), *Peasant Struggles in India,* Bombay, 1979 and 'Popular Movements, National leadership and the Coming of Freedom with Partition, 1945-47,' *Economic and Political Weekly,* Annual Number, 1982; R.P. Dutt, *India Today,* London, 1940; Sunil Sen, *Agrarian Struggle in* Bengal, 1896-1947, New Delhi, 1972; D.H. Dhanagare, 'Social Origins of Peasant Insurrections in Telengana' in A.R. Desai (ed.), *Peasant Struggles.*

16. See Gyanendra Pandey, *The Construction of Communalism in Colonial North India,* New Delhi, 1990; 'The colonial Construction of Communalism : British Writings on Banaras in the Nineteenth Century,' in Ranjit Guha (ed.), *Subaltern Studies* Vol. VI, New Delhi, 1989 and 'The Prose of otherness,' *Subaltern Studies, Essays in Honour of Ranjit Guha,* Vol. VIII, New Delhi, 1994; Ranjit Guha, 'On

some Aspects of the Historiography of Colonial India,' in *Suhaltern Studies* Vol. I, 1982; Gyan Pandey, 'Rallying Round the Cow : Sectarian Strife in the Bhojpuri Region, 1888-1917,' in *Subaltern Studies,* Vol. II, New Delhi, 1983; Shail Mayaram, 'Speech, Silence and the Making of Partition Violence in Mewat,' in *Subaltern Studies,* Vol. IX, New Delhi, 1996; Partha Chaterjee, *The Nation and its Fragments,* New Delhi, 1994, etc.

Till date eleven Vols. of *Subaltern Studies* have been published under the caption, *Writings on South Asian History and Society.* It is the brainchild of Ranjit Guha and company.

17. See the writings of H.M. Elliot, Dawson, W.W. Hunter, etc.
18. See the writings of Penderal Moon and R.J. Moore.
19. Sumanta Niyogi. *op. cit.*
20. Especially see P.N.S. Mansergh, 'Some Reflections on the Transfer of Power in Plural Societies,' in C.H. Philips and M.D. Wainwright (eds.), *op. cit.*
21. Penderal Moon, *Divide and Quit,* London, 1961.
22. H.V. Hodson, *The Great Divide : Britain, India, Pakistan,* London, 1969. David Page, *Prelude to Partition,* Oxford, 1982; Percival Spear, *India, Pakistan and West,* London, 1952.
23. Especially see R.J. Moore, *Endgames of Empire : Studies of Britain's India Problem,* Delhi, 1988; and Percival Spear, *The Oxford History of Modern India, 1740-1975'* (Second edn.) Oxford, 1978.
24. See Penderal Moon, *Gandhi and Modern India,* London, 1968; and Allen Campbell Johnson, *Mission with Mountbatten,* London, 1972.
25. Especially see the writings of R.J. Moore and R. Coupland.
26. Hector Bolitho, *Jinnah : Creator* of *Pakistan,* London, 1954.
27. See Anil Seal, *The Emergence of Nationalism,* London, 1968; Benedict Anderson, *Imagined Communities, Reflections on the Origin and Spread of Nationalism,* London, 1991; J. Gallagher, G. Johnson and Anil Seal (eds.), *Locality, Province and Nation : Essays on Indian Politics 1870-1940,* Cambridge, 1973; Sugata Bose and Ayesha Jalal (eds.), *National Democracy and Development : State and Politics in India,* Delhi, 1997.
28. See B.R. Tomlinson, *The Political Economy of the Raj, 1914-1947 : The Economic Decolonisation of India,* London, 1979; Bernard Porter and A.J. Stockwell, *British Imperial Policy and Decolonisation,* Vol. I, 1938-51, Houndmills, 1987; David Porter, 'Manpower Shortage and the End of Colonisation : The case of the Indian Civil Service,' in *Modern Asian Studies* 7(1), 1973, 47-73.

29. Sugata Bose and Ayesha Jalal, *Modern South Asia, History, Culture, Political Economy,* pp. 156-64.

30. See Leonard Mosley, *Last Days of the Raj*; R.J. Moore, *Escape from Empire : The Attlee Government and the Indian Problem,* Oxford, 1983; H.V. Hodson, 'The Role of Lord Mountbatten,' in C.H. Philips and M.D. Wainwright, *op. cit.* and Percival Spear, *India : A Modern History,* Michigan, 1961.

31. His writings on India include : *Delhi : A Historical Sketch,* London, 1937; *Communal Harmony,* London, 1940; *India, Pakistan and West,* London, 1952; *Delhi : Its Monuments and History,* London, 1945; *Nabob's,* Karachi, 1955; *India : A Modern History; Master of Bengal : Clive and His India,* London, 1975; *The Oxford History of Modern India, 1740-1975.*

    He has edited with S.M. Ikram, *Cultural Heritage of Pakistan,* Karachi, 1955 and with Spear Margaret, *India Remembered,* New Delhi, 1961.

32. He has written his memoirs under the title *The Mission with Mountbatten,* London, 1972.

33. His important works are : *The Great Divide : Britain, India and Pakistan; Twentieth Century Empire,* London, 1966 and 'The Role of Lord Mountbatten' in C.H. Philips and M.D. Wainwright (eds.), *op. cit.*

34. He has written extensively on India. For instance, *Strangers in India,* London, 1943; *Future of India,* London, 1945; *Divide and Quit,* London, 1961; *Warren Hastings and British India,* London, 1961; *Warren Hastings and British India,* London, 1968; 'May God be with you Always,' *The Round Table,* July, 1971; *Plain Tales from the Raj,* London, 1973 (edn.); *Wavell : The Viceroy's Journal,* London, 1973; and *The British Conquest and Dominion of India,* London, 1989. He has also been the co-editor of multivolume, *Constitutional Relations between Britain and India, The Transfer of Power 1942-1947.*

35. He has written mainly on the Commonwealth and has produced Indian conditions in details. His works are — *The Name and Nature of Commonwealth,* Cambridge, 1955; *Commonwealth and the Nations,* London, 1968; *Commonwealth Experience,* London, 1969; *Prelude to Partition : Concepts and Aims in Ireland and India,* Cambridge, 1978, and 'Some Reflections on the Transfer of Power in Plural Societies' in C.H. Philips and M.D. Wainwright (eds.), *op. cit.* He has been the editor-in-chief of twelve volumes, documents published by the British Government under the title *The Constitutional Relation between Britain and India, 1942-1947, The Transfer of Power,* London, 1970-1983.

36. Moore has been most important imperialist historians on India's partition. His writings include, *Liberalism and Indian Politics, 1872-1977,* London, 1966; *Crisis of Indian Unity,* Oxford, 1974; *Churchill, Cripps and India, 1939-45,* Oxford, 1979; *Endgames of Empire : Studies of Britain's Indian Problem,* Oxford, 1988; *Escape from Empire : The Attlee Government and the Indian Problem,* Oxford 1983; (ed.), *Tradition and Politics in South Asia,* New Delhi, 1979; *Making of the New Commonwealth,* Oxford, 1987; 'The Mystery of Cripps Mission' *Journal of Commonwealth Political Studies,* XI (03), November, 1973; 'Recent Historical Writings on the Modern British Empire and Commonwealth; Later Imperial India,' *Journal of Imperial and Commonwealth History,* 4(1) October, 1975; 'Mountbatten, India and Commonwealth,' *Journal of Commonwealth and Comparative Politics,* 19(1) March, 1981; 'Towards Partition and Independence in India,' *Jounral of Commonwealth and Comparative Politics,* 20(2), July, 1982; and 'Mountbatten Viceroyalty,' *Journal of Commonwealth and Comparative Politics,* (22) (2), 1984.
37. See Percival Spear, *India, Pakistan and West*; and H.V. Hodson, *The Great Divide : Britain, India and Pakistan.*
38. The Muslim League's demand for Pakistan has been generalised as the demand by the Muslims in general.
39. The acceptance of the June Plan of Mountbatten by the Congress and the Muslim League is taken as proof that both the parties accepted partition. But the context has not been explained in these writings. The reasons and reservations put forward by the Congress and its leaders have been deliberately deleted. See Sucheta Mahajan, *Independence and Partition, The Erosion of Colonial Power in India,* pp. 205-332.
40. The Congress had to accept the partition demanded by the League and proposed by the British Indian Government as a solution to the widespread violence and as a final settlement to the communal problem. But the violence which coincided the partition belied the Congress expectations and calculations. See Sucheta Mahajan, *Independence and Partition,* pp. 333-81.
41. See Penderal Moon, *Divide and Quit.*
42. See Swarna Aiyar, 'August Anarchy : The Partition Massacres in Punjab, 1947,' *South Asia,* Special Issue, 18, 1995 and Vinita Damodaran, 'Bihar in 1940s, Communities, Riots and the State,' *South Asia,* Special Issue, 10, 1995.
43. Anita Inder Singh, *The Origins of the Partition of India, 1936-47.* Delhi, 1990, pp. 250-51.
44. Sueheta Mahajan, *op. cit.,* p. 389.

45. Swarna Aiyer, *op. cit.*

46. See G. Adhikari, 'Year of Unprecedented Revolutionary Upsurge : 1946' in *Review People's Age* 5(30), 26 January, 1947; Gautam Chattopadhyay, 'The Almost Revolution : A Case Study of India in February, 1946,' in *Essays in Honour of Prof. S.C. Sarkar,* New Delhi, 1976; A.R. Desai, 'Introduction in A.R. Desai (ed.) *Peasant Struggles in India;* Mohan Rau,' The Telengana Peasant Armed Struggle, 1946-51,' *Economic and Political Weekly,* 8 (23) January, 1973; and Sumit Sarkar, 'Popular Movements and National Leadership, 1945-47' *Economic and Political Weekly,* 17(14 & 15), 1982.

47. Mushirul Hasan, *Nationalism and Communal Politics in India, 1916-23,* New Delhi, 1979; and (ed.), *Communal and Pan-Islamic Trends in Colonial India,* New Delhi, 1981; Prabha Dixit, *Communalism — A Struggle for Power,* New Delhi, 1974; Humayun Kabir, *Muslim Politics and Other Essays,* Calcutta, 1969; Bipan Chandra, *Communalism in Modern,* India (2nd edn.), New Delhi, 1987; K.N. Panikkar, *Communalism in India : History, Politics and Culture,* Delhi, 1993; W.W. Hunter, *Indian Musalmans* (reprinted), Delhi, 1969; William Cantwell Smith, *Modern Islam in India,* Lahore, 1963; G.R. Thursby, *Hindu-Muslim Relations in British India,* London, 1975; M.S. Golwalker, *We or Our Nationhood Defined,* Nagpur, 1939; V.D. Savarkar, *Hindutva,* Poona, 1923; *Hindu Sangathan,* Bombay, 1940; and *Hindu Rashtra Darshan : A Collection of His Presidential Speeches,* Bombay, 1949, etc.

48. P.C. Joshi, 'The Economic Background of Communalism in India — A Model of Analysis,' in B.R. Nanda (ed.), *Essays in Modern Indian History;* Ashgar Ali Engineer, 'Genesis of Communal Violence,' *Economic and Political Weekly,* Vol. 27, No. 5, February 01, 1992; and *Communal Violence in Post-Independence India,* New Delhi, 1984, Prahha Dixit, *op. cit.*; K.N. Panikkar, *Communalism in India : Indian History, Politics and Culture,* and Bipan Chandra, *Communalism in Modern India.*

49. *History of British India,* 2 Vols., London, 1970.

50. *Early History of India,* Oxford, 1904 and *Oxford History of India,* Oxford, 1919.

51. *A View of the History, Literature and Religion of the Hindus,* London, 1820.

52. *A History of India from the Earliest Period to the Close of Lord Dalhausie's Administration,* 3 Vols., London, 1867.

53. *Principle of Political Economy,* Vol. II, London, 1848.

54. *Indian Musalmans,* London, 1871 and *History of British India,* London, 1899.

55. *Indian Unrest,* London, 1910; and *India,* London, 1926.
56. See Percival Spear, *India, Pakistan and West;* Penderal Moon, *Divide and Quit;* and H.V. Hodson, *The Great Divide : Britain, India and Pakistan.*
57. Syed Ahmad Khan, *Writings, and Speeches,* edited by Mohammad Sham, Bombay, 1972; *The Present state of Indian Politics,* 1888; F.K. Khan Durrani, *The Meaning of Pakistan,* Lahore, 1944; M.A. Jinnah, *Speeches and Writings,* 2 Vols., edited by Jamiluddin Ahmad, Lahore, 1960.
58. See V.D. Savarkar, *op. cit.,* and M.S. Golwalker *op. cit.,* and Swami Dayanand Sarswati, *Satyarth Prakash,* 1875.
59. See Chaudhuri Khaliquzzaman, *Pathway to Pakistan.*
60. Ram Gopal, *Indian Muslims : A Political History, 1858-1947,* Bombay, 1959.
61. Mahmud Hussain, *et al., History of the Freedom Movement,* Vols. IV and V.
62. See Mahmud Hussain, *et al., History of the Freedom Movement,* Vol. VI.
63. Periodisation of Indian history in imperial writings has been done in a biased manner. See James Mill, *op. cit.*
64. See M.A. Jinnah, *Speeches and Writings, op. cit.*
65. See the writings of Ashirvadi Lal Srivastava, R.C. Majumdar and J.L. Mehta.
66. See Romila Thapar, Harbans Mukhia, and Bipan Chandra, *Communalism and the Writings of Indian History,* New Delhi, (Fourth Print), 1984; Romila Thapar, *The Past and Prejudice,* New Delhi, 1975; R.S. Sharma, *Communal History and Rama's Ayodhya,* New Delhi, 1997, (Rev. Edn.).
67. See the writings of R.J. Moore, *op. cit.;* Sugata Bose and Ayesha Jalal, *op. cit.*
68. See especially, Percival Spear, *India, Pakistan and West;* and H.V. Hodson; *The Great Divide : Britain, India and Pakistan.*
69. Archival materials related with the transfer of power have been published in 12 Volumes by the British Government under the chief editorship of Professor Mansergh.
70. See Hugh Russell Tinker, *India and Pakistan : A Political Analysis,* London, 1902 and *Experiment with Freedom : India and Pakistan,* London, 1967; R.J. Moore, *op. cit.,* and David Page, *Prelude to Partition.*

71. See S. Gopal, *Minds of Nehru*; and Ayesha Jalal, *op. cit.*

72. Sugata Bose and Ayesha Jalal, *op. cit.*, p. 191.

73. The writings of Percival Spear, Penderal Moon, H.V. Hodson, Allen Campbell Johnson, P.N.S. Mansergh and R.J. Moore, have been analysed here. This group includes administrator turned historians like Hodson, and Johnson, participant observers and critique like Penderal Moon, professional historians like Spear and Moore and official historians like Mansergh. Thus, these writings may be regarded as representative of its group.

2

Traditional Views

(I) PERCIVAL SPEAR : COMMUNALISM AND THE PAKISTAN MOVEMENT

The communal approach to the modern Indian history has been adopted both deliberately and unconsciously by the historians belonging to different schools and generations. The traditional or classical imperialist historians, writing on modern India in general and on the Indian freedom struggle in particular have been engaged in introducing communal approach to historical interpretations. The British rule in India right from its inception was supported, justified and given ideological, theoretical and moral support, by the imperial ideologues. When the nationalism was emerging in the second half of the nineteenth century in opposition to the colonialism, the communal ideology became a major tool in the hands of British policy-makers and its ideologues. Percival Spear belongs to the group of professional imperial historians who have touched upon one of the important issues of colonial and post-colonial India.

Spear is well-known for his writings on Indian history especially on modern Indian history. He stayed in India for long time and remained associated with the teaching of history at St. Stephen's College, Delhi up to 1940. He served under colonial regime during World War II. As Spear puts it, the social composition of Delhi in general and of Stephen's College in particular represented by and large the national configuration. The geographical location and historical importance of Delhi made it more important in the northern part of Indian subcontinent. Therefore, a professional historian with sound academic record and keen observer like Spear should have been an objective interpreter of the contemporary socio-political reality. But his active participation in the colonial governance and ideological affiliation and compulsions of imperialist historiography resulted into biased explanations of India's recent past and its implications for the present.

While, analyzing Spear's writings it seems that a number of factors shaped his approach to historical reconstructions. Firstly, he stayed in India during the period, when the Indian national movement under the dynamic and charismatic leadership of Mahatma Gandhi had entered into its mass phase and the colonial hegemony — physical and ideological — was slowly but gradually being eroded. Therefore, the colonial set-up badly needed ideological support. Secondly, the communalism, a direct product of colonial regime, was entering into violent phase. Hence, its theorisation was required, so that it could be shown that it was a pre-colonial legacy. Thirdly, the successful socialist revolution in Russia and its opposition to imperialism sounded alarm among the imperialists. That is why, they needed fresh justification of their rule. And the fact that "the classical imperialist historiography is mainly concerned with the rise, expansion and fulfilment of the British rule"[1] is manifested naturally in his writings.

In order to justify the phenomenon of communalism, Spear tries to trace its origin in pre-colonial India and says that it was produced in the process of cultural evolution in India. He talks about heterogenetic culture, where the great tradition of a country is the product of imposition of superior culture from outside. This cultural conflict results into compromises, adjustments and impacts. As India had to face continuous cultural invasions, its culture represents complicity. "One who looks on the surface of Indian affairs is likely to be baffled by the complexity of detail and apparent incompatibility of rival interests and ideas." Thus, he treats India as melting pot of cultures and asserts that in spite of several cultural invasions, India has maintained its uniqueness. At the same time, he talks about strains and stresses produced due to cultural interactions, which inevitably lead to territorial divisions, like that of 1947.

Spear's analysis of the history of medieval India smacks of a typical colonial mindset. He calls it "Muslim Period" and traces separate identity for the Muslim community right from the Arab invasion of Sind in A.D. 712. "Muslims in India require a separate treatment"[2] because they are different from Hindus. "Muslims are not mere exceptions here and there to general rule of Hinduism, they are a large and compact body of people who exist in their own right and have to be considered independently of the Hindus."[3] Unlike earlier invaders, Muslims could not be assimilated in the mainstream of Hinduism, through the process of cultural adjustments and assimilation. He calls Rajputs invaders, who had been assimilated in the fold of Hinduism.[4] However, this assimilation was not possible for later Turkish invaders, because they brought with them their own religion and culture.[5]

While talking about the modernising effect of colonial regime, Spear analyses the interaction between Western ideas and institutions and its Indian counterpart but in a distorted way. He discusses the process of 'Westernisation'[6] through the introduction of English as medium of instruction.[7] But the response of Indians to western influences, he writes, differ on religious lines. In the process of accommodation and acceptance, he observes, synthetic movements were started by Hindus and Muslims. These movements asserted the legitimacy and values of Hindu and Muslim civilisations respectively. The political manifestations of these movements, he writes, were the Indian National Congress and the Muslim League, which spoke for two nationalisms. In this way, the author has attempted to label the Indian National Congress as Hindu organisation and absolved the colonial regime from any responsibility in the formation of the Muslim League.

Spear's explanation of the emergence of communalism is a biased interpretation. He tries to trace its origin in pre-colonial period and blames Islam as well as Hinduism for it. "On the Indian side we must recognise that the idea of an Indian nation embracing all inhabitants of the subcontinent was a new and from the point of orthodox Hinduism, a wrong one. Orthodoxy regarded India as *Aryavarta,* the land of Aryans, which automatically excluded the Muslim."[8] Thus, he is trying to show that the Muslims were excluded from the Hindu's concept of nation. At the same time he suggests that the Muslims tried to maintain their separate and independent identity which led to the beginning of communalism. The

Mughal period (A.D. 1526-1707), according to him was the classical phase of Islam of India and its decline had made Muslim community impoverished, divided and directionless.[9] Muslims, he says, had no middle class, though on other occasions he says that Muslims were being led by an "Articulate Group."[10] "To arouse Muslim's feelings, they must be made to feel that Islam was in danger for which their antipathy to certain aspects of Hinduism was an instrument."[11] This call, he feels, was the most important cause of emergence of communalism and separatism. "Hindus, feelings about the cow are as untranslatable into Western terms as are Muslim feelings about idolatry and they are no less strong."[12] In this way, Spear has tried his best to relate the communalism with the existing social milieu. In fact, communalism was not a pre-colonial legacy, rather it was a direct product of colonial policies especially of "Divide and Rule."[13] Therefore, the colonial regime should share the larger responsibility for the emergence and intensification of communalism.

The term "Pakistan"[14] was coined in 1933 and the demand for Pakistan was fulfilled in 1947. Spear's explanation of the Pakistan movement can be located in the conservative imperial model. The short gap between the coining of the term and fulfilment of the idea of Pakistan is regarded as proof of culmination of a process, rooted in Indian tradition itself. "Clearly such a rapid growth leading to such a spectacular success must have sprung from roots deeper than purely political motives and stretching far beyond the twenties of the twentieth century."[15] The strength of the Muslim community in Spear's view was not however in exact proportion to their numbers. Dispersion sapped their strength and was indeed one of the "fundamental causes of the communal problem."[16] In this manner, like all other scholars of the imperialist school, Spear, too, gives a distorted picture of Pakistan movement and locates it in Indian tradition itself.

In his answer to the question, "Why Muslims demanded a separate nation state?", Spear has attempted to differentiate Muslims from their Hindu neighbours. "Muslims are sufficiently different to consider themselves a separate nation; they differ from the Hindus not only in belief, but also in culture, tradition and above all in their sense of value."[17] Thus, Spear asserts that Muslims were not a minority at all, but a separate nation and it is this fact which may serve as a first clue to an understanding of Pakistan movement.[18] It is clear from the descriptions that Spear is trying to overlook the inter-community similarities which are more pronounced and highlights differences which are sometimes unintelligible.

The nature of Islamisation of Indian populace and the role of leadership have been highlighted by Spear for the separatist tendency among the Muslims. The Pakistan movement threw the cloak of Western nationalism over the Islamic conception of separate culture and so converted a cultural and religious entity into a separatist political force. While describing the processes of Islamisation operatives in India, he says that one of them being the marriages between Central Asian Muslims and Indian women. These Muslims were dissociated themselves from their original homeland and it is probably from this class, that most of the later Muslim leadership emerged.[19] Further he says that the Sufi saints as class who were responsible for the large scale conversion into Islamic faith were responsible for the sense of separateness and sense of mission which tended to bind together people of the most diverse racial and social origin into cultural religious unity.[20] Spear has classified the Muslim articulate class into different categories and says that one group saw Indian Islam as a community within India, but separate from the Hindus and not to be swallowed up by them. Sir Syed Ahmad represented this view which promoted the formations of the Muslim league and led on to the Pakistan movement.[21] Thus, he has tried his best to project that the colonial regime had nothing to do with the formation of the Muslim League and Pakistan movement.

The class conflict between the ruler and the ruled, between imperialist and nationalist among the elites, etc. have been interpreted unhistorically. Spear regards these contradictions based not on class but on religion. He writes that incompatibility of religious, economic, political and cultural interest encouraged separatism. "To the Muslims an industrialised India meant a Hindu India, because the Hindu was a financier and businessman, the Muslim in general an agriculturist and soldier."[22] Spear imphasizes that due to strong cultural traditions of both the communities, 'permanent fissure'[23] between Hindus and

Muslims continued, which manifested in separatist movement. He concludes that it was therefore not surprising that when the Hindu stretched out his hand for the sceptre, the Muslims cried out for Pakistan.[24] Thus, the class conflict has been coloured in religious shade.

In the second half of the nineteenth century, nationalism emerged which posed a challenge to the colonial regime. The latter took recourse to the promotion of communal feelings in order to weaken the former. However, Spear has tried his best to conceal the official encouragement given to the Pakistan movement. He writes that the separatist tendency was a consequence of the reform movements that were initiated by different communities. "The Islam in India was politically depressed and culturally isolated in the eighteenth century."[25] It was in this condition of political eclipse and cultural depression that Islam had to face the onslaught of Western ideas. But the Muslims' progress towards an Anglo-Islamic synthesis lagged a good generation behind that of Anglo-Hindus.[26] Spear further opines that two parallel movements started in Islam — one was the internal movement or movement of body aimed at purifying Islam and second was movement among leaders under Western influence. It was under Pakistan movement which finally welded the two together into a national movement comparable to that of the Indian National Congress.[27] He further argues that since the Hinduism and Islam were different in fundamentals, internal movements produced different results. Sayed Ahmad Khan's refusal to join the Congress on its foundation in 1885 was the first concrete sign of divergence. The second was the formation of the Muslim League in 1906 and the third was its insistence on separate electorates. Thus, Spear has praised the modernising effect of colonial regime and wrongly interpreted the formation of the Indian National Congress and the Muslim League. These two organisations — one leading the national movement and other a separatist movement — have been said to be the result of religious reform movements.

It is an open secret now that the Muslim League was formed on official instance and it worked in collaboration with colonialism to hamper the freedom struggle. However, this collaboration among the opponents of Indian national movement has been defended by Percival Spear who opines that it was a consequence of cultural similarities. "Sir Sayyed Ahamad's movement was inspired by the thought that the Muslims of India were a separate people or nation who must not be absorbed into Hinduism and that the essence of Islam was consistent with the best that the West had to offer."[28] Another reason for this collaboration, in Spear's view, was the Indian National Congress because it became both cultural and political voice of the new 'Hindu India.'[29] This is the reason he says, the Muslims preferred British to Hindu or Sikh rule, they felt the weight of Western challenge less keenly because they possessed more of "Western outlook in their own tradition."[30] Thus, he is trying to project the Indian National Congress as a Hindu body and opines that Muslims collaborated with the British due to fear from the Congress and this collaboration became possible due to similarities between the West and Islam.

The Indian freedom struggle was taking a definite shape towards the end of the nineteenth century. This initial phase has been interpreted ahistorically. He opines that the Muslims did not join the Indian National Congress and allowed it to become dominantly Hindu in character through their abstention.[31] Thus, he bypasses the fact that the Third Session of the Indian National Congress itself was presided over by a Muslim, Badruddin Tyabji. Spear argues that the Muslims were alarmed in the beginning of the twentieth century and organised and formed the All India Muslim League in 1906. They demanded separate electorate and got it through the Morley-Minto Reforms of 1909. In this way, Spear has been trying to conceal the fact that the elites among the Muslims were encouraged by the colonial authority to form the Muslim League. It was due to official encouragement that they got what they demanded in the form of separate electorate.[32]

In spite of the fact that the colonial authority promoted the Muslim League, the latter came closer to the Indian National Congress due to national and international realities of the initial years of twentieth century. Both cooperated and fought against the regime under the Gandhian leadership. But this cooperation has been painted in religious colour by Spear. He asserts that international political development and nascent Muslim nationalism brought Muslims nearer to Indian National

Congress resulting into "Lucknow Pact of 1916."[33] Thus, he tries to subordinate nationalism to religion. He goes on saying that among the Muslim articulate class, there were those, more traditionally minded, for whom Muslim India was a province of world Islam and for whom nationalism was subordinate to religion. Ali Brothers were connected with this view. They found convenient bridge between nationalism and pan-Islam in the Khilafat movement and when they broke down, tended actively to promote 'Muslim separatism.'[34] At another place, Spear says that the Muslims cooperated with the Congress to save Islam from Western onslaught. The Muslim cooperation continued till Non-cooperation Movement. However, the end of the Non-cooperation and the Khilafat movements proved a turning point in the development of separatism.[35] The passing storm of the Non-cooperation left the Muslims as a whole disillusioned and fearful of their future. For this state of affairs he blames Gandhian leadership and the Congress. "In the post-Khilafat period of the Hindu majority personified in the enigmatic figure of Gandhi, seemed to be the main threat to a Muslim existence."[36] Now the Indian Islam needed a more dynamic creed and larger vision and found it in the writings of Muhammed Iqbal. "Sayyed Ahmad gave Indian Islam a sense of separate existence, Iqbal a sense of separate destiny."[37] Thus, in Spear's opinion Pakistan movement got a definite direction in the post-Khilafat — Non-cooperation period.

By 1920, several constitutional reforms had been introduced and several political institutions were in the making. The elites now became conscious of their position in power politics. Henceforth, the making and working of constitutional reforms witnessed elites' struggle over power-sharing. This elite consciousness has been given religious colour. Spear opines that in the background of 'Simon Commission,'[38] heightened apprehension quickened the urge to unity and also the search for a practical policy. The search for unity lead to the reorganization of the Muslim League under the leadership of Muhammed Ali Jinnah. The search for positive programme followed two directions. First was the safeguard of Muslim interests and second was the autonomy of Muslim majority areas. "The ideology of Iqbal,[39] the vision of Rahmat Ali[40] and fears of Muslims were thus united by the practical genius of

Jinnah to bind Muslims together as never before during the British period and lead to effect an act of political creation."[41] Thus, Spear has tried to show that in the 1930s, Muslims united due to this consciousness towards their separate identity and fears of the impending Hindu Raj. He has deliberately ignored the British role in accelerating the Pakistan movement.

Furthermore, Spear has tried to explain the Pakistan movement in terms of power politics. He opines that the growth of the Indian national movement and struggle to capture power further widened the Hindu-Muslim divide. "By late 1930s the Congress was thinking not merely of getting rid of British but of controlling India which would be left to them. Here the Muslims came in and henceforward the Congress was fighting on two fronts."[42] He is talking as if the Congress did not have Muslims. Therefore, they were alarmed. The Government of India Act 1935 did gave momentum to the Muslim separatist tendency, but the explanation given by Spear is one-sided and full of biases. He opines that this Act gave to the majority the power of cultural as well as political dominance over any minority. Thus, it increased Muslims' fear. The fear of dominance by one community over the other created an atmosphere which made the partition inevitable. In fact, the colonial authority in collusion with the anti-nationals tried to contain the freedom movement and for this purpose it took recourse to constitutionalism. The occasions of constitutional reforms were utilised by the Government to check the freedom struggle and strengthen the divisive forces. But Spear has described it in reverse way.

The British Government tried to delegate powers gradually but in Spear's view the Congress policy gave momentum to Pakistan movement especially in the last decade of the Raj. This is the reason, he says, that the Muslims desired freedom from British as well as Hindus.[43] He calls the Congress a Hindu organisation and regards the Muslim League the representative of all Indian Muslims. In proportion, as the prospect of British departure brightened, suspicions of Hindu intentions deepened.[44] The Congress has been blamed for the divergence with the League when it refused to share power with the League in the provinces. The Congress policy of absorption instead of cooperation particularly in the United Provinces in 1937 was a bitter blow to the policy of cooperation and coalition of the Muslim League. The Congress did not form a coalition government with the League, but Spear regards it as a proof of Hindu absorptive tendencies. At the sametime, he equates the Congress Raj with the Hindu Raj. "The Congress Raj means Hindu Raj and not all the charm of Mahatmaji and the Congress Working Committee will disabuse them of this notion."[45]

The Congress policy of non-cooperation with the League, compelled the latter to widen its bargaining power. Hence, in post-1937 period, the League started mass politics. This is regarded as the political foundation of Pakistan and the Congress has been blamed by Spear for this. He writes, "This converted the middle class nationalist movement into a popular Muslim resurgence and so laid the political foundation of Pakistan."[46] In this way, Spear defends the colonial authority as well as the separatist tendency of the Muslim League.

When the World War II broke out in 1939 and India was declared on war without taking its consent, the Indian National Congress opposed it and the Congress ministries in provinces resigned from the office in protest. The resignation of Congress ministries was a relief for colonial and communal ideologues and activists. Now both joined hand and blamed the Congress for it. Spear in a typical imperial tone says that the Muslim League demanded separate Pakistan in 1940[47] because Jinnah realised the distinct response of Hinduism and Islam to Western influence, so each must in consequence seek a "separate political and cultural expression."[48]

The Indian National Congress demanded full responsibility before sharing the War effort. However, the colonial regime under the guidance of Churchill did not want to delegate any more power. Therefore, the colonial Government promoted the League which was gradually strengthened. But Spear blames the Congress for constitutional deadlock and this deadlock steadily deepened the suspicions between the League and the Congress.[49] The British Government in order to obtain Indian support in War sent the Cripps Mission in 1942.[50] This Mission was made to fail by the colonial authority but Spear blames Indians for its failure. He opines that the constitutional as well as communal deadlock was complete than ever.[51] So, with the failure of the Cripps Mission, the golden moment passed and with it the last real chance of establishing a united independent India. The rejection of the offer was the prelude to partition.

The British attitude towards Indian problems convinced the nationalists that constitutional path would not work. Therefore, they turned towards struggle. The Congress under the leadership of Gandhiji gave the clarion call of "Quit India"[52] which marked the beginning of a revolution from 9 August 1942. Obviously, Spear is very critical towards the Congress especially at this juncture. He calls the Quit India Movement a rebellion and its failure, he asserts, discredited the Congress. "The congress had not only acted wrongly, they had made a mistake, they had backed wrong horse."[53] Now, he feels that the Muslim separatism had gained unprecedented strength and the League would not accept anything short of partition. Thus, he negates the role of struggle for freedom and highlights the Muslim separatism. But he has not written a single word against the colonial regime.

Being an active participant in the colonial regime during the War, Spear would like us to impress that due to the Congress and League antithetical policies, the regime faced greatest challenge in solving Indian problems. Wavell's task was to ensure cooperation between two highly suspicious bodies, the failure of which would mean partition. This became true after the failure of the Simla Conference in 1945.[54]

In the post-World War II period, the anti-colonial movements in India got momentum. At the sametime, political and economic realities of Britain compelled the colonial regime to take definite steps. The newly-elected British Labour Government intervened directly and sent the "Cabinet Mission"[55] in 1946. The aim was to preserve a united India while giving 'reasonable' satisfaction to Muslim claims of autonomy. Again attempt of reconciliation failed over communal allotment of seats. The ambiguity of provisions created problems. Ultimately, the Congress formed the Interim Government, while the Muslim League started 'Direct Action' from 16 August 1946. The colonial regime did not show any interest in containing the communal riots. The terror that was unleashed could not be restrained within peaceful bounds. Spear argues that the hope of united independent India was extinguished in the blood and monsoon passion of 1946.[56] Now, partition was the only solution to the prolonged civil war.

The Viceroy, Mountbatten announced his plan of partition and freedom on 3 June 1947. Both the Congress and the League professed dissatisfaction but each believed that they would gain nothing from fighting. Hence, they accepted it. The plan was implemented with the lightning speed. India won freedom on 15 August 1947 but only after the tragic event of partition. Spear, in this way, would like us to believe that the British Government implemented what the Indians demanded. His ideological commitment and affiliation makes him blind. Therefore, he cannot see the catalytic and most decisive role played by the colonial authority in the whole drama of partition.

Thus, Spear has explained the ideology and phenomenon of the communalism and Pakistan movement, in a typical imperialist fashion. His writings are overburdened with intense and indelineable ideological pressure, symptomatic of an imperial mindset. Since he was a part and parcel of the colonial regime in India, he is not critical of the colonial policies, rather he tries his best to defend it. He locates the beginning of communalism in the Indian cultural and social milieu, so much so that he ignores intra-community differences and inter-community similarities. In India, he suggests the communal affiliation was stronger than class affiliation.[57] Spear, too, like other scholars of this school has praised Jinnah and tried to malign Gandhian leadership. He writes, "The differences of community and religion were elevated by the Qaid-I-Azam into the fundamental divisions of the country. As oil and water, so the Hindus and Muslims can never mix."[58] Thus, Spear's aim is to blame Indians for the partition and absolve the Britishers of their responsibility in it.

(II) H.V. HODSON : THE DETERMINIST APPROACH TO PARTITION

In view of historians' national and ideological affiliation, the vivisection of Indian subcontinent in 1947 is viewed either as a tragedy or as natural and necessary event or as the fulfilment of a national movement. The historians belonging to the imperialist school constitute an important academic circle, comprising generations of historians who have shown a keen interest in this sensitive issue from the very beginning. On the whole, scholars of this school in general would like us to believe that partition which coincided with the independence of India was not a handiwork of Britishers, they were only mediating or even trying their best to avert it. However, they could not succeed because there was a great divide in the Indian society. H.V. Hodson, the administrator-turned historian,[59] belonging to this school has tried his best to put the old wine in a new bottle. He has constructed the myth of inevitability of the partition of India deliberately and consciously.

The partition of India, argues Hodson, was inevitable. Therefore, it could not be averted or converted into other options. He holds the Indian social milieu and the role of the Indian National Congress responsible for it and tries to give a clean cheat to the colonial regime. He writes, "What happened in 1947 was nearly a by-play : that the die was cast much further back, when the Cabinet Mission persisted in seeking consent to compromise, rather than imposing compromise by arbitration, or when Lord Wavell failed to secure a national Government at Shimla conference or when the Congress rejected Cripps Offer in 1942 or when the Muslim League adopted Pakistan as its goal or when they failed to admit the Muslim League ministers in 1937 or at other dates perhaps earlier."[60] Thus, Hodson approaches this issue with a predetermined conclusion and has produced one-sided accounts of events preceding the partition.

A man of letters, H.V. Hodson remained associated with the British Indian affairs since 1930 and served in different capacities. The most important portfolio that he held was that of the Reform Commissioner, Government of India (1941-42). This period itself was very important. The World War II was at its peak, the British imperialism was at its zenith under Winston Churchill, national freedom movement of India was also in its decisive phase and to top it all, the Muslim separatism had just taken a new turn, positively supported by the colonial regime. This association with colonial regime is possibly the reason that he frequently takes the side of the Conservative Party.

The main emphasis of Hodson is on events of 1947, but in order to support his views, he moves back to eleventh century. "The tale that ended in 1947 can be said to have had its beginning eight or nine centuries earlier. The transfer of power to two successor states was the end of the story, the preface of which was the annexation of the Punjab by Mahmood Ghazni in A.D. 1018 and which began in earnest with the defeat of Prithvi Raj by Muhammad Ghori in A.D. 1192."[61] But the chief defect of his analysis here is that he does not say even a single word about the intervening 'eight' or 'nine' centuries. He again starts from 1935 with the premise that Hindus and Muslims could not mix together and remained on opposite poles.

Right from the beginning Hodson frees Britishers from their catalytic role in partition. He points out the short- and long-term British policy. "British policy aimed at leading the peoples of India to a condition in which they would be able to govern themselves and grow out of imperial tutelage."[62] This is the sophisticated version of 'civilising mission' and 'white man's burden' theory.[63] However, the material self-interest of British and strategic importance of India shaped the short-term British policy. "Without Indian empire the concept of pax-Britannica would have been a hollow claim. So they tried to maintain its hold over India."[64] He would like us to believe that Britain left India on its own will. "Britain granted India national independence because of the development of public opinion along liberal lines both in Britain itself and countries whose goodwill was important to her."[65] Thus, he negates the role of Indian national movement in India's liberation.

The creation of Pakistan, he regards, was the result of strains in Indian Muslim attitudes, which gave the communal division a peculiar political importance and objective. "They had been settled in India as rulers and wanted to remain so. For Muslims, to roll back history by removing the European invaders could not mean a restoration of Hindu rule rather a revival of their own."[66]

Hodson tries to prove the inevitability of partition by completely negating the inter-community similarities and intra-community differences. "Hindus and Muslims lived in a village separated not only by religious creed and rituals but by whole modes of life and attitudes of mind, each a permanent hereditary group without inter-marriage or mutual absorption."[67] This explanation negates the known reality. Although, sense of social division in religious terms was pervasive in Indian society, Hindus and Muslims belonging to the same class or locality often had more in common with each other than with their co-religionists in "sections of society."[68]

In order to give his thesis wider horizon, Hodson compares the Hindu-Muslim conflict with the Protestant-Catholic conflict and say that "the former was far deeper than the latter."[69] He further says that there was conflict between the British Government and the Indian National Congress. This conflict became triangular when the Muslim League emerged with its clear objective. And it was this triangle, which was resolved only by the partition of India.[70] He is saying that what happened in 1947 was bound to happen. "Linlithgow and Wavell, Mountbatten and Cripps, Gandhi and Jinnah, Sikandar Hyat Khan and Jawaharlal Nehru and all the others-were mere puppets moved by historical forces which they had no power to deflect."[71]

In a typical imperial fashion, Hodson defends the British policies which let loose the divisive and separatist forces in Indian society. For example, he defends the policy of communal representation, which is a typical example of 'divide and rule' policy followed deliberately by the colonial authority. In his words, "Aware of the risk that one class or community might, by virtue of its superior numbers, wealth and education come to dominate India's nascent political life and the counsels of government, successive Viceroys supported the policy of separate communal or class representation."[72] However, he accepts that Britain did use the Hindu-Muslim rivalry for her own interest, but says that they did not invent it. For him it was necessary and logical if the pattern of Indian life was to be represented in the counsels of Government.

Starting his discussion from A.D. 1018 he takes a long jump and comes to 1935. The Government of India Act 1935 was a turning point for him in the Indian National Congress and the Muslim League *vis-a-vis* Hindu-Muslim relation. The elections in provinces to implement provincial autonomy proposed by this Act and its result left the League in wilderness in six provinces and thenceforward accepted the Congress as its mortal foe. The cry of 'Islam was in danger' was raised and Congress Raj to the Mussalmans became a worse bogey than the British Raj had ever been. This view is supported by other imperialist historians as well. Percival Spear, too, accepts that "political foundation of Pakistan was laid down in 1937, when the Congress failed to accept the League as a coalition partner in United Provinces."[73] Hodson further argues that even the implementation of federal scheme proposed by the Act, could not have averted the partition. However it is rejected by R.J. Moore.[74]

Muslims, Hodson says, realised their weakness — disunity and lack of mass base. Hence they tried to remedy it under the leadership of Mohammed Ali Jinnah. In 1936 Jinnah talked of organising Hindu and Muslims separately, so that they could understand each other better. In 1937 he charged the Congress of pursuing Hindu policy. Hodson says that the religious or quasi-religious provocations now combined with political and administrative accusation resulted into Muslim apathy towards the Congress. In 1938 at Lucknow Jinnah spoke significantly of the Muslim 'nation' that would emerge from the struggle with majority community who had clearly shown their hand that Hindustan is for the Hindus.[75]

The so-called 'dictatorship' by the High Command of Congress heightened Muslims' fear. Above all, the future majority rule was seen to be Congress rule, exerted from centre dominated by the Hindu majority, through an organisation which brooked no opposition and refused to share its power. There is no doubt that the conduct of the provincial self-governments from 1937 to 1939 was a major cause of spread of two-nation theory and the Pakistan movement.[76] Thus, while dealing with the Congress High Command, he forgets that the Congress was leading a movement and strict discipline was necessary to achieve this higher goal. The beginning of World War II in 1939 provided Muslim League its long desired opportunity.

The Congress ministries resigned from provinces and Congress demanded immediate national government. However, the Muslim League under Jinnah promised Muslim support in the War effort on two conditions — in the present 'justice and fairplay' for Muslims in Congress provinces, for the future an assurance that no constitutional advance for India should be made nor any Indian constitution 'framed' or 'adopted' without the consent and approval of the Muslim League. In March 1940 at Lahore, the League adopted the 'Pakistan Resolution.' In August Offer (1940). Lord Linlithgow promised full weightage to minorities. Henceforth Jinnah behaved like a typical Western dictator but Hodson has nothing to say about it.

The period when Hodson was Reform Commissioner in India (1941-42) provided best opportunity for Indians in the form of Cripps proposals. The Cripps proposals proposed enlargement of Governor General's Executive Council, Dominion Status on unspecified date when the War is over and accepted Muslim League's demand as well, though implicitly. The Congress rejected it which was followed by the League, though both had different reasons for the rejection. Still, the negotiation was going on when Cripps received 'return' telegram. Thus, Cripps Mission was sabotaged by the Churchillian imperialism. However, Hodson's affiliation with the Conservatives comes in to rescue Churchill. "The Cripps Mission failed due to differences among the Viceroy, Cripps and War Cabinet as well as among Indian leaders."[77]

"The effect of Cripps Mission, says Hodson, was that it widened the gulf between the Congress and the Government and created frustration among Congressmen."[78] And it was this frustration and reaction which compelled the Congress to start Quit India 'insurrection.' It led to serious disorder and disturbance. "Nevertheless within about three weeks the situation was everywhere under control and it was clear that insurrection had failed."[79] Thus, Hodson speaks in classical imperialist tone. The movement could be suppressed only utilising the War preparations, but Hodson says that it proved the strength of existing authority. The movement proved that the days of the British in India were numbered. However, Hodson says that the Britain's will to stay had gone. Thus, by denying the Indian national movement its due place, Hodson is interpreting events in typical colonial model.

Hodson pulls legs of the new Viceroy Wavell, the Secretary of State for India and leaders of main political parties of India when he deals with Shimla Plan. "The new Viceroy tried to solve the constitutional problem of India, while the Secretary of State for India had his own formula to solve it."[80] Lord Wavell organised Shimla Conference to discuss the formation of a 'politically representative' council.[81] Hodson calls the proposed council politically representative, which was in reality communal because it was to include equal proportion of caste Hindus and Muslims. This plan failed because Jinnah demanded the right to nominate all the Muslim members. "If the Viceroy had been adamant as Mr. Jinnah, the latter would have obliged himself to give in."[82] Again Hodson views it from inevitable angle. In his words, "All this may have been inevitable because the Muslim League's demand of Pakistan and the Congress' demand of united India were incompatible."[83]

In Hodson's view post-War developments hastened the pace of events. On 26 July 1945, Labour Government took office in Britain under Mr. Attlee. In August, the War was over. He says, "These changes of fortune heightened the hopes and shortened the patience of Indian politicians."[84] The Cabinet Mission came to India to seek agreement with Indian leaders, the subject of the agreement being constitutional 'principles and procedures.' Hodson has criticised the Labour Government. "They were not enjoined to impose any solution."[85] The recommendations of Mission proved apple of discord. The Muslim League and the Congress took different stands. The latter formed Interim Government while the former involved in 'Direct Action Day' on 16 August 1946. This resulted in unprecedented violence. This is skilfully neglected by Hodson because it does not suit his predetermined model.

By the end of 1946, His Majesty's Government decided to replace Lord Wavell. The 'natural option' was Mountbatten. Hodson has very soft corner for Mountbatten.[86] Mr. Attlee's declaration in British parliament that His Majesty's Government would transfer the power in responsible Indian hands by a date not later than June 1948, is regarded as an open licence for Pakistan in some form or the other. He says, "The creation of Pakistan and the transfer of power well before 1947 were implicitly but plainly written in the statement of 20th February 1947."[87]

Thus, started the mission of Mountbatten aiming at transfer of power to Indians with or without agreement among themselves. Hodson says that people who were to decide the fate of India were to be Britishers.[88]

The partition of India, Hodson concludes, was compiled by political forces, not by official advice.[89] "Lord Mountbatten wanted to have a United India but it was impossible."[90] Hodson says that Jinnah declared that once partition had been decided upon, all trouble would cease and people would live happily. Jinnah called upon Viceroy to hand over power as soon as possible.[91] Hodson further says that Viceroy's discussion with Congress leaders other than Gandhi, also tended to lead in the "same direction."[92] Mountbatten discussed the matter with other leaders as well. After this protracted discussion Hodson opined, "Only partition into two sovereign nations was the solution; because the Congress and the Muslim League were looking in different directions. The Congress said that better partition than any dilution of the Cabinet Mission plan and the Muslim League said that "no Cabinet Mission plan at any price."[93] Thus, the responsibility for partition and the speed with which it was implemented rested on Indian parties, not on the British as detailed by Hodson.

Hodson has tried his best to absolve Mountbatten of his responsibility in India's partition. He says that it was the need of the hour when Mountbatten came to the stage. He writes, "Whatever other criticism may be made of Lord Mountbatten's Plan for transfer of power, it certainly can't be said that it was imposed without the fullest consultation with India's political leaders or that it was contrary to the ultimate consensus of their views. It may certainly be said that it was not he but the Indians who divided India."[94]

On 3 June 1947, Mountbatten's Plan was announced and India was partitioned and freed on 14-15 August of the same year. This plan was initially rejected by the Congress as well as by the League. Hodson argues that, "Mountbatten took Gandhi's consent by convincing him that the new plan was the only possible way to achieve an early and peaceful transfer of power."[95]

In response to the question as to why British Government was in hurry to transfer the power, Hodson says that the partition was panacea of all evils. Therefore, it was administered at the earliest possible date. "The difficulties in governing India between the date of announcement and the effective establishment of the successor authorities rendered it advisable to make the transition period as short as possible."[96] Hodson does not answer, why and how this date was selected? He only says that the final date was declared by accident.

Even the last days of British Raj in Indian subcontinent have been explained by Hodson in an ideal imperial version like all other traditional imperialist historians. He completely devalued the Indian national movement and its fulfilment. What India achieved on the night of 14-15 August 1947; was not the fulfilment of its long cherished goal rather it was the culmination of British long-term policy of granting India self-rule which had been promised by Montague in 1917. This interpretation is the climax of Hodson's imperial attitude.

H.V. Hodson describes the partition of India in the above-mentioned way. In this pursuit he differs slightly with some other historians of imperialist group, like Percival Spear,[97] A.C. Jonson,[98] P.N.S. Mensergh,[99] E.W.R. Lumby,[100] R.J. Moore,[101] Penderal Moon[102] and Hugh Tinker.[103] However, he is similar to other ideologues of his school, when he concludes. Thus, he is true representative of his group. The distinction of H.V. Hodson lies in the fact that he was the first to utilise some primary sources, which were not published by then. He has utilised Mountbatten's private papers and his documents of the period when the latter was Governor-General of free India. Hodson was lucky to have interview with Mountbatten and Ismay. He himself has first hand knowledge of events when he was Reform Commissioner of the Government of India during 1941-42. Thus, he does not have the problem of scarcity of sources. However the abundance of sources, and ideological compulsion definitely created problems for him. These problems manifest in his confused writing. He is totally irregular in chronological sequence. He does not seem to be technically sound.

Thus, while describing the partition of India, Hodson has followed the pattern of elite historiography, in which the task of elites is to justify the mistakes of the present by citing only suitable examples from the recent and distant past. In this intellectual pursuit, aspirations and activities of masses are totally neglected. Hodson, being a part and parcel of regime in the last phase, has exaggerated the British rule. He goes up to the extent of saying that the British rule gave India unity such as it had never previously known.[104] He deliberately ignores and sometimes even defends the 'divide and rule' policy of the colonial regime. He also blames the Congress for the division of India because it was the Congress which led the mainline anti-colonial movement. He argues, "The aim and the ideal of the Indian National Congress was to unite Indians of all castes, classes and creeds for the effort of political advance but while the Congress had retained its ideals, it failed in practice because once the advance began, the conditions of the former unity disappeared. Once political power was to be had by Indians, the questions 'which Indians?' inflamed ambitions among majorities and jealousy among minorities and awakened all the dulled historical memories to conflict. It is first the prospect and now actuality of supreme power which has disunited India and will work to keep it disunited."[105] Thus, his writings seem to be the official history of the British India which is obsessed with historical inevitability.

(III) ALLEN CAMPBELL JOHNSON : A PRESSMAN'S INTERPRETATION OF PARTITION

Historians with imperialist orientation have been busy in interpreting the Indian history in general, right from the beginning of the British rule over the Indian subcontinent. In particular, they have been approaching the theme of partition of India with a predetermined purpose.[106] These historians are of different generations and varied sub-categories. 'Administrator-turned historians'[107] form a special sub-category among the British historians who have shown keen interest in Indian history. These scholars have touched upon different issues, parties and personalities involved in the partition. Allen Campbell Johnson[108] belongs to this sub-category of imperialist scholars. He occupies a significant place in this line-up. Since he was an active participant in the "operation winding up of the Raj" in the Indian subcontinent, he was in a position to have first-hand experience and knowledge of the events and processes taking turn hour by hour and day by day. Therefore, his collection of facts should be regarded as primary and may be helpful in filling up some important gaps in the study on partition.

Allen Campbell Johnson was son of a military officer. He completed his study at Christ Church, Oxford. He was an Honours in Modern History. After the completion of study, he became Political Secretary to the Leader of Parliament, Liberal Party, Sir Archibald Sinclair. He served this post for over three years (1937-40). But when the World War II started in 1939, his army background compelled him to join military service. He joined Royal Air Force and was posted in South East Asia as Wing Commander, Inter-Allied Record Section. Thus, he came in contact with India directly. When the war was over, he joined active politics and contested the parliamentary elections twice. His familiarity with Indian conditions and interest in contemporary world affairs, helped in his appointment a Press Attache to the last Viceroy, Mountbatten. Thus, he was in a position to witness the whole drama of partition and the role played by different parties and personalities in it. Since, he had been trained in the historian's craft, he could have produced an impartial and objective account of the events just preceding and coinciding the partition. But the effect of alma mater and commitment to ideology checked his pen from going much ahead against the set pattern of the imperialist or Oxbridge writings.

In this way, we may say that Johnson was capable of describing the events and process historically, which contributed to the making of events like partition and the upheavals which coincided with it. He has discussed the Indian matter from 19 December 1946 to 28 June 1948. As a Press Attache to Viceroy he attended all the seventy staff meetings which Mountbatten convened in order to arrive at a formula in accordance with the Attlee's Declaration of 20 February 1947.[109] It were at these staff meetings that the fate of India and Indians was decided. In the light of this, the description of Johnson could have been of greater significance. But he does not give the detail of discussions. He prefers to mention only the decision taken or policy decided. Seldom he comments from a historian's angle. By and large, he has not used the causation in his writings.[110] However, he seems to be adept in selecting the facts for the set goal. To top it all, he is very cautious in using appropriate words and phrases on the occasions. Therefore, his description is a classic memoirs by an expert news-reporter.

Allen Campbell Johnson starts his discussion with the British Parliamentary debate over Attlee's Declaration.[111] "During this debate," he writes, "Churchill said that India was to be subjected not merely to partition but to fragmentation and to haphazard fragmentation."[112] In fact, this was the real face of Britain's long cherished policy towards India. Instead of highlighting this statement, Johnson emphasized the assertion of Attlee. He writes, "The definite objective of the British Government is to obtain a unitary government for British India and Indian states, if possible within the British Commonwealth through the medium of a Constituent Assembly set up and run in accordance with the Cabinet Mission Plan."[113] Thus, at the very outset, Johnson tries to conceal the real motive of the metropolitan Government and to defend the colonial policy.

Johnson, along with Mountbatten and company arrived in New Delhi on 22 March, 1947. He is trying to give impression that he had appropriate knowledge of the Indian situation and regards it a revolutionary condition. He further argues, "We have inherited inter alia communal rioting, which is spreading as though by chain reaction, the key province of the Punjab with its threefold Hindu, Muslim and Sikh communal problem [...]. So, in short we have the people rioting, the princes falling out among themselves, entire Indian Civil Service and police running down and the British who are left sceptical and full of foreboding."[114] By explaining this way, he wants to show that in India the situation was out of control and in this situation no one but Mountbatten could succeed. This would also justify Mountbatten's approach to Indian problems. He completely ignores the strength of the national movement at this juncture. Conscious of the fact that the British policies had been important factors in such developments, he refrains from explaining the causes of it.

Mountbatten after his arrival in India and oath, started long and protracted discussion with leaders from British India and Princely States including Gandhi, Nehru, Patel, Jinnah and Baldev Singh. Johnson praised this way of functioning. He writes that in Nehru's view, Wavell had made one serious blunder by inviting the Muslim League to come into the Interim Government, instead of waiting a little longer for them to ask to be brought in.[115] But he does not explains as to why this blunder was not undone by Mountbatten? He argues that Lord Mountbatten had discovered from personal discussion with the leaders of the Muslim League and the Congress that the partition was inevitable.[116] In order to support this conclusion, he cites the 'March Resolution'[117] of the Congress and Patel's assertion during meeting with Mountbatten.[118] He further writes that Nehru's tripartite proposals for the Punjab were first sign of the Congress acceptance of the Hindustan-Pakistan division.[119] In this way, through generalisation and distortion he opines that the inevitability of the partition had been accepted by the Indians as well.

It should be noted here that at this juncture the pressure from below was nearing its climax. It was indicated by J.J. Singh, an influential Sikh with powerful American connections, who spoke of anti-British feeling in India and of the possibility of revolution.[120] But Johnson has ignored it completely. He also ignores the separatist nature of the Muslim League and calls it a representative of national aspirations.[121] Thus, omission is aimed at interpreting the transfer of power as voluntary from British Raj to India and Pakistan.[122] Thus, Johnson comes very close to the classic imperial ideologues.

Undoubtedly, the situation in India was very grim. The colonial regime had deliberately allowed the situation to deteriorate. The authorities were not taking effective steps to check it. Johnson explains this inactivity in an imperialist tone. He writes, "Mountbatten hopes that the diplomacy of discussion will have the effect of playing down the communal tension."[123] He also supports the deadly speed of Mountbatten in moving towards his goal on the pretext that the urgency of the situation demanded it. He writes, "Mountbatten has been convinced that the June 1948 time limit far from being not long enough is already too remote a deadline; a quick political solution was needed."[124] Thus, he regards the quickness of decision as a solution to Indian problem.

Having made himself familiar with the views of Indian leaders, Mountbatten convened Governors' Conference on 11 April 1947. On the eve of this Conference, he outlined the broad principles of his incipient plan.[125] In this way, it becomes clear that Mountbatten was preoccupied with dividing India on religious lines. But he was projecting it in a way that it seemed to be demanded by the Indians themselves. Even after this, Johnson tries to show that Mountbatten was favouring unity on the basis of the Cabinet Mission Plan.[126] Johnson himself opines that the Cabinet Mission Plan was the last attempt to achieve a unitary system for India.[127] After Governors' Conference, Johnson concludes that by far the greater part of the subcontinent is calm and quiet and ready to accept any reasonable solution.[128] Thus, the imperialist mindset of Johnson prevents him to see the speedily deteriorating law and order throughout the north and north-western part of Indian subcontinent.

Towards the end of April, Mountbatten and company toured the Frontier Province and the Punjab and *en route* had first hand knowledge of communal riots and forcible conversions. This tour should have been followed by firm action to check it. But Johnson has utilised it to justify the lightning speed which was adopted by Mountbatten henceforth. He writes, "The whole visit has brought home to us the need for achieving the wider agreement on India's future as quickly as possible. If we don't, there will be a complete disintegration of what remains of law and order, both in the Frontier and the Punjab, not to speak of the other northern provinces."[129]

In this background the whole colonial set-up was diverted to the making of what came to be known as Mountbatten's Plan or 3 June Plan.[130] Mountbatten convened an all-party meeting on 2 June at the Viceroy House for the acceptance of this Plan. He said clearly that he was not forcing the pace against their will. A terrific sense of urgency had been pressed upon him by everybody to whom he had spoken. They had wanted the present state of uncertainty to cease, therefore, the sooner the power was transferred, the better for all.[131]

This Plan provided for the partition of India before the transfer of power. Johnson opines that Mountbatten thought of transferring power on 15 August 1947 and hinted on it during these meetings. This indecent haste has been supported by Johnson on the ground that everybody was asking for speedy solution of the Indian problem. But it should be noted here that except Jinnah and his League and some Hindu fundamentalists, everybody was looking for solution other than partition as well. Therefore, this justification put forward by Johnson for June Plan is not fully justified. Rather the 3 June Plan should be taken as the symbolic victory of the colonial regime and the Muslim League. Johnson himself asserts that Jinnah had left himself at Mountbatten's disposal.[132] And possibly this is the reason that Mountbatten did not ask Jinnah to stop "Direct Action."[133] The continuation of communal violence compelled even the secular nationalists to accepts the 3 June Plan. Obviously, therefore, the Plan has been interpreted as a master stroke of Mountbatten and panacea to all ills.

It is true that this June Plan was accepted by the Congress though unwillingly while the League accepted it in obvious way. The Congress had to accept because in the face of Muslim separatist and colonial connivance, it was the only option to get independence and to get rid of communal frenzy.[134] This Plan was designed to fulfill the League's demand of separate Pakistan, though smaller in area, than it had been projected. So, it was accepted by Jinnah. But one question comes obviously as to why Jinnah accepted this motheaten, mutilated and maimed Pakistan? Was there any secret deal between Jinnah and Mountbatten? Because, it was this Jinnah, who had until then demanded the whole six provinces. The possibility of a secret deal cannot be neglected on the basis of circumstantial evidence. While presenting the Plan before the leaders of all-party meeting, Mountbatten was speaking very confidently and in a virtually threatening tone. Johnson writes that while presenting the plan, Mountbatten had said, "He was merely asking them to accept the Plan in a peaceful spirit."[135] Thus, a big gap remains in the writing of Johnson on this point.

Johnson, too, like other scholars of his school has praised Mountbatten for his statesmanship especially for the 3 June Plan. Johnson wrote a long letter to his mother from "The Retreat" Mashobra, Simla.[136] He writes, "Mountbatten's diplomacy had succeeded for several reasons but primarily because of his own personality."[137] In fact, it was the context which played a decisive role in the acceptance of the Plan by the Indian leaders. But Johnson gives undue importance to the role of individuals in the making of history.

Thus, after the 3 June Plan it became crystal clear that India would be partitioned before the actual transfer of power.

Therefore, a boundary would be demarcated. On 27 June, Jinnah proposed that Sir Cyril Redcliff should be invited to serve as the Chairman of the Punjab and Bengal Boundary Commissions.[138] This proposal was accepted by Mountbatten. Johnson remains silent over this issue.

On the basis of Mountbatten Plan, Indian Independence Bill was proposed by the Labour Government and passed by the British Parliament almost unanimously.[139] It got Crown's assent on 18 July. It should be noted here that until then the British Government had been accepting that their aim was to have a united India. Then, why accepted a plan which devised division. Therefore this unanimity should be taken as evidence that this Bill was not a break from past but a continuation and climaxing of the divide and rule policy. Johnson who was in London during this period does not explain it in the way it should have been.

The Indian Independence Act was implemented on 14-15 August 1947. This otherwise important occasion coincided with and was marred by the unprecedented violence and unplanned dislocation of men and materials. Johnson gives a detail of this black spot on the golden occasion.[140] This was the result of the partition and the way it was thrust upon. Though the Punjab and Bengal Boundary Awards had been ready by 12 August yet they were not made public.[141] Therefore, uncertainty prevailed and this delay created chaos. Definitely, Mountbatten should share responsibility. But Johnson does not write even a single word against his master or the regime.

In this way, India was divided and freed from colonial yoke. Pakistan celebrated its Independence Day on 14 August in Karachi. Johnson along with Mountbatten participated in this function. The presence of small crowd and the absence of popular enthusiasm, as witnessed by Johnson, was the negation of the opinion that Pakistan had been demanded by the Muslims in general. Johnson writes, "I had never dreamt that the creator of a nation at the moment of reaching the promised land could, when surrounded by his devoted followers be at such a distance from them." He further says, "Neither the scale nor the enthusiasm of the crowd was anything like as great as I had expected."[142] Thus, Johnson though unwillingly has shown that Jinnah and his long cherished theory had lesser popular base.

India won independence on 15 August 1947. On this day message from Mountbatten was broadcast in America which had been recorded on 8 August. It goes, "Two years ago I had just returned from the Potsdam Conference and was in the Prime Minister's room in 10, Downing Street when the news of Japanese surrender came through. Here as I speak to you tonight in Delhi, we are celebrating an event no less momentous for the future of the world — India's Independence Day. In the Atlantic Charter, we the British and Americans dedicated ourselves to champion the self-determination of peoples and the independence of nations. Bitter experience has taught us that it was often easier to win a war than to achieve a war aim; so let us remember August 15 as very Important Day, not only as the celebration of victory but also the fulfilment of a pledge."[143] It is the complete negation of the role of the national movement in the liberation of India. It is also a sophisticated version of the 'civilising mission' theory. This is well supported by Johnson.

In India, the Independence Day was celebrated throughout the length and breadth of the country. However, New Delhi was the focal point. Johnson gives an impressive picture of this ceremony.[144] The massive crowd and unparallel enthusiasm were indicative of the strength and the popularity of the national movement in India. But Johnson does not point out this.

Johnson gives detailed account of the communal violence which accompanied the partition especially in the North-West and North-East India. He himself had witnessed the effect of violence from air while returning from Karachi to Delhi on 16 August. He writes, "As we passed over the boundary areas of the Punjab, we could see several large fires, beacons of ill-omen dominating the landscape for miles around."[145] But while dealing with communal violence in Bengal, he praised Gandhi for the latter's effort in checking the violence in this part. He calls it the result of "Miracle of Gandhi's moral influence."[146]

In this way, we see that Johnson's uniqueness lies in the fact that he had witnessed the partition in person and had utilised official and private letters while interpreting the partition. He is first among his school who has utilised such primary sources. It is also important to note that he has not resorted to illogical generalisations.

However, like most other colleagues, Johnson, too, refrains from writing even a single word about the British policy of divide and rule and its different manifestations. He asserts that unity had been ever greatest legislative and administrative achievement in India but by March 1947, the only alternative was Pakistan or chaos.[147] In this way, he gives a clean chit to Mountbatten from his responsibility in the partition. He further argues that what Mountbatten proposed through the 3 June Plan was the demand of the Indian leaders.[148] Thus, he attempts to absolve the British in general of any responsibility in the vivisection of India.

To top it all, he locates the roots of divisions in the pre-British India. He suggests, "Independence through the partition was not the culmination of long cherished aim but it was nonetheless the response to a challenge as real as it was to many surprising. It is not sufficient to say that if the requisite statesmanship had been forthcoming, unity could have been preserved. A wealth of British genius and eminence, talent and service had been thrown into the task of its nourishment. The conflict that had preceded Warren Hastings was not to be liquidated with the departure of Mountbatten, but a *modus vivendi* was achieved based upon equity compromise and acceptance, if not agreement after discussion."[149] Thus, Johnson like a classic imperialist scholar sees a permanent divide in the Indian society and it was this divide which resulted into the division of India.

(IV) P.N.S. MANSERGH : ATTEMPT TO REVIVE CLASSIC IMPERIALIST ASSUMPTIONS

Great events stimulate great historical works. Such a great epoch-making event for the historians is the partition of India which preceded the independence from colonial yoke on 15 August 1947. This bifurcation of the Indian subcontinent has been a continuous source for controversies in the academic and political circles, since it was imposed on this zone. So much so, that even the terms used for this tragic finale of the

Raj differ according to the national, ideological and group affiliations of the scholars concerned. For instance, Jinnah called it partition and the Muslim League regarded it as compromise,[150] while Jawaharlal Nehru called it division and the Congress regarded it as final settlement.[151] To top it all, the British scholars regard it natural and inevitable which fulfilled the national aspirations of the Muslims.

Historians in general and British scholars in particular have approached the theme of the partition mainly due to its relevance for the present-day South Asia. The scholars are busy in the their effort to solve the controversies pertaining to the role and responsibilities of individuals and parties in the vivisection. Among the British scholars P.N.S. Mansergh[152] occupies a prominent place.

Mansergh[153] was educated at Oxford College, Pembroke. He started his career in the Ministry of Commonwealth since 1934. In 1935, he wrote *Irish Free State : Its Government and Politics.* While working in this department he familiarised himself with the developments in India. In 1941, he joined the Ministry of Information. He paid his attention towards Indian affairs. In 1944, he was promoted to the post of the Head of Empire Division in this Ministry. Two years later, he accepted senior appointment in the Dominion Office. In this way, he gradually specialised in British foreign relations especially the Commonwealth affairs. His familiarity with the subject led to his election as the Chairman of the British Commonwealth Relation at the Chattam House in 1947. In the same year, India won independence after the shock-therapy of partition. Thus, the events preceding and succeeding the partition left deeper influence over his mind.

In 1953, Mansergh got the distinction of being the first Smut Professor of the History of Commonwealth at Cambridge. In this way, he came in contact with the other prominent centre producing imperial ideologues. He came to be associated with reading and teaching the history of colonial and post-colonial era. He was also the Visiting Professor at the Indian School of International Studies, Jawaharlal Nehru University, Delhi. Thus, he also came in direct contact with India and Indians. When the British Government decided to publish the archival materials related to the transfer of power, Mansergh was appointed as

Editor-in-Chief. He along with E.W.R. Lumby[154] and Penderal Moon,[155] documented the official documents and records in twelve big size volumes covering the period of 1 January 1942 to 15 August 1947. Finally, he retired as Master of John's College, Cambridge in 1980. Thus, we see that Mansergh was capable of interpreting the partition theme on methodologically sound basis. But his association with Oxford and Cambridge and the imperial set-up, shaped his mindset in a classical imperial framework. Therefore, his writings are overburdened with the imperialist mindset.

The 1930s witnessed decisive shifts in the Indian nationalist movement, colonialism and communalism. Incidentally, it was during this period that Mansergh started his career. Possibly this is the reason that Mansergh starts his discussion on India from this point. Secondly, in recent decades, the focus has shifted towards the last decades of the Raj. The scholars lay emphasis, while interpreting the partition, on the events just preceding it. These factors helped Mansergh in the selection of the period for the documentation of the archival materials. However, he himself accepts that the selection of the date was arbitrary.[156] Thus, he starts his discussion with the making and the working of the Government of India Act, 1935.

Mansergh, like most of the scholars of his school, has approached the theme of partition with a predetermined mindset. He regards the partition inevitable. He refutes the charge that the British Indian Government introduced and promoted the policy of *divide et empera.* He cites an example from the Round Table Conference 1931. He argues that one Indian delegate during the conference had replaced the Congress blame of 'divide and rule' by the phrase 'we divide you rule.'[157] He has generalised this statement, even if it was correct. He delivered a judgement that pushed to its logical conclusion meant the divisions at root were domestic. In this way, the divisions were natural which culminated into the partition. What British did, in his words, ensured peaceful transfer of power, which is remarkable. Thus, Mansergh has generalised a doubtful statement and tried to absolve the Britishers not only of their responsibilities in partition but also to ignore the 'unprecedented violence that coincided the transfer of power.'[158]

By 1930, the Indian national movement had become a truly mass movement mainly due to efforts made by Gandhiji. This exerted great pressure on the colonial set-up. Therefore, the latter took recourse to constitutionalism because on the one hand, it was thought that it would reconcile the liberal elements, while on the other hand, it would give new dimension to the divide and rule policy. Henceforth, the Princely States were encouraged against the national movement. The Government of India Act, 1935 was designed to fulfil these colonial aspirations. It proposed for an All India Federation comprising British India and willing Princely States and introduced Provincial Autonomy in British India. Mansergh blames the Congress that it was due to latter's policy that these two provisions encouraged the Muslim separatism and proved decisive in the partition of India. In this way, he defends the British Government which had given undue weightage to the minorities and the Princely States in this Act.

In 1936-37, elections were held to implement the Provincial Autonomy section of the Act. In these elections, the Congress popularity resulted into its massive victory. The Congress formed ministries in seven out of eleven provinces on its own. It did not form coalition government with the Muslim League especially in the United Provinces. Mansergh like other imperial ideologues, argues that this decision of the Congress was ill-advised. In his words, "The way in which those governments were formed, proved to be a major source of the Muslim League's grievances against the Congress. The nature of that grievance is not in dispute. It lay in the fact that the Congress after its massive victory in 1937 provincial elections, had formed one-party governments in provinces, in which the Muslim League had expected coalitions in which they would be partners. This repudiation and the rejection of the League derived fundamentally from the Congress conviction that it represented all India."[159]

Thus, Mansergh like other ideologues of Oxbridge group, asserts that the policies of the Congress leaders were responsible for the critical change in the Muslim sentiments from readiness to cooperate to insistence upon separation. On the basis of Maulana Abul Kalam Azad's autobiography,[160] he holds Jawaharlal Nehru and Rajendra Prasad responsible for this. But it should be noted here that the Congress and the League were parties with different rather mutually antagonistic aims and objectives. Therefore to think of a coalition between these two parties, that too in case one party gets clear majority, is illogical. Secondly, there was no pre-poll agreement between these two parties. Thirdly, it was the decision of the Provincial units and the Congress High Command, not the decision of Jawaharlal Nehru or Rajendra Prasad. To top it all, the authenticity of the *India Wins Freedom* itself is doubtful. In this way, it is illogical and ahistrorical to blame the Congress and the national leadership for not forming coalition with the League. What is the guarantee that this coalitions had not worked in a way that the coalition Interim Government at the centre worked during 1946-47.

However, Mansergh asserts that the Indian social milieu was the natural fertile track for the growing rift between the Congress and the League. He argues that there is a greater element of determinism or alternatively a more limited freedom of manoeuvre in situation where there is latent or actual tension between communities, expressing their will through a parliamentary franchise and preoccupied with a prospective transfer of power than is apt to be allowed by contemporary observers and leaders.[161] In this way, he tries to impress that it was the quest of power and inherent Hindu-Muslim conflict, which gave momentum to the Muslim separatism.

In a likewise manner he explained the federal part of the Act. He argues that the federal scheme was bound to collapse in view of the prevailing situation. He writes, "Nationalists, it might be argued in situation such as the Irish and the Indians were bound to make mistakes or a mistake alleged to be conclusive. But were such mistakes the necessary product of a historical situation the contours of which were determined not merely by the interaction of majority and minority aspirations and fear but also by the nature of the imperial factors?"[162] Thus, he blames the Indian situation for the collapse of the federal scheme. However, he criticises the imperial set-up as well for its failure but in a defensive mood. He further argues that the federal scheme was designed to preserve the unity but it could not fulfil the aspirations of the Hindus and the Muslims. In practical terms, it was a second best to the majority who preferred unity and also to minority who preferred partition.[163] Thus, he is ahead of other ideologues in tracing the definite course of partition right from 1935. In fact, the Congress rejected the federal part because the Muslims and the Native States had been granted undue weightage in order to act as a counterweight against the Congress.[164] Therefore, it was bound to be rejected by the Congress. But Mansergh, on the basis of Canadian and Australian experiences, expresses the probability that the federalism could have succeeded. Thus, like Moon, he talks in terms of 'ifs and buts.'

During the World War II (1939-45), the Muslim separatism got active support from the colonial regime and was strengthened considerably. But Mansergh blames the Congress leaders and the pluralistic nature of the Indian society.[165] He considers the Lahore Resolution of the Muslims League as a definite demand of a separate sovereign Pakistan.[166] Further, he asks a question and then answers it. Whether the Muslims were a community, the second largest within India or they a separate nation? If they were the former then the pattern of a self-protective policy might have been expected to be, as indeed it was least down to 1940. But if the Muslims were not the second largest community in India but a separate nation then the demand for a separate homeland was preliminary. On this dichotomy, he asserts that the Pakistan Resolution symbolised the conversion of a community into the nation and it led to the closing of different options before the policy-makers. Thus, the Pakistan Resolution was the climaxing of the earlier trend of Muslim separatism. But, Mansergh calls it national aspiration.

During the World War II, the Congress was opposing the war efforts of the British Indian Government. The then Governor General, Linlithgow made a declaration in form of the August Offer.[167] Its aim was to obtain Congress cooperation in the war effort but due to its shortcomings it was rejected by the Congress. Henceforth, the colonial regime relied heavily on the League and regional Muslim parties in the war effort. This, in turn, strengthened the League. But, Mansergh blames the Congress for it on ahistorical basis. He does not give logical evidence to emphasise this hypothesis. He also bypasses the collusion between the Muslim League and the colonial regime.

Towards the end of 1941, the War entered into more intense phase. The British Prime Minister sent Cripps Mission[168] to India in 1942 to obtain India's co-operation in the war effort and to show that he was interested to solve the Indian problems. The Cripps Mission failed. The Linlithgow — Churchill — Amery circle made this Mission a failure. However, Mansergh blames Gandhi individually for its failure. He writes, "On 8 April, Mahatma, in his two hours, conversation with the members of the Congress Working Committee, urged them to reject the Cripps proposals. The telephonic conversation was intercepted by the Intelligence Service".[169] But R.J. Moore does not talk about this document or Report.[170] In this way, Mansergh holds Gandhi responsible for the failure of the Cripps Mission on the basis of a doubtful evidence.

The constitutional and communal problem had been further complicated during the World War II. The new Governor-General Wavell tried to solve it and convened an all-Party Conference at Simla in 1945. This Wavell Plan failed because Jinnah demanded the Hindu — Muslim parity in the Council and that all the Muslim members would be the League nominees. The British Indian Government could have implemented this plan. But it allowed it to collapse without pressurising Jinnah. Thus, this Simla Conference and the failure of the Wavell Plan enhanced the prestige of Jinnah and the League. But Mansergh while defending the colonial regime argues, "The transfer of power to two as distinct from one successor authority carried the implication of equality between the two successor states. Prior to the transfer, the League had to be equated with the Congress, or as Jinnah would have phrased it, Pakistan with Hindustan. In numerical terms, this meant the equation of minority with majority. It had happened in plural societies elsewhere."[171] In this way, he attempts to justify the colonial support given to Jinnah through inaction.

Thus, Mansergh has tried to defend the imperial policy of appeasement towards the League, which slowly but gradually intensified the divisive forces. It should be noted here that in 1945, Jinnah and the League could have been pressurised by the government. Had the British good intentions, the Wavell Plan would have been implemented. But this was not to be. Mansergh supports this action of the government and says that the imposition of any order to ensure unity could have resulted in disturbance. He writes, "Had the British indeed succeeded in imposing, then the consequences, again accepting the fundamentals of Jinnah's analysis might well have been, as he threatened in 1947, the bloodiest civil war in the history of Asia."[172] However, the very next year, the Muslim League under the guidance of Jinnah started the 'Direct Action' from 16 August and a civil war situation emerged. Thus, the above logic of Mansergh is not satisfactory.

In the post-War period, the British Government under Attlee showed its interest in solving the Indian problems. In March 1946, the Cabinet Mission was sent to India for this purpose. Last six Volumes of the *Transfer of Power* series cover the period from 23 March 1946 to 15 August 1947. The documented records in these volumes unfold as to how the British policy on India was hammered out under extreme pressure, week by week, day by day and hour by hour.

Like all earlier plans and offers, the Cabinet Mission Plan, too, failed to solve the Indian problems rather it gave new dimensions to the Muslim separatism. The Congress, too, made mistakes. The Muslim League under Jinnah rejected the Plan and started Direct Action from 16 August. The colonial government remained silent spectator and allowed the riots to spread and intensify. Mansergh's explanations of these riots are reflective of typical imperial mindset. He opines that these riots were natural in the Indian situation because it was the unity of India that was artificial and imposed, the division natural.[173]

The increasing 'pressure from below' in India compelled the British Government to decide to wind up the Raj as early as possible. The British Prime Minister, Attlee made this public in his famous Declaration on 20 February, 1947. Mansergh writes, "Attlee's Declaration had transformed the political atmosphere in India and made change in the highest office seem natural and appropriate."[174] So, Mountbatten replaced Wavell in March 1947. He proposed the partition and independence of India in his '3 June Plan.'[175] Mansergh has attempted to provide justification for this climax of the policy of 'divide and rule.' He writes, "By March 1947, the partition had become inevitable. The League was satisfactorily holding its position emphatic in its insistence that there had never been one India, that the unity was the creation of the British Raj."[176] Thus, he tries to impress that when Mountbatten reached India, other options had been closed, the only alternative, the partition was open. Now, the partition must be accepted to avoid Civil war. This is the reason, he opines, that the partition preceded the transfer of power.

Mansergh justifies the partition on other grounds as well. He argues that both the British and the Congress wanted united India but to solve the communal and constitutional deadlock, the British had to offer and the Congress had to accept the partiton.[177] He further argues, "The Congress failed to achieve united India because activities and the interests of the Congress leaders were diverse, while those of the League were concentrated wholly on the creation of Muslim State." Thus, he holds the leaders of the Congress and the League responsible for the June Plan and the ultimate partition.[178]

The power was transferred on 15 August 1947, prior to over ten months of the proposed last date in the Attlee's Declaration.[179] The lightning speed at which the power was transferred has been defended by Mansergh. He opines that it was in the interest of the subcontinent that power was transferred as soon as possible, even at the cost of partition. Responsibility without power is not an inevitable situation and had the transfer of power been long protracted, that is, the fate which would certainly have overtaken the army and administration.[180]

Thus, Mansergh by training and experience, was in a position to describe the end of the Raj in Indian subcontinent in an objective manner. But the legacy of imperial writings had deep influence over his writings. His works, though remarkable, are full of gaps. One, he, like other ideologues of this group sees the partition from inevitable angle. His main hypothesis is that in all plural societies like that of India, it was bound to happen. Second, the selection of the period for the documentation of records and documents in the transfer of power project is not fully justified. He lays emphasis on the Cripps Mission to justify it in the very first volume. He says that it was a turning point in the transfer of power but he does not mention the role that it played in the partition. Third, Mansergh has not recorded all the documents. Possibly he has been advised by the British Government not to publish such documents that could malign the British image. It has been emphatically demonstrated by V.N. Datta.[181]

Moreover, it becomes evident that considerable documentary materials had been destroyed before partition. For instance when Wavell at a dinner party asked Vallabhbhai Patel, how he was getting on with his work. Patel replied that he had wanted to see the intelligence reports on the Congress. Wavell said that he had ordered them to be destroyed. The discussion held in the War Cabinet has been totally eliminated. It could have provided vital clues in solving some of the controversies. Last but not least, Mountbatten — Jinnah encounter has not been recorded. Therefore, it is difficult to explain as to why Jinnah agreed to have a 'moth-eaten' Pakistan. In this way, we find some vital gaps in the writings of Mansergh, which are in typical imperial framework.

NOTES AND REFERENCES

1. A.T. Embree, *Imagining India, Essays on Indian History,* Delhi, 1989, p. 54.
2. Percival Spear, 'A third force in India, 1920-47 : A Study in Political Analysis', in C.H. Philips and M.D. Wainwright (eds.) *The Partition of India : Policies and Perspectives 1935-1947,* London, 1970.
3. Percival Spear, *India, Pakistan and West,* London, 1952, p. 77.
4. Percival Spear, *The Oxford History of Modern India, 1740-1975,* Delhi, 1951, p. 87.
5. Therefore, it is argued by the imperialist school that the Muslims remained separate as a distinct community. Hence, communalism was the natural corollary of the social milieu of India. Contrary to it, the nationalist historians blame colonial authority for the emergence of communalism. Another section of historians views it as a game of elites — alien and indigenous.
6. It refers to a process of change brought about in Indian society and culture as a result of over 150 years of British and the term subsumes changes occurring at different levels — technology, institution, ideology and values. This concept was propounded by the eminent sociologist, M.N. Srinivas. See *Social Change in Modern India,* New Delhi, 1972.
7. Percival Spear, *India, Pakistan and West,* p. 88.

8. Percival Spear, *India, A Modern History,* Michigan, 1961, p. 330.
9. Percival Spear, *The Oxford History of Modern India,* p. 354.
10. C.H. Philips and M.D. Wainwright (eds.), *op. cit.,* pp. 496-97.
11. *Ibid.,* p. 497.
12. Percival Spear, *India, Pakistan and West,* p. 90.
13. See Bipan Chandra, *Communalism in Modern India,* New Delhi, 1984.
14. In 1933, Chaudhri Rahmat Ali, a student at Cambridge coined the word 'Pakistan' etymologically, the land of the pure. 'P' stood for Punjab, 'A' for Afghan (North West Frontier Province), 'K' for Kashmir, 'S' for Sind and 'tan' for Baluchistan. See Sugata Bose and Ayesha Jalal, *Modern South Asia : History, Culture, Political Economy,* Delhi, 1999.
15. Percival Spear, *The Oxford History of Modern India,* p. 355.
16. Percival Spear, *India, Pakistan and West,* p. 79.
17. *Ibid.,* p. 79.
18. Percival Spear, *The Oxford History of Modern India,* p. 355.
19. *Ibid.,* p. 356.
20. *Ibid.,* p. 357.
21. C.H. Philips and M.D. Wainwright (eds.), *op. cit.,* p. 497.
22. Percival Spear, *India, Pakistan and West,* p. 91.
23. *Ibid.,* p. 91.
24. *Ibid.,* p. 91.
25. Percival Spear, *The Oxford History of Modern India,* p. 358.
26. Percival Spear, *India, Pakistan and West,* p. 206.
27. Percival Spear, *The Oxford History of Modern India,* p. 358.
28. *Ibid.,* p. 360.
29. Percival Spear, *India, Pakistan and West,* p. 200.
30. *Ibid.,* p. 206.
31. Percival Spear, *The Oxford History of Modern India,* p. 362.
32. See S.R. Mehrotra, *Towards India's Freedom and Partition,* New Delhi, 1979.
33. At Lucknow, the two main parties adopted a joint scheme of reforms known as the Congress-League scheme. Its adoption was a result of bargain between them. The Congress accepted the separate electorate for the Muslims which proved fatal in the long run. See J.P. Suda, *Indian Constitutional Development and National Movement,* Meerut, 1956.

34. C.H. Philips and M.D. Wainwright (eds.), *op. cit.*, p. 497.
35. Percival Spear, *The Oxford History of Modern India*, p. 362.
36. *Ibid.*, p. 361.
37. *Ibid.*, p. 362.
38. In 1927 an all-white men Commission under the chairmanship of John Simon was appointed to look into the working of the Indian Council Act, 1919 and to report on the further constitutional reforms. See Prakash Chandra, *History of the Indian National Movement*, New Delhi, 1997.
39. In 1930, Iqbal suggested the union of Frontier Province, Baluchistan, Sind and Kashmir as a Muslim state within a federation. It has been interpreted by the imperialist historians as a definite case of Muslim separatism.
40. Chaudhri Rahmat Ali coined the word 'Pakistan' in 1933 at Cambridge. How far he had been encouraged by the British policy-makers and colonial ideologues is yet to be explored.
41. Percival Spear, *The Oxford History of Modern India*, p. 363.
42. Percival Spear, *India, Pakistan and West*, p. 203.
43. Percival Spear, *The Oxford History of Modern India*, p. 374.
44. *Ibid.*, p. 377.
45. Percival Spear, *Communal Harmony*, London, 1940, p. 6.
46. Percival Spear, *The Oxford History of Modern India*, p. 375.
47. Jinnah in his presidential address to the Lahore session of the Muslim League, March 1940, said, 'Islam and Hinduism are not religions in the strict sense of the word, but are in fact different and distinct social orders and it is only a dream that the Hindus and the Muslims can ever evolve a common nationality. The Muslims are a nation, according to any definition of a nation and they must have their homeland, their territory and their state.'

    Thus, he demanded 'Pakistan' in ambiguous terms. This should not be regarded as the demand of the Muslims of India because it was opposed by the other Muslim groups. In April 1940, Azad Muslim Conference held in Delhi under the Presidentship of Allah Baksh, the premier of Sind, condemned this Pakistan Resolution. See V.P. Menon, *The Transfer of Power in India*, Madras, 1957.
48. Percival Spear, *India, Pakistan and West*, p. 208.
49. Percival Spear, *The Oxford History of Modern India*, p. 382.
50. The aim of the Cripps Mission was to break the constitutional and communal deadlock and obtain India's full cooperation in the War effort. However, the secret motive was only to show the world that

Britain was sincere to Indian problems. Therefore, it was made to fail by its originators. Thus, it could not break the communal deadlock but definitely accelerated the Pakistan movement by including it in the official document for the first time, though implicitly. See Maulana Abul Kalam Azad, *India Wins Freedom (The complete version)*, Delhi, 1988.

51. Percival Spear, *The Oxford History of Modern India*, p. 382.
52. The Quit India Movement was a national mass movement which horizontally and vertically engulfed all India and Indians. It proved to be the climax of India's freedom struggle. That is why, it has been denounced in imperialist writings. See Mridula Mukherjee, 'The Quit India Movement and the INA', in Bipan Chandra and others (eds.), *India's Struggle for Freedom*, pp. 457-72.
53. Percival Spear, *The Oxford History of Modern India*, p. 384.
54. The Governor-General Wavell proposed the constitution of the Executive Council on the basis of communal parity. Jinnah demanded that all the Muslim members would be the League nominees. It was opposed by the Congress. Wavell declared the failure of the plan but it gave veto power to Jinnah in constitutional reforms and indirectly accepted the Muslim League as the sole representative of Indian Muslims. See Maulana Abul Kalam Azad, *op. cit.*
55. The Cabinet Mission followed the policy of appeasement towards the Muslim separatist movement. In order to appease the League, it provided the grouping of British Indian Provinces — Group 'A' included the Hindu Majority Provinces, Group 'B' that of the Muslim Majority Provinces of the North-West and Group 'C' that of the Muslim Majority Provinces of the North-East India. This proved to be the bone of contention between the Congress and the League. Obviously, the colonial regime sided with the League.
56. Percival Spear, *The Oxford History of Modern India*, p. 388.
57. C.H. Philips and M.D. Wainwright (eds.), *op, cit.*, p. 497.
58. Percival Spear, *Communal Harmony*, p. 6.
59. H.V. Hodson remained associated with the colonial Government from 1930 up to 1945 in different capacities. He had been an expert in world economy but he wrote Indian history of modern times in detail.
60. H.V. Hodson, *The Great Divide* : *Britain, India and Pakistan*, Karachi, 1969, p. 181.
61. *Ibid.*, p. 9.
62. *Ibid.*, p. 3.
63. Sumanta Niyogi, 'Colonial Historiography : Its Intellectual Origins and

Perspectives on Indian Nationalism', *Journal of Historical Studies,* Patna University, Patna, No. 1, 1995, pp. 48-75.

64. H.V. Hodson, *op. cit.,* p. 3.
65. *Ibid.,* p. 4.
66. *Ibid.,* p. 11.
67. *Ibid.,* p. 10.
68. Anita Inder Singh, *The Origins of the Partition of India,* Delhi, 1987, p. 230.
69. H.V. Hodson, *op. cit.,* p. 3.
70. *Ibid.,* p. 12.
71. *Ibid.,* p. 13.
72. *Ibid.,* p. 13.
73. Percival Spear, *The Oxford History of Modern India, 1740-1975,* p. 375.
74. C.H. Philips and M.D. Wainwright (eds.), *The Partition of India, Policies, and Perspectives, 1935-1947,* pp. 54-94.
75. H.V. Hodson, *op. cit.,* p. 41.
76. *Ibid.,* p. 75.
77. *Ibid.,* p. 103.
78. *Ibid.,* p. 105.
79. *Ibid.,* p. 107.
80. *Ibid.,* p. 116.
81. *Ibid.,* p. 120.
82. *Ibid.,* p. 125.
83. *Ibid.,* p. 128.
84. *Ibid.,* p. 129.
85. *Ibid.,* p. 133.
86. H.V. Hodsan, 'The Role of Lord Mountbatten,' in C.H. Philips and M.D. Wainwright (eds.), *op. cit.,* pp. 117-26.
87. H.V. Hodson, *The Great Divide : Britain, India and Pakistan,* p. 203.
88. *Ibid.,* pp. 207-8.
89. *Ibid.,* p. 210.
90. *Ibid.,* p. 228.
91. *Ibid.,* p. 232.
92. *Ibid.,* p. 225.
93. *Ibid.,* p. 245.
94. *Ibid.,* p. 247.

95. *Ibid.*, p. 317.
96. *Ibid.*, p. 319.
97. Percival Spear, *India, Pakistan and West*, London, 1952.
98. See A.C. Johnson, *The Mission with Mountbatten*, London, 1995.
99. P.N.S. Mansergh, 'Some Reflections on the Transfer of Power in Pluralistic Societies', in C.H. Philips and M.D. Wainwright (eds.), *op. cit.*, pp. 43-53.
100. E.W.R. Lumby, *Transfer of Power in India, 1945-47*, London, 1954.
101. R.J. Moore, *Endgames of Empire — Studies of Britain's Indian Problem*, Delhi, 1988.
102. Penderal Moon, *Divide and Quit*, London, 1961.
103. Hugh Tinker, *Experiment with Freedom* : *India and Pakistan, 1947*, London, 1961.
104. H.V. Hodson, *Twentieth Centrury Empires*, London, 1966, p. 104.
105. *Ibid.*, p. 105.
106. The imperialist writers attempt to give ideological support to the colonial regime and to defend its policies. See Sumanta Niyogi, 'Colonial Historiography : Its Intellectual Origins and Perspective on Indian Nationalism', in *Journal of Historical Studies*, Patna University, Patna, No. 1, 1995, pp. 48-75.
107. The administrator-turned historians formed a compact group within the imperialist school. These scholars had observed the Indian society from within and were fully aware of the adverse effect of the colonial policies. Therefore, when they tried to interpret the Indian history, they utilised Indian subjective-objective conditions for their purpose.
108. The writings of Allen Campbell Johnson include : *Growing Opinions*, London, 1935; *Peace Offerings*, London, 1936; *Anthony Eden — A Biography*, London, 1938; *Viscount Halifax — A Biography*, London, 1941; and *Mission with Mountbatten*, London, 1951.
109. See A.C. Johnson, *Mission with Mountbatten.*
110. Broadly speaking, he does not talk in terms of cause and effect but he has detailed the possible effects of partition. *Ibid.*, pp. 356-58.
111. On 20 February 1947, British Prime Minister Attlee declared that the British would quit India by June 1948, if necessary without achieving agreement between Indian parties and without a defence treaty. The power would be transferred to the best successor authorities available at that time. See R.J. Moore, *Endgames of Empire* : *Studies of Britain's Indian Problem*, p. 6.
112. Allen Campbell Johson, *Mission with Mountbatten*, p. 28.
113. *Ibid.*, p. 31.

114. *Ibid.*, p. 40.

115. *Ibid.*, p. 44.

116. *Ibid.*, p. 354.

117. With the League's intentions clear in the Punjab after 3 March, the Congress Working Committee passed on 9 March a resolution calling for the partition of the Punjab. See Anita Inder Singh, *op. cit.*, p. 226.

118. Allen Campbell Johnson quotes Patel as saying that India must get rid of the Muslim League. See *Mission with Mountbatten*, p. 46.

119. *Ibid.*, p. 47.

120. *Ibid.*, p. 54.

121. *Ibid.*, p. 53.

122. *Ibid.*, p. 363.

123. *Ibid.*, p. 56.

124. *Ibid.*, pp. 55-56.

125. On the eve of the Conference, the broad principles of Mountbatten Plan are :

    (1) that the responsibility for partition, if it comes, is to rest fairly upon the Indians themselves;

    (2) the Provinces, generally speaking, shall have the right to determine their own future;

    (3) Bengal and the Punjab are to be rationally partitioned for voting purposes;

    (4) the predominantly Moslem Sylhet district in Assam is to be given the option of joining the Moslem province created by a partitioned Bengal and

    (5) General Elections are to he held in the North-West Frontier Province. *Ibid.*, p. 62.

126. *Ibid.*, p. 59.

127. *Ibid.*, p. 354.

128. *Ibid.*, p. 65.

129. *Ibid.*, p. 80.

130. See B.N. Pandey, *The Breaking of British India*, pp. 202-3.

131. Allen Campbell Johnson, *Mission with Mountbatten*, p. 99.

132. *Ibid.*, p. 56.

133. Jinnah withdrew the League's acceptance of the Cabinet Mission Plan, on 29 July 1946, and decided to celebrate 16 August 1946 as 'Direct Action Day.' From this day the Muslim League's National Guard started killing Hindus and Sikhs and the latter retaliated in the same way.

Thus, near a civil war situation prevailed. See Sucheta Mahajan, 'Freedom and Partition,' in Bipan Chandra *et al.*, *India's Struggle for Independence*, pp. 487-504.

134. Sucheta Mahajan, *Independence and Partition*, pp. 333-59.
135. Allen Campbell Johnson, *Mission with Mountbatten*, p. 100.
136. Since the 3 June Plan and its acceptance by Indian parties was a real victory for the colonial regime, Mountbatten along with other staff went on excursion to celebrate this victory.
137. Allen Campbell Johnson, *Mission with Mountbatten*, p. 117.
138. *Ibid.*, p. 126.
139. *Ibid.*, p. 134.
140. In the Punjab, twelve million Hindus, Sikhs and Muslims were involved in the communal violence erupted in the wake of partition and migration of some nine million people began overnight in area, the size of Wales. *Ibid.*, pp. 355-56.
141. John Christee and Johnson met Redcliff on 12 August 1947. The latter said that both the Punjab and Bengal Awards were complete and ready. *Ibid.*, p. 153.
142. *Ibid.*, p. 155.
143. *Ibid.*, p. 151.
144. *Ibid.*, pp. 158-69.
145. *Ibid.*, p. 156.
146. *Ibid.*, p. 357.
147. *Ibid.*, p. 354.
148. *Ibid.*, pp. 354-55.
149. *Ibid.*, p. 363.
150. For further details see, Multi-Volume : *A History of the Freedom Movement 1707-1947*, prepared under the leadership of Mahmud Hussain. This series was sponsored by Pakistan government. Also see K.B. Sayed, *Pakistan : The Formative Phase* 1857-1958, London, 1968; Choudhary Khaliquzzaman, *Pathway to Pakistan*, Lahore, 1961; and Waheed Ahamad, 'Historiorgraphy of Partition', in Ramakant and Rajan Mahan (eds.), *op. cit.*, pp. 84-94.
151. See Tarachand, *History of Freedom Movement*, Vol. IV, New Delhi, 1967; Pattabhi Sitaramayya, *The History of the Indian National Congress*, Vol. II, Bombay, 1946; and Ram Gopal, *How India Struggled for Freedom*, Bombay, 1967.
152. Nicholas Mansergh, *Irish Free State : Its Government and Politics*, London, 1935; *Commonwealth Experience; Commonwealth and the Nation; Name*

and the Nature of the Commonwealth; Prelude to Partition; Concepts and Aims in Ireland and India; 'Some Reflections on the Transfer of Power in Plural Societies,' in C.H. Philips and M.D. Wainwright (eds.), *op. cit.*, and Chief Editor of official documents under the title, *The Constitutional Relations between Britain and India 1942-47, The Transfer of Power*, XII Vols.

153. For biographical details, see Norman Hillover and Philip Wiglay (eds.), *The First British Commonwealth : Essays in Honour of Nicholas Mansergh*, London, 1980.

154. E.W.R. Lumby is another important pillar of the Oxbridge group of intellectuals. His *magnum opus* is the *Transfer of Power in India, 1945-47,* London, 1954.

155. He is administrator-turned historian, who has written widely on India and partition.

156. See introduction to the First volume of documents of the *Transfer of Power,* London, 1970.

157. C.H. Philips and M.D. Wainwright (eds.), *op. cit.,* p. 50.

158. See Ayesha Jalal and Sugata Bose, *op. cit.*

159. C.H. Philips and M.D. Wainwright (eds.), *op. cit.,* p. 47.

160. In this book he asserts that he himself proposed well-thought and farsighted views but they were rejected by other Congress leaders, which proved fatal for the Hindu-Muslim unity. For further details, see *India Wins Freedom.*

161. C.H. Philips and M.D. Wainwright (eds.), *op. cit.,* p. 48.

162. *Ibid.,* p. 49.

163. *Ibid.,* p. 46.

164. See Bipan Chandra, *et al., op. cit.*

165. C.H. Philips and M.D. Wainwright (eds.), *op. cit.,* p. 51.

166. Mansergh, *Prelude to Partition : Concept and Aims in Ireland and India,* p. 27.

167. The August Offer proposed for the enlargement of the Executive Council and appointment of all Indians but the Governor-General and the Commander-in-chief. But the Congress was demanding a national Government of sort. Therefore, the latter rejected it.

168. It accepted the League's demand of Pakistan for the first time. Therefore, it was bound to be rejected. But Churchill called Cripps back when the negotiation was in progress. Thus, it broke down. For detail see Bipan Chandra, *et al.,* (eds.), *India's Strugge for Independence,* pp. 443-56.

169. See *The Transfer of Power,* Vol. I.

170. See R.J. Moore, *Churchill, Cripps and India, 1939-45.*
171. C.H. Philips and M.D. Wainwright (eds.), *op. cit.*, pp. 51-52.
172. Mansergh, *Commonwealth Experience,* p. 124.
173. See B.N. Pandey, *op. cit.*, pp. 202-03.
174. N. Mansergh, *Commonwealth Experience,* pp. 135-36.
175. C.H. Philips and M.D. Wainwright (eds.), *op. cit.*, pp. 49-50.
176. N. Mansergh, *Commonwealth Experience,* pp. 131-32.
177. In Attlee Declaration, the British government had decided to wind up the Raj by June 1948.
178. N. Mansergh, *Commonwealth Experience,* p. 125.
179. No government publishes all the documents it possesses and government wants the public to know the truth. Mansergh volumes were subject to the inter-party agreement through the group of Privy Counsellors. We do not know the terms of reference given to him as the chief editor. V.N. Datta, 'Interpreting Partition,' in the *Proceedings of the Indian History Congress,* 57th session, 1996, p. 8.
180. Penderal Moon (ed.), *Wavell*: *The Viceroy Journal,* p. 347.
181. N. Mansergh, 'Introduction' to *Transfer of Power*, Vol. I.

3

Critique of Colonial Policies

(I) PENDERAL MOON : THE ROLE OF MAHATMA IN THE PARTITION

The vivisection of Indian subcontinent into two sovereign states of Pakistan and the Indian Union has been an issue of lively debate since 1947, when it was thrust upon "the people" of this zone of South Asia by the elites — alien and indigenous. Interestingly, this debate is still inconclusive. Historians, both professional and amateur, have produced a huge corpus of literature on this theme. Historians with different ideological preoccupations and national affiliations differ over the role played by different personalities, parties and organisations in the process of partition. The British historians during colonial and post-colonial era have approached this issue with a typical mindset. Their sole aim is to defend and legitimize the colonial policy of *divide at empera* and absolve the Britishers of their responsibility in partition, which was accompanied with uncounted massacres and displacement of the masses. In order to achieve their goal, the imperialist historians have blamed the objective-subjective socio-cultural milieu and the nature of contemporary leadership for the partition. Obviously, their main target has been Gandhi, who happened to be the most dangerous opponent of colonial regime. Penderal Moon,[1] the administrator-turned historian, is a true representative of this school.

Moon, with a sound family background, was educated at Winchester and subsequently at Oxford. He passed the Indian Civil Service examination in 1928 and in his own words, he had been attracted to this profession due to the scope of the service in India and a very idealistic picture of the sort of work to be done. He was deeply influenced by R. Coupland,[2] a prominent imperial ideologue. In India, Moon was in close contact with Raj Kumari Amrit Kaur, the Mahatma's Secretary during the Quit India Movement. He had mainly served in the Punjab zone and was the Revenue Minister of Bahawalpur State. He had witnessed the communal riots in person, before, during and after the partition. Finally, back in England he became an Assistant Editor in the Historical Section of the India Office Library and Records where Professor Nicholas Mansergh[3] and his colleagues were engaged in editing of the India Office documents on the transfer of power.[4] His career as a historian spread over nearly half a century, *i.e.,* from 1944[5] till his demise in 1987.[6] Thus, he was in a position and capable to detail the authentic and objective accounts of events that preceded and followed the partition, but his national affiliation and ideological preoccupation induced him to produce a biased and one-sided history in a non-empirical fashion sometimes differing on some issues from other ideologues of his own school.

Mohandas Karamchand Gandhi — a product of the half-hearted modernising effort of the colonial regime but deeply rooted in his own cultural context — started his anti-colonial campaign through mobilisation of the masses. The colonial regime perceived the danger of erosion of its hegemony and, therefore, in order to weaken this movement, started promoting the anti-national elements present in Indian society. Penderal Moon started his career as a civil servant in this condition and witnessed the Mahatma and his "modes of opposition" in action. Possibly this is the reason that Moon, like other historians of his school, has tried his best to defend the colonial regime and its policies by blaming Gandhi personally for the partition. However, in reality, the partition was one among the several adverse impacts of colonial policy, of course, supported by the power-hungry Indian elites cutting across communities. Penderal Moon, too, like other scholars of his school, has misinterpreted the objective social conditions of this subcontinent and tried to show that it was a divided society having mutually antagonistic interests. Of several differences, the most serious according to him, was the clash of Hinduism with Islam and these two groups constituted two distinct and often antagonistic communities. Thus, he ignores the fact that it were Britishers who made these two communities antagonistic at the elite level.

While explaining the emergence of Gandhi as the national leader, he negates the personality and techniques of the former. He argues that Indian society with ancient outlook and mild British rule helped Gandhi's emergence at the national political horizon.[7] Actually, Gandhian leadership and modes of opposition aroused consciousness among the masses against the exploitative and oppressive British rule and the masses accepted him as their leader. In this way, Moon has attempted to undermine the Gandhian leadership and to conceal the exploitative nature of colonial rule by blaming Gandhian modes of opposition which, we are told, widened the gulf between the Hindus and the Muslims which culminated into the partition.

Broadly speaking India, like other nation-states of the late nineteenth century and early twentieth century consisted of manifold divisions. But some divisions have been highlighted and while negating the underlying unity, some new divisions have been artificially imposed by the imperial ideologues. Moon highlights the Hindu-Muslim divide and says that this conflict is the real threat to India's future peace and thus provides justification for the British rule.[8] Thus, Moon has tried to defend the divisive role of and justify the existence of the colonial regime.

In the second decade of the twentieth century, the Indian National Congress was still an elite organisation despite getting support from different sections of the society, but the All India Muslim League was purely elitist having no popular support. The colonial regime was opposing the former right from its inception. Gandhiji started his political career in India in this situation and attempted to unite all such groups so that the colonial regime could be challenged unitedly. But Gandhiji has been blamed for Hinduising the national movement which widened the gulf between the Hindus and the Muslims. Moon argues that the Hinduising of the national movement which Gandhian leadership promoted and symbolised was injurious and ultimately fatal to the Hindu-Muslim unity, but Gandhi failed to see the dangers. He supports his argument on the basis that Gandhi's basic concepts, his moral values and ideals, even his fads and fables were of Hindu origin, in his writings and speeches he constantly employed language, imagery and symbolism that were undisguisedly derived from Hinduism.[9]

Thus, Moon tries to portray Gandhi as a typical Hindu leader, contrary to the fact that he was a mass leader. In order to show that Gandhi was never accepted by the Muslims, Moon argues that they had formed their own organisation.[10] He denies the Government role in the formation of the Muslim League.[11] He is so obsessed with his ideology that he even extends his full support to the 'Separate Electorate'[12] system introduced by the Morley-Minto Reforms, 1909. He regards this as an indispensable safeguard of Muslim interests.[13] It is clear that when Gandhi started his Indian campaign, the colonial regime through its divide and rule policy and with the help of the indigenous elite, had sown the seeds of mutual rivalry which culminated into the partition of India. Therefore, it is illogical to blame Gandhiji for widening the gulf between the Hindus and the Muslims.

The Non-cooperation Movement (1920-22) was the first all-India movement, started by Gandhi, which in combination with the Pan-Islamic Khilafat Movement became a real challenge to the colonial regime. This unprecedented show of the Hindu-Muslim unity was a real danger to it. That is why, the colonial ideologues vehemently criticise this. Moon goes to the extent of saying that this action of Gandhi set Congress on a course that led to disunity.[14] In order to prove his hypothesis, he tries to colour even the Mopilah revolt in a communal colour.[15] He further argues that due to the Mopilah rebellion, the Muslims turned toward the Government and the Hindu-Muslim unity began to crumble.[16] In fact, the colonial regime, which was afraid of the Hindu-Muslim unity, intensified its policy of communalisation of Indian politics and society and sided with the communal forces.

The colonial regime promoted the divisive forces through constitutionalism which became crystal clear in the early decades of the twentieth century especially after 1909.[17] The same motive was behind the appointment of Simon Commission in

1927. The Indian National Congress challenged it and produced the Nehru Report but ultimately it failed to satisfy Jinnah's demand because the Hindu fundamentalists opposed more concessions. This was "parting of ways" writes Moon, between the League and the Congress.[18] He holds Gandhi responsible for the failure of the Report on the basis that the latter ought to have made attempts to get the Report modified, so as to meet Jinnah's demand. But it was not possible because Gandhi had no control over the all-parties conference. Secondly, it widened the gulf between the elites of the League and the Congress, therefore it should not be taken as the parting of ways between the Hindus and the Muslims as Moon has explained.

Gandhiji being a true mass leader, gauging the level of mass-consciousness started the Civil Disobedience movement in 1930. It had also become a necessity in the changed context of the late 1920s. Though the League denounced it, the nationalist Muslim leaders and masses participated wholeheartedly. However, Moon citing the instance of Kanpur, argues that this movement far from uniting the two communities had windened the gulf between them. He says that the Muslims' contempt for the movement was resented to by the Hindus, which created tension.[19] He nowhere mentions the role of three consecutive Round Table Conferences and the subsequent "Communal Award,"[20] through which the Metropolitan Government and the colonial set-up attempted further communalisation of Indian politics. Thus, Moon is involved in the concealment and distortion of facts.

The elections of 1936-37 clearly established the fact that the Congress was a national body and the League had no popular support. Henceforth, the League took recourse to communal politics aimed at gaining public support and the colonial regime extended its direct support in this effort. However, Moon has a different biased story to tell. He says that the Congress's refusal to form a coalition government in the United Provinces and the Congress government's policies made the Muslims apprehensive of the 'Congress Raj' and this influenced the Muslim thinking. Moon suggests that by 1939 Muslims all over India gathered under the League.[21] He further writes, "Through generalisation of the Congress policies, the

League denounced the federal part of the Government of India Act 1935 and Jinnah was accepted as the sole Muslim leader."[22] Moon in this way, blames Gandhi and the Congress for the so-called policy of absorption in place of coalition.[23] But how could a coalition government be formed between two diametrically opposite parties and that too without any pre-election agreements?

Moon's hypothetical equation is that the Congress and Gandhi did not recognise the League as the only authoritative and representative organisation of the Muslim India. Therefore, Jinnah's anti-Congress propaganda continued and the growing rift between the Congress and the League differences, was not healed.[24] In support of this hypothesis, he says that the main theme of Gandhi's preaching to the public was derived from the Hindu rather than the Muslim tradition thereby, representing the spirit of Hindu revivalism. In his opinion, the communal deadlock became the prime national question but Gandhi and most of the Congress leaders failed to see it.[25]

The Congress opposed the colonial Government's declaration of India being on war in 1939 and decided to cooperate conditionally. Moon, like other historians of this group, has denounced the Congress attitude and praised the League which was cooperating in the war effort. Moreover, he blames the Congress and Gandhi for the 'Pakistan-Resolution'[26] passed by the League in 1940. He says, "Had the Congress formed a coalition government during War along with the League, the mutual differences could have been healed." But he fails to see that the League was marching rapidly on the path of separatism with the colonial support.

The "Cripps Proposals"[27] provided a golden opportunity which was not availed by the Congress under the Gandhian leadership. Moon also criticises Gandhi for not accepting the 'Rajaji Formula.'[28] But it should be noted here that the Congress Working Committee repudiated the "Rajaji Formula." Therefore, Gandhi should not be blamed for it. But Moon is determined to hold Gandhi responsible for the partition. He says, "Thus Gandhi became a party to rejecting the Muslims' right of self-determination, the one condition on which the Hindu-Muslim accord was possible at this stage. Unwillingly by counselling the rejection of the Cripps Offer and Rajaji Formula, he had paved the way for Pakistan."[29] Since, the colonial regime was not ready to accept India's right to self-determination, Gandhi took recourse to active opposition. In spite of the fact that some leaders of the Congress opposed it, he got the 'Quit India' resolution passed. Moon designates the Quit India Movement as "a campaign of violence and sabotage."[30] He further says that in the absence of Congress leaders, Jinnah consolidated his position. But he does not refer to the active role of the British regime in the process.

Gandhi met Jinnah in 1944 when the former was released from jail. As expected this meeting failed to yield any result. Moon again blames Gandhi of offering only "a shadow and husk, a maimed, mutilated and moth-eaten Pakistan." It was rejected by Jinnah because at this stage he was asking for six provinces. Moreover, Jinnah saw in it a plan to evade the demand of Pakistan.[31] Moon holds Gandhi and the Congress responsible for the division but praises the Wavell Plan which gave veto power to Jinnah in the constitutional matters.

In the post-War period, due to its own compulsion and increasing pressure from below in India, the Metropolis Government sent Cabinet Mission to India in order to decide Indian issues. The League accepted the long-term provisions of the Cabinet Mission Plan as it had definite hope of the creation of Pakistan. The Congress accepted it conditionally. These two parties differed on the 'Grouping of provinces'[32] and 'parity in the proposed Executive Council.'[33] Obviously, the colonial regime sided with the League. In Moon's opinion Gandhi ought to have tried to persuade the Working Committee to concede the League's demand of parity at the new Executive Council and its sole right to nominate all the Muslim members. How illogical this argument is? This would have meant the acceptance of the League as sole representative of the Muslims and thereby sacrificing the nationalist Muslim leaders and masses on the altar of elite interests. Moon regards Gandhi's interventions 'decisive and disastrous'[34] though Gandhi never intervened or directed the Working Committee. On flimsy grounds, he blames Gandhi for the Working Committee's rejection of the Viceroy's proposal of the Council on communal basis.[35] This is quite ahistorical to blame Gandhiji for the decision taken by the Working Committee on democratic basis. Moon argues that the League's withdrawal of its acceptance of the Mission Plan and declaration of 16 August as the 'Direct Action Day' were the aftermath of Nehru's statement regarding long-term provisions of the Plan. He opines that the disorders that followed the Direct Action Day made the partition inevitable[36] and Gandhi is personally and fully responsible for it.

Gandhi being a mass leader now tried to protect them from the ill-designs of both the colonial regime and the indigenous elites. He tried to mitigate the adverse effect of communal riots. But Moon makes a mockery of him. He writes, "Amid the gloom Gandhi still nursed the hope that if in Bengal, Hindus and Muslim could be persuaded after recent upheavals, to live in goodwill and amity, then the whole of India might be saved and partition avoided."[37] On this basis, Moon opines that Gandhi should have accepted the League as the representative of Muslim India.

In order to buttress his long cherished hypothesis, Moon made the elections of 1946 his main plank. In this election, the League got 75 per cent of the votes in Muslim constituencies. Therefore, Moon says that it was a clear proof that the Muslims were in full support of the League and its main demand *i.e.*, the partition. But it should be noted here that the total vote cast in all Muslim seats all over the subcontinent was only 6 million, while the Muslims had a population of 79 million according to the Census of 1941.[38] Therefore, only 7.6 per cent of the total Muslim population had voted. Assuming that half of the total Muslim population would have been adult, merely 16 per cent of the adult Muslim population voted. Therefore, the conclusion that the Muslim (masses) had voted for Pakistan is ahistorical and illogical because it was the elite Muslims who had voted. Thus, Gandhi's belief that Muslim masses were still in favour of unity was not illogical.

The transfer of power became certain after Attlee's Declaration of 20 February 1947, but the Congress-League feud, in Moon's opinion, made it certain that the partition must precede the transfer of power. Gandhi advised the incoming Viceroy Mountbatten, to give up the attempt to appease both the parties simultaneously and leave India even at the risk of anarchy. But the colonial regime turned a deaf ear to this advice because it would have been a betrayal to the League. Moon would like us to believe that the colonial regime now decided to divide India in the interest of its inhabitants. The regime, he suggests, true to its benevolent nature could not leave its subjects to die.

The colonial regime now headed by Mountbatten acted at a lightning speed and proposed June Plan[39] to divide India and quit, which was accepted by the elite of both the parties though this plan was not in line with their demands. Being a philosopher in action, Gandhi could see nothing but evil in the partition. For him, partition was a calamity but since this calamity could not be averted, he began to think as to how it could be mitigated or even turned into a blessing. Therefore, separating himself from the self-interested elites and the adamant regime, he started a single-man mission for this cause. The events that followed shows that Gandhi's conclusions were not ill-founded.

Moon, in a typical imperial model, asserts that the communal divide was a pre-colonial truth and it was not the Britishers but Indians like Gandhi who widened the breach. He writes, "Gandhi's appeal to the mass-feeling aroused communal passion that existed at mass level and thus thwarted his own aim of Hindu-Muslim unity."[40] Moon also tries to reduce the role of the Gandhian era in the national movement. He argues that had Gandhi followed the constitutional path, independence would have been achieved earlier and with less disturbance and disorder, perhaps even without the disaster of partition. This statement is so funny and childish that it needs no comment. Thus, Moon has credited the colonial regime and metropolis for granting independence to India but blamed Indian social milieu and Gandhi for the partition.

To sum up, Penderal Moon's interpretation of the colonial regime and its impact on India is perfectly in tune with the elite historiography of the imperial model in which the aspirations, expectations and activities of the masses and their leader have been either totally neglected or at least undermined and distorted. In this scheme Gandhi, 'the Asian of the Century',[41] has been squarely blamed for the division of this subcontinent which was in fact imposed by the colonial set-up in collusion with the power-hungry elites of this zone of the Orient. Moon suggests that the inevitable consequence of Gandhian personality was the intensification of the Hinduisation of the Congress and the national movement which was injurious and ultimately fatal to the Hindu-Muslim unity.[42] He further blames Gandhi of his ignorance of the emergence of the League as the sole representative organisation of the Muslims. Actually, the metropolis was worried about its interests in the post-colonial phase and the indigenous elites were afraid of the mass consciousness aroused by the Gandhian mode of opposition, ideologies and strategy. They are still trying to undermine Gandhi's revolutionary ideas through negating his role and by blaming him for mistakes that he never committed. Therefore, Moon's conclusion that the largest share of responsibility for the failure to reach an agreement that could have preserved Indian unity falls on Gandhi[43] is biased and symptomatic of the classical imperial mindset.

(II) PENDERAL MOON : A MILD CRITIQUE OF IMPERIAL POLICY

Indian nationalism and the national movement had taken a new turn under the able guidance of Gandhiji, which had become visible from the last years of the second decade of twentieth century. The colonial regime had been facing 'physical'[44] as well as 'ideological'[45] challenge. It was in this situation that Penderal Moon started his career as an Indian Civil Servant with high hopes. He witnessed in person, the communal riots and human sufferings, before during and after the partition. Therefore, this administrator-turned historian was in a position to explain the events of last few decades of the Raj. In spite of the fact that he is also an ideal representative of the Oxbridge circle, he is critical of the imperial policy on some occasions. However, in ultimate analysis, he resembles with the other scholars of his school. Therefore, in tune with the imperial writings, he has tried to absolve the colonial regime of its blunders by blaming Indians and the Indian socio-cultural milieu.

Penderal Moon completed his education at the New College, Oxford. Having a good academic record and being ambitious, he appeared at the Indian Civil Services examination and qualified it in 1928 when he was only twenty two-years old. He maintained afterward that he had been the victim of propaganda. When he was a schoolboy, he had heard of this covenant service and inspired by the scope for the service in India. He was very much impressed by the nature of job to be done which had been painted in idealistic colours. Thus, Moon came to India partly from a sense of idealism believing that his work here would improve the lot of Indian masses. He liked to take responsibility and to do the things in his own way. Sometimes he liked, in Jenkin's phrase, to bait his superiors.

Moon came to India when the Simon Commission[46] was being boycotted throughout India. Possibly this is the reason that he hoped that the Raj would come to an end before his career in the ICS was over. After watching the situation in India, he felt that the 'well-intentioned' but alien administrative and judicial machinery which the British Raj had imposed on India, did more to obstruct than to promote economic progress and real justice. In this way, at the very outset, he ignores the exploitative and the oppressive nature of the British rule.

In 1938, Moon became the Private Secretary to the Governor of the Punjab. In 1941, he returned to the district work on the important post of Deputy Commissioner, Amritsar. He did not, however, keep his disagreement with the government to himself. He even expressed it in correspondence with Rajkumari Amrit Kaur. This unconventional and indecent criticism led ultimately to his resignation in 1943. Back in England, Moon started expressing his Indian experience and observations, in writings and produced his first book, *Stranger in India* (1944). In 1945 he wrote, *The Future of India.* These books deal with the contemporary Indian problems especially the constitutional problem. These works reveal the unmistakable influence of an eminent constitutional expert on India and imperial ideologue, R. Coupland.[47] Moon had come under Coupland's influence during his college days at Oxford. That is why, he joined the small compact circle of imperialist ideologues in defending the colonial regime though in a different way.

In London, Moon was associated with a small group of intellectuals centered at Chatham House. He began to advise Stafford Cripps from behind the curtain since 1945. Possibly due to this association with Cripps, Moon was appointed Secretary to the Development Board and Planning Advisory Board in 1946.

In 1947, Moon became Revenue Minister of Bahawalpur state. It was in this capacity that he witnessed the unparallel upheavals of 1947 which accompanied the end of the Raj in the Indian subcontinent. He writes that he had tried to control the disturbances which had erupted during the partition in the state. He has left a graphic and moving account of the disturbances.[48]

In 1948, he joined the service of the Independent Government of India. He served in different capacities like the Chief Commissioner, Himachal Pradesh, Chief Commissioner, Manipur and Advisor to the Planning Commission. After retirement from India, there followed a knighthood (1962) and appointment with the World Bank and the National Economic Development Board of Siam.

In 1965, he again turned to academic activities and became a fellow and also Bursar of All Souls. He introduced a new vigour in the college. It was here that he produced his *magnum opus.*[49] In 1972, he retired from All Souls but was almost immediately offered the vacant post of Assistant Editor in the Historical Section of the India Office Library and Records. During this period Mansergh[50] and his group was engaged in editing the India Office Documents on the transfer of power, 1942-47 for publication. For the next ten years (*i.e.,* up to 1982) Moon commuted two or three days a week from his farm to the Indian Office Library and Records to supervise the editorial team which benefited greatly both from his personal knowledge of men and events recorded in the documents and at a deeper level from contacts with such able minds.

In this way, it is clear from above description that Moon was a man of action with keen mind. *The Times* obituarist thought that he was basically an academic but this is a misconception. At the bottom he preferred action to contemplation. This predilection was expressed at the outset of his career by his decision to join ICS and at the end an active management of his farm at Wottom Underwood near Aylesbury. It may be said that he belonged to the tradition of gentleman scholar rather than the professional academic. He preferred to write mainly about the political foreground than the economic background, about great events rather than local conditions. His last book exemplifies his gift of presenting a clear and intelligible account of major themes, of course, with biases and gaps.[51]

Penderal Moon starts his discussion on the partition of India from the post-World War I scenario. At the very beginning he starts praising the British rule in India and negating India's freedom struggle. Like other scholars of his group, he asserts that the British were on a civilizing mission. He writes, "The emergence of India as a free self-governing country had been foreseen more than a hundred years before 1947. By the turn of the present century (twentieth) it had become an avowed object of Indian nationalists and by the World War I it was recognized by British statesmen as the inevitable outcome of the British Raj."[52] Thus, he tries to justify the British conquest and continuation of British rule. Indeed, he presents a more sophisticated version of white man's burden theory.

Being a keen and sensitive observer, Moon traces the origin of division of India not in distant past but in the recent past. He takes it back only to 1870. He tries to compartmentalize the Hindus and the Muslims. He opines that the Muslims had been much slower than the Hindus to avail themselves of Western education, to train as teachers and lawyers and to enter government services. By the time they were setting up the first Anglo-Oriental College for Mohammedans at Aligarh in 1877, S.N. Banerjee had already organised his middle-class Indian Association.[53] In this way, he is trying to show that the founder of Aligarh School, Syed Ahmad Khan was working only and only for the Muslims, right from the beginning, because they had been neglected not by the Britishers but by the Hindus. At the same time, he clearly labels the Indian Association as a Hindu middle-class organisation. He has done so primarily to justify his hypothesis that the Indian National Congress was mainly a Hindu body because in the process of evolution of nationalist organisations, the Indian

Association was the precursor of the Congress. Thus, Moon, too, starts writing on India with a typical colonial mindset. As we shall see that though he criticizes the British policy on some occasions, his aim remains constantly to defend the colonial regime and blame Indian leaders, organisations and conditions for the dark side of the British imperialism in India.

Moon has been an eye-witness to the nationalist challenge and the colonial counterattack on physical and ideological level. But instead of giving objective description, he relies on the writings on India by the West. This is the reason that he, too, like other Western scholars, sees only divisions in the Indian society. He asserts, "India's divisions are many and deep. These are caste divisions, economic divisions and political divisions. But all pale into insignificance beside the great divisions between the Hindus and Muslims. It is the conflict between these two communities which is the real barrier to liberation."[54]

In this way, Moon provides justification to the continuation of the British rule. Also, due to these divisions he regards the partition a necessity. He argues, "Unification in an Indian context must be understood very loosely as meaning the healing of divisions. In as much as India's divisions are the main obstacle to her liberation, unification in this sense is a primary political objective — even though the healing of divisions may in fact only be obtainable at the unhappy sacrifice of political unity."[55]

India's division in Moon's opinion was necessary also because the Muslims in India were a distinct community. He argues, "Though the groups lived side by side, the rigour of religious institutions had kept even neighbours apart with the result that Hindus and Muslims constituted two distinct and often antagonistic communities."[56] While on another occasion, he says that to a surprising degree Muslims are at once intermingled and yet separate and distinct.[57] In this way, he is trying to make it clear that the Hindu-Muslim division and antagonism were natural.

It should be noted here that the colonial regime resorted to constitutionalism and communalism, when the national movement began to take shape in the second half of the nineteenth century. The indigenous elites of both the communities fell victim of the communal trap laid down by the colonizers.[58] But all the imperial ideologues including Moon have denied the divisive roles played by the British. However, sometimes Moon blames some Englishmen for this. It is an open secret that the Britishers provided moral and material support to Syed Ahmad Khan. But Moon denies it simply. Ho opines that under the influence of their great leader Syed Ahmad Khan, Muslims held aloof from political organisations believing that their welfare was better protected under British rule than it would be if the Hindu dominated Congress achieved political influence.[59] Thus, speaking in a classical imperialist tone, he tries to impress that the Muslims sided with the Britishers due to their own interest. The Muslim fear of Hindu-domination was further enlarged when the nationalist movement took extremist form which took recourse to glorify India's past. This fear, he argues, manifested in abstention of Muslims from the Congress.[60]

The colonial regime introduced constitutional reforms in a way that it unfolded some new divisions and widened the existing ones. But Moon says that the British started introducing parliamentary system step by step because their aim was to train Indians in self-governance. But the Muslims were not attracted to the parliamentary system because of the dilemma inherent in it. Therefore, these reforms, he says inspired Muslims of independent action. Consequently in 1905 they formed a separate political organisation of their own, the All India Muslim League.[61] It should be noted here that the then Governor-General Minto II had actively supported the formation of the League by the Muslim elites in 1906, not in 1905. But Moon ignores it completely. Thus, Moon has tried to impress that the Muslim League was formed by the Muslims due to their consciousness and antipathy towards the Congress.

The British Government adopted the policy of carrot and stick which manifested in the Indian Council Act, 1909. But Moon regards it a great advance towards the parliamentary self-government on the British model.[62] The most notorious provision of this Act 'Separate electorate system'[63] has been defended by Moon. "It insured that the Muslims would be represented not by compromising candidate dependent on

Hindu votes but by whole-hearted champions of the Muslim interest."[64] However, he makes it clear that Minto supported the separate electorate because it would act as a counterpoise to the Congress.[65] He further criticises by arguing that the Western education might also have led young Muslims into the ranks of the liberal nationalists if Minto had not encouraged the Muslims to regard themselves as a separate community.[66] It, is clear that Moon is impartial while detailing the Act of 1909. Though he supports the separate electorate by giving it a new dimension but he also clarifies the implicit motives of the policy-makers. In this way, he differs slightly from the other scholars of his school.

The imperial capital was shifted from Calcutta to Delhi in 1911 and the partition of Bengal was annulled. Since Bengal had been partitioned to weaken the national movement and to appease the Muslim elites, the capital was shifted to conciliate Muslims. Moon writes, "Calcutta had always particularly since the partition, been a major centre of nationalist activities. It was therefore peculiarly unsuitable as an imperial capital. At the sametime Hardinge expected that establishing the imperial capital in Delhi, the seat of Mughals, would conciliate Muslim sentiments."[67] In the same manner, contrary to imperialist writings, he highlights other instances of British encouragement extended to the Muslim League. He writes, "In 1910 the Lt. Governor of U.P., J.P. Huvett, with the help of the Agha Khan, succeeded in moving the League's headquarter to Lucknow where it could be expected to be more conservative and stable."[68]

The entrance of Mahatma Gandhi into the Indian freedom struggle widened its social base horizontally and vertically and gave a new ideological dimension to it. The first all-India Gandhian movement — the Non-cooperation — proved to be the first real all-India anti-colonial mass movement.[69] This is the reason that Gandhiji had been attacked by the imperialist ideologues of different generations. In a likewise manner, Moon blames Gandhi for 'Hinduising the national movement'[70] and holds him individually responsible for the partition. He misinterprets the Mopilah rebellion and on this basis concludes that the Non-cooperation movement widened the gulf between the Hindus and the Muslims. It should be noted here that

Mopilah rebellion was out and out an agrarian movement.[71] It got communal colour only when the landlords and colonial state used unprecedented violence against them. Moon, like many other imperialist and communalist historians, calls it a Muslim holy war (*Jehad*) against the Hindus.[72] He further argues, though illogically and ahistorically, that the Muslim confidence in the Government of India began to revive and the Hindu-Muslim alliance resting on the shaky foundation of the Khilafat issue began to crumble. The Mopilah rebellion had dealt it the first blow.[73] In this way, Moon deals with Gandhiji and his movements from imperial bent of Mind.

The second half of the 1920s witnessed further intensification of the national movement. This was the reason that the British Government appointed a statutory commission in 1927, two years earlier than the scheduled date. The Secretary of State, Birkenhead, while defending this all-white, Simon Commission had challenged the Indians to produce a constitution. Indian nationalists produced 'Nehru Report' after several rounds of all-party meetings. But it could not be passed due to objections raised and concessions demanded by the fundamentalists of both the major communities. It definitely widened the gulf between the Congress and the League. But Moon blames Gandhiji personally for missing this chance of Hindu-Muslim unity.[74] In this way, Moon passes the verdict on the Nehru Report like other scholars of his group but he is critical to the Simon Commission which is rare in imperialist writings. He regards this Commission a first-class blunder and holds Irwin responsible for it.[75]

By 1930, Moon suggests the gulf between the Hindus and the Muslims had considerably widened. He assigns different contributing factors like the policy of Congress, Indian socio-cultural milieu and Gandhian leadership. Moon argues that even by 1930, the Pakistan idea was not thought of.[76] However, he traces the origin of two-nation theory from Syed Ahmad Khan and says that the latter by implication had hinted at possible division.[77] But he nowhere mentions the role of the colonial regime in it.

Thus the aim of this whole mental exercise is to show as to how the idea of Pakistan was not familiar with the three main parties — the Muslim League, the Congress (which is a

Hindu body in his words) and the British. In his words, "To the Hindu nationalists, the idea of dividing India was anathema. To the British, deemly conscious that the unification of India was one of the greatest achievements of their rule, it was not in the least attractive. And finally the Muslims saw practical difficulties in it." This was the response of Moon to 'Iqbal's proposals'[78] and 'Rahmat Ali's word Pakistan.'[79] But, Moon does not refer to them directly. However, the latent aim of Moon here is to show how the idea of Pakistan got momentum due to ill-conceived policies of the Congress.

In 1930, Gandhiji started Civil Disobedience movement mainly due to increasing pressure from below and to unite the nationalists in anti-colonial movement. The Congress popularity and erosion of colonial hegemony resulting from this movement have persuaded the imperial ideologues to criticize Gandhi and this movement.[80] In a likewise manner Moon opines, "The civil disobedience far from uniting the two communities had widened the breach between them. Muslims every where except in the Frontier Province had openly shown their contempt for the movement and their pleasure at the discomfiture of those participating in it. This attitude was resented by Hindus and tension thus created between the two communities was the background to the rioting in Kanpur."[81] This is the classical example of misuse of the history by the imperialist scholars. Moon has tried to depict Muslims in general as anti-national and attempted to show that the Hindus reacted against this attitude of the Muslims.

It should be noted here that in the 1930s, the Muslim separatism began to take definite shape. In this process, the colonial regime assisted through the Round Table Conferences (1930-32) and subsequently through the Communal Award. But Moon has bypassed all these points.

The British policy of divide and rule got definite manifestation in the Government of India Act, 1935. This Act provided for, among many things, the Provincial Autonomy for the British Indian provinces and proposed for an All India Federation comprising the British India and willing Native States. Moon gives clean chit to the British policy-makers on the ground that this Act took no account of the Pakistan chimera.[82] But he argues that due to Congress policy, this Act changed the attitude of the Muslims and position of the League and proved decisive in the partition.[83] Like other historians of his school and Pakistanese historians, Moon too, considers the failure of the Congress in forming coalition governments with the League in provinces especially in the United Provinces, the prime cause of the creation of Pakistan.[84] It should be noted here that the coalition government between the Congress and the League was not possible because both had different aims. Secondly, there was no pre-poll agreement for this between these parties. Therefore, to blame the Congress for disappointing the Muslims on this basis is not logical. Thus, we find big gap in the Moon's writings as well.

Moon further extends this argument and says that it became the main reason of growing uneasiness among the Muslims and a tendency to rally to the League and ultimately the League became in effect the only Muslim party.[85] In a likewise manner, he also blames the Congress for its policy towards the States. It should be noted here that the Congress after long debate intervened in States People Movement because of increasing pressure.[86] Moon argues that the significance of the Congress policy towards the States did not escape the notice of Muslim leaders. Jinnah termed it a camouflage to secure numerical majority in the Central Assembly. It was one of the several factors that combined at this time (1937-39) to fill the Muslims with apprehension of the Congress Raj and to cause a revolution in Muslim thinking.[87] However, on the other occasion, Moon asserts that the Muslims and States together could check the Congress domination at the centre.[88]

In this way, Moon holds the Congress responsible for the rejection of the federal section of the Act by the Muslim League and the native States. He writes that the Congress policies had scared the Muslims and the Princes into opposition to the proposed federal scheme.[89] He also holds the Congress responsible for not recognising Jinnah's legitimate claim that the League represented all-India Muslims. Therefore, the rift between the Congress and the League could not be healed.[90] In this situation, the launching of mass contact programme among the Muslims by the Congress further worsened the condition.[91] Thus, the gulf widened and culminated into the partition. He also gives supernatural reason which made the partition inevitable.[92]

In this way, the working of the Act of 1935 and the Congress policies, in Moon's opinion, strengthened the League and changed its attitude. This changed attitude reflected in the Lahore Resolution of the League in March 1940. Moon regards this resolution spontaneous and sudden.[93] Moon still has hope of regulation and compromise[94] but on the other hand regards this transition logical, and the demand for Pakistan the only alternative.[95] In the whole discussion, he nowhere mentions the British policy in strengthening the League.

It should be noted here that the Muslim League widened its base during the World War II and its demand crystallized. He holds the 'Congress'[96] as well as the 'British Policy'[97] responsible for it. He writes that had the Viceroy proclaimed that the War for freedom would end only in the freedom of India, the Congress would have been swung in favour of cooperation; in that case Jinnah would have had to cooperate too. Thus, unlike his colleagues he attacks the British Government policy but his ideological commitment and affiliations stop him from going ahead. Therefore, he returns to the stands taken by his group and blames the Congress and Gandhi for growing Muslim separatism.

The War progressed and the Congress non-cooperation in the British war effort continued. Linlithgow, in order to obtain the Congress support, made declaration of the 'August Offer'[98] in 1940. But it was rejected by the Congress because it made little advance on what had been said before. Thus, the communal and the constitutional deadlock remained as it was.

The year 1941 passed without the slightest rapprochement between the Congress and the League. Moon asserts rightly that there were several obstacles to any rapprochement, the greatest being the mutually opposite aims of the two parties.[99] Thus, the optimist Moon correctly perceived the nature of Muslim League's politics.

The year 1942 is very significant for more than one reasons in Indian and world context. The anti-colonial feeling in India was rising to the revolutionary level.[100] On the other hand, the War had also entered into a decisive phase. Therefore, Britain under international pressure, sent Cripps Mission to India. Moon explains the real motive of the Cripps proposals. He writes that the possibility of partition through the non-accession of some of the Muslim majority provinces, was for the first time publicly acknowledged by the British.[101] This attitude of the British policy, Moon asserts, increased the prestige of Jinnah even among the Muslims who did not want Pakistan because it increased the former's bargaining power.[102] These proposals could never be acceptable to the Congress.

Thus, Moon's description of the Cripps proposals is against the tradition of imperialist historiography. It seems to be objective and non-biased. But on its failure, he joins his school in denouncing Indian parties and leaders. He blames Gandhi individually for the rejection of the proposals by the Congress[103] but at another place praises Gandhi for the rejection.[104] Thus, we find Moon in dilemma. This becomes clear when he himself says that the negotiation broke down because Jawaharlal Nehru and Maulana Abul Kalam Azad wanted the Viceroy to become a constitutional head of the Government.[105] At another place, he argues that the Hindus rejected it because it had accepted the principle of partition.[106]

It should be noted here that the Cripps Mission did not fail due to Indians but it was sabotaged by Linlithgow-Amery-Churchill axis. The contemporary official correspondence shows it clearly.[107] But as we have seen Moon has blamed the Congress in general and Gandhi, Nehru and Azad in particular for the failure of the Cripps Mission. He has asserted that with its failure went the last chance of bringing the Congress and the League together.[108] As it has been shown earlier, Moon later on advised Stafford Cripps on policies. This is the reason that he is sympathetic towards Cripps and his Mission.

Moon has discussed the 'Rajaji Formula'[109] in detail. This formula was initially opposed by Gandhi and ultimately it was defeated at the Congress meeting. Moon has admired Rajgopalachari and has denounced Gandhi. Moon concludes that by rejecting Cripps proposals and Rajaji Formula, Gandhi had paved the way for Pakistan.[110]

In face of Churchillian imperialism and India's conditions, the nationalists had no option but to protest for the fulfilment of popular aspirations. Therefore, Gandhi proposed, the Congress passed and common people started and took part in the Quit India Movement which proved to be the climaxing of liberation movement. That is why, Moon like other scholars with imperial affiliations criticises Gandhi and the Congress for the call given. He uses phrases like, 'insane rebellion'[111] and 'campaign of violence and sabotage'[112] for this movement. But Moon is silent over the violent mechanisms used by the colonial regime in suppressing the movement. He also tries to minimize its role in the liberation. So much so, that he writes that it played important role in the partition. He opines, "The greatest gainers from the 1942 rebellion apart from the British authorities were Jinnah and the Muslim League. They steadily consolidated their position in the Muslim majority provinces in which they had hitherto been weakest and by the end of War were able to substantiate the claim that only the League could speak for the Muslims."[113] Thus, in describing the Quit India Movement, Moon is perfectly in tune with his group.

Mahatma Gandhi met Jinnah in 1944 but this long protracted talk (from September 9 to 27) failed to achieve any break-through. Moon opines that Gandhi was ready to offer a shadow and a husk, a maimed, mutilated and moth-eaten Pakistan.[114] Therefore, Jinnah rejected it. He further says that had it been offered in 1940 or even in 1942, Jinnah might have accepted. In this way, he is trying to impress that due to wrong strategy of the Congress and its leaders, Jinnah had become ambitious.

Moon, while discussing the post-War India, raises Wavell to high pedestal because the latter tries to solve communal and constitutional deadlock.[115] Wavell tried to reconcile conflicting aims of the Congress and the League within a united India through his plan at the Simla Conference. But his plan failed due to Jinnah's undue demands. Wavell could have implemented it but he did not do so. On the other hand, this plan even after its failure gave veto power to Jinnah in the constitutional development. But Moon does not mention it at all.[116]

The post-War period finds due echo in the writings of Moon as well. He argues that the elections of 1945-46 triumphantly vindicated Jinnah's claim to speak for the Muslims of India.[117] He has made generalisation on the basis of the fact that the League won all the Muslim seats in Central Assembly and in the Provincial Assemblies 446 out of a total of 495 Muslim seats.[118] In fact, the Muslim elites (voters) had voted for the League but Moon interprets it as if it were accepted by the Muslims in general.[119] Therefore, the generalisation is a serious mistake on the part of Moon as a historian.

The newly-elected Labour Government under the leadership of Attlee sent Cabinet Mission in 1946 to solve the Indian problems. Moon opines that the prospect of avoiding partition had considerably worsened. Therefore, the Mission did not succeed in preserving the unity of India.[120] While on the another occasion, he asserts that it failed due to its wrong approach.[121] At the sametime, he says that it failed because its rejection by the Congress and the League and its failure made the partition inevitable. Thus, he seems to be confused over the Cabinet Mission Plan.

The Muslim League started 'Direct Action' from 16 August 1946 and the colonial regime remained silent spectator. Moon has given the regional details of this violence and criticised the British officials for not controlling the violence. It should be noted here that the League had been strengthened due to active support of the regime but now it reached near its goal due to Government inaction. But Moon has escaped this point deliberately. Moreover, it is yet to be deplored whether there was any agreement or understanding between the League and the colonial regime on which basis the League members were inducted into Council without suspending the 'direct action.'

In this charged situation, the British Prime Minister Attlee made a declaration on 20 February 1947, that the British would leave India by June 1948. Moon is of the opinion that this declaration meant partition and partition within next seventeen months.[122] Now Mountbatten replaced Wavell to implement this declaration. Thus, for Moon, the partition could not be avoided now.

The viceroyalty of Wavell gets mild and almost impartial treatment in Moon's writings. He asserts that it was during Wavell's reign that decisions were taken to divide and quit. Wavell failed because he was trying to preserve the unity of

India, which was almost impossible. At the same time, Moon says that Wavell was continuously obstructed and thwarted, first by Churchill's predominantly Tory Government and then by the Labour Government of Mr. Attlee. This disharmony between Wavell and the successive British Governments was frustrating for him personally and calamitous for India. Moon concludes, "It made partition with all its disasters inevitable."[123] Thus, unconventionally, he holds the British Government especially Churchill's Government responsible for the partition.[124] In this way, he occupies a unique place in the row of imperialist ideologues.

Thus, Moon has tried to impress that when Mountbatten arrived in India, a firm basis for agreement between the parties already existed. This is the reason that Mountbatten acted at the lightning speed for the end of the Raj. Moon criticizes this 'indecent haste.'[125] But Moon's failure as a historian lies in the fact that he fails to answer as to why the June Plan was accepted by the Congress and Gandhi. He also fails to explain the reason for preponing the date for the transfer of power from June 1948 to August 15, 1947.[126]

Thus, it becomes clear that while interpreting the partition of the Indian subcontinent, Moon blames different parties at different points of time. He writes, "The Congress must share the blame and, of course, blame also attaches to the Muslim politicians and to some extent to the British who at a critical time showed little interest in bringing the parties together. But the largest share of responsibility for the failure to reach an agreement that could have preserved Indian unity appears to fall on Gandhi and the Congress though it were they who desired to prevent it."[127] He too, like other scholars of Oxbridge school, sees partition from necessary and inevitable angle.[128]

(III) R.J. MOORE : CONSTITUTIONAL REFORMS AND PARTITION OF INDIA

The colonial regime, faced with nationalist challenge, refined and gave definite and refined shape to its long cherished policy of divide and rule. Communalism, the most important among divisive forces and a direct product of colonial India, proved to be a fruitful tool for the colonial rulers in sustaining their rule, had to be reconciled with the nationalists' demand. Therefore, they took recourse to constitutionalism. But it were colonial and communal factors which decided the timing and shaped the nature of the constitutional reforms especially in the twentieth century. That is why, constitutionalism was designed in order to cater to the minimal nationalist demand and at the same time to intensify communalism. The colonial regime devised gradual devolution of power against the nationalist demand of Swaraj at once. This stage-wise devolution generated a crisis which was partially resolved by thrusting the partition upon the people of the Indian subcontinent in 1947.

This constitutionalism has been interpreted differently by the historians of different schools. The historians of imperial school — both amateurs and professionals belonging to different generations — have pondered over this issue. R.J. Moore[129] occupies prominent place among such historians. It has been attempted here to analyse his writings on historigraphical line, so that the gap between his professed objectivity and actual work could be ascertained and bridged and his place among imperial ideologues could be determined.

R.J. Moore starts his discussion from 1917, when the Secretary of State for India, Montague made a declaration in the British Parliament pertaining to the aim of British Policy on India. This August Declaration has been regarded as 'revolutionary' because it has been argued that the process of devolution started henceforth. This process pushed Indian parties apart.[130] The process inaugurated in 1917 largely with an aim to rally support in World War I time, was only completed thirty years later when the Second World War had exposed the palpable inadequacy of British resources in sustaining the Empire.[131] Moore opines that the main Indian problem was freedom with unity, which also came into focus since Montague's revolutionary declaration of 1917.[132] This devolutionary process intensified crisis in terms of Indian unity, which was resolved through the partition of India in 1947.[133]

Thus, Moore has deliberately neglected the "Separate electorate system"[134] which was introduced in 1909 through Indian Council Act and perpetuated thereafter. Henceforth, it became a major tool to further the imperial policy of 'divide and rule.' Actually, it was not the devolutionary process which created crisis, rather it intensified the divide. It was the separate electorate system which gave birth to new and nourished older divisions which complicated the constitutional problem.

The Mountague-Chelmsford Reform of 1919 and its reverberations found loud echoes in Moore's writings in typical imperial framework. Moore says that the Act of 1919 devolved real power, which introduced several cleavages in Indian politics. It were the separate electorate and the dyarchy provisions of the Act which widened the gulf but, these have been defended by him. He says that the failure of the Congress to respond to the policy of devolution by stages had resulted in a series of fissures. Groups not entirely satisfied with the strategy or leadership of the Congress, emerged one by one to take advantage of the new opportunities.[135]

In the Act of 1919 separate electorate system was further expanded. But Moore argues that it was the implementation in substance of the Congress-League scheme of representation envisaged in the Lucknow Pact.[136] In his opinion, the dyarchy gave Indian ministers power and privilege to extend patronage in important departments of State.[137] The Muslims, who supported the Act, have been praised as "farsighted." In Moore's opinion these Muslims developed a constitutional scheme at variance with the Congress because they enjoyed the fruits of devolution in their majority provinces.[138] The lesson was clear : Muslims should press for further Muslim majority provinces to be carved out of British India and for steady devolution of central authority upon autonomous provinces.[139] The intensification of communalism has been explained in terms of Congress non-cooperation to constitutional reform.[140]

The hollowness of the Act of 1919 and the success of Swarajist politics played decisive role in the appointment of a statutory commission in 1927, two year earlier than the scheduled date. This Simon Commission was boycotted by Indians with few exceptions. However, Moore has converted this exception into norms. He opines that the Secretary of State's announcement regarding the appointment of Simon Commission was to sound the depth of cleavages caused by the strains of a decade of devolution.[141] Except a section of the Hindu Mahasabha, a section of the Muslim League and the Justice

Party, all other parties and groups resolved to boycott the Commission. But Moore suggests that only the Hindus boycotted.[142] Moreover, the Shafi faction of the Muslim League, which did not boycott the Commission, has been equated with the general opinion of the Muslims in majority provinces of Bengal and the Punjab.[143]

In response to the Simon Commission and the challenge of Birkenhead, the Indian nationalists united and the Nehru Report was prepared. It was the first attempt of Indians to frame their own constitution. But Moore's imperial affiliation compels him to label the Report as essentially a nationalist Hindu Plan.[144] This is the reason, he argues, that it alienated not only Jinnah's League but also the Princes. In December 1928, at the All-Party Conference held in Calcutta, Jinnah rejected the Report mainly due to opposition of the Mahasabhites. The Muslim League rejected the Report, but Moore opines that actually the Muslims rejected Nehru Report.[145] Thus, he equates the Muslim League with Muslims of India and concludes that a decade of devolution had sharpened the conflict between the majority community in British India and the minorities.[146] And the bargaining position of the Muslims and the Hindus left no room for communal agreement.

In order to mobilise support for the Simon Commission, Irwin declared grant of Dominion Status as the aim of the Raj and announced a conference in London to discuss constitutional advance. Some prominent leaders of the Congress met at Delhi and issued a manifesto offering cooperation with Britain in framing the proposed constitution. The manifesto interpreted Irwin's declaration to mean that the conference was to meet not to discuss when the Dominion Status was to be established but to frame a scheme of Dominion constitution for India. This interpretation was rejected by Irwin as well as His Majesty Government. For the imperial authority, the conference was to be the means of ascertaining views, not an organ for negotiation. Therefore, the Congress decided not to attend the conference.

The Congress declared complete independence (*Purna Swaraj*) as its goal in the Lahore session in 1929. Moore argues that Gandhi preserved substantial unity of the Congress by bowing to the younger Nehru, though older Congressmen — Moderates, Muslims, Hindu communalists and industrialists

— regarded the resolution as a mistake.[147] In this way, he tries to show that the Congress' rejection of the conference method and adoption of agitational method created disunity. In reality, the Congress decided to start a movement due to the Government's denial of dominionhood.[148] Between 1930 and 1932 three Round Table Conferences were organised to discuss constitutional concessions for India. The British Government utilised this opportunity to foster disunity in India. Three Round Table Conferences and many less formal gatherings failed to produce a federal structure with attractions sufficient to ensure the Princely accession that were required for India's safe and steady advance to central responsibility.[149] The Hindu-Muslim dispute over residuary power was not resolved.

The Act of 1935 has been interpreted as a decisive factor in the partition of India. In the absence of the Congress, the constitution that was developed between 1930 and 1935 favoured the Princes and the Muslims. It seemed to take India closer to responsible self-government but it really contributed to further dissent. While it did provide a central responsibility within a strong federation, it allowed the Princes to veto this step and the Muslims to posit themselves against it.[150] Like other imperialist historians Moore, too, blames Congress for the failure of the two most important provisions of the Act which, in turn, stimulated separatism. He opines that, in order to explain the Princes' failure to accede to all India Federation, it is unnecessary in final analysis to look beyond the policies that Congress developed towards the States.[151]

The Congress contested elections to the new provincial councils in 1936-37 and accepted office but, in Moore's view, with disastrous consequences for all-India Federation.[152] He further says that the Congress denied the Muslim population any say in the government. A sense of exclusion and even persecution drove the Muslims into hostility against the Act.[153] From the time of the Congress' election triumph and the formation of the Provincial ministries, the ambassador of the Hindu-Muslim unity and the Muslim League became steadily more separatist in outlook.[154] Thus, Moore falls in line with typical imperialist ideologues.

The Congress was leading a national movement and therefore, it was necessary to ensure unity and discipline in the party. But all imperialist historians blame Congress for it. The Congress' attempt to overturn the balance of federal constitution by seeking to impose uniform policies upon the Congress provinces through the Congress Working Committee also stimulated the growth of Muslim separatism.[155] Moore would like to give the impression that the failure of the Congress to include the Muslim League in the provincial ministries, especially in United Provinces, played an important role in Muslim separatism.[156] By 1939, the Muslim League condemned responsible self-government as a constitutional ideal, unsuited to the realities of Indian politics.[157] Thus, the devolution of power by stages, coupled with the uncooperative and unconciliatory policies of the Congress, enlarged the obstacles to the achievement of Dominionhood by a united India.

In Moore's opinion, the Conservative Government policy along with the Congress, made Pakistan a possibility in the 1930s. Between 1930 and 1935, Britain brought into being a powerful block of autonomous Muslim provinces in eastern and north-west India, a strong base for Muslim bargaining when the question of Central Government emerged in more real terms after the Federal scheme collapsed. It made Pakistan plausible.[158] He further argues that if Britain wanted Indian unity, her main problem in early thirties was to achieve an accord between the two communities. This may not have been impossible. Amity might have been encouraged.[159] Indeed the tendency of the policy was to alienate rather than reconcile the communities.[160] In 1938 itself, Zetland concluded that the dominant factor in determining the future form of Government of India would prove to be the All India Muslim League.[161] In this way, separate electorate in combination with devolutionary process, stimulated separatism. The separate electorate of Minto introduced at least in part out of a respect for minority interest, had been perpetuated by Montague and Chelmsford. The Communal Award embodied in the Act of 1935, wove together the strands of communalism and separatism by giving the Muslims virtually perpetual majorities in the legislature of the Punjab, Sind, the North-West Frontier Province and Bengal.[162]

The complex constitutional problem was further complicated due to the outbreak of the Second World War in September

1939. His Majesty's Government misjudged Indian situation and announced India on war without taking its consent. The Congress again returned to the policy of non-cooperation. The crystallisation of demands of the Congress and the Muslim League, made Linlithgow aware of the true nature of the Indian problem soon after the outbreak of the War. But in the absence of effective diplomacy during the first year of the War, the gap between British policy and Congress demands became a gulf, the communal rift became a chasm and party resolutions hardened into ultimata.[163] The Congress demanded a national government and British declaration of War aim for India, while the League demanded that it should be regarded as the only organisation that could speak for the Muslim India. Thus, British Government was on the horn of a painful dilemma.

Moore argues that during the War, the Conservative Home Government and Linlithgow did little to solve the communal deadlock. The Ramgarh demand of the Congress for 'complete independence,' was the result of Britain's failure to have amicable relations with the Congress and it was quickly followed by the Lahore Resolution of the Muslim League. Thus, the Congress and the League took extreme positions. Moore emphatically argues that perhaps Ramgarh and Lahore resolutions marked the beginning of the end of Indian unity.[164]

The British Government in order to solve the constitutional deadlock, made several attempts but failed. The first concerted effort resulted in the August Offer of Linlithgow in 1940.[165] It was rejected by all parties. In 1942 international pressure and Labour initiative produced Cripps Mission.[166] Moore blames Linlithgow-Churchill-Amery axis for the failure of this Labour initiative.[167] The defeat of the Cripps Offer in 1942 was a watershed in the history of the partition of India.[168] The constitutional deadlock that followed the failure of the Cripps Mission gave Jinnah and the League three years in which to strengthen their organisation and extend their influence.[169] Moore holds Churchill responsible for partition on several counts including his onslaught on Cripps. The repudiation of Cripps in 1942 was one of many bricks that Churchill placed in the walls of partition.[170] Moreover, Moore argues that success of Cripps Mission could have averted the partition.[171] The indefinite postponement of national government at the centre, the removal of the Congress from competition in provincial politics and the recognition of Jinnah as the Muslim spokesman on all India problems encouraged and enabled the League to capture power by constitutional process in all but one of the component provinces of the putative Pakistan. "The Cripps Offer was the only War-time attempt to arrest the trend."[172]

The Labour Government tried to solve the Indian problem from post-imperial perspectives and despatched the Cabinet Mission in 1946.[173] The League was ready to accept the Cabinet Mission plan on the assumption that grouping of Muslim provinces into sections B and C was compulsory and the League would enjoy parity with the Congress in an Interim Government. Moore says that the League's strategy was frustrated by the Congress and His Majesty's Government. In August 1946 Jinnah was driven to a course of 'Direct Action' by his mistrust of the Congress and His Majesty's Government infirmity.[174]

In September the Muslim League joined Interim Government to wreck it from within. The situation further worsened. Moore opines that the outcome of negotiations in 1947, a dual transfer of power to a single truncated Pakistan dominion and a single Indian dominion, flowed from the Congress policy and His Majesty Government's acquiescence in it.[175] Before the arrival of Mountbatten, the Congress had reconciled itself to the partition.[176] The achievement of Mountbatten is that the elusive condition of a successful transfer of power, *i.e.*, the agreement between the Congress and the League, had at last been fulfilled.[177]

To sum up, R.J. Moore, like other prominent ideologues of the imperial school, has interpreted the partition with a predetermined and preoccupied mindset. His aim is to justify the colonial policy and absolve it of any reponsibility in the partition. He defends the colonial policy of divide and rule and constitutionalism and blames the Congress and Indian condition for the partition. "The devolution of power by stages was bound to involve the attachment to the Raj of individuals or communities whose interests were served by collaboration. 'Attaching in order to devolve' is not necessarily the same as 'dividing in order to rule.' However, the devolution of power by stages did contribute substantially to the eventual partition of India. This was largely because the Congress refused to cooperate with the Raj unless it was accorded plenipotentiary status, yet failed to secure a mandate from the Muslims."[178]

(IV) R.J. MOORE : THE NEO-IMPERIAL APPROACH TO PARTITION

R.J. Moore's writings represent the recent imperialist approach to the modern Indian history in general and the partition of India in particular. While maintaining the tradition of British historiography, he has analysed the last four decades of the British Raj in the Indian subcontinent in a more critical way. He has some significant advantage over the other historians of his school. By the time he started his writings on India, the British Government had started publishing the Documents and Records of the India Office Library. By that time, other writings on the partition had either become obsolete or had exhibited their relevance in understanding the dynamics of historical events. To top it all, East Pakistan had declared independence, therefore some of the earlier assumptions had been weakened or disappeared. In this background, Moore has utilised his genius and available sources to produce a series of works covering the period 1917 to 1947. He occupies an important place among the imperialist scholars writing on partition.[179]

Unlike other ideologues of his school, Moore has tried to explain different factors and parallel processes contributing to the partition. For instance, he interprets the 'Separate Electorate'[180] as an important factor responsible for the perpetuation of communalism and separatism through different constitutional attempts. He writes "The separate electorate of Minto introduced at least in part out of a respect for minority interest, had been perpetuated by Montague-Chelmsford. The Communal Award embodied in the Act of 1935 wove together the strands of communalism and separatism by giving the Muslims virtually perpetual majorities in the legislatures of the Punjab, Sind, the North-West Frontier Province and Bengal."[181] He further holds the imperial regime responsible for the partition. He opines, "From 1917 to 1945 British constitutional strategies and the Viceregal diplomacy were concerned primarily with underpining imperial governance with Indian collaborative structures. In the process legitimacy was accorded to blocks in the Congress path to national freedom with unity.[182] In this way, as we shall see in the following pages, Moore has tried his best to evaluate more objectively the role played by the British, the Congress and the Muslim League in the partition of India.

R.J. Moore starts his discussion in the background of the World War I and opines that the core of the British policy towards India was the reconciliation of the principles of freedom and unity.[183] In accordance with this broad policy and other unavoidable reasons, the British Government took recourse to the process of gradual devolution of power. This gradual devolution, as opposed to the Congress demand of freedom at once, created a crisis of unity which could be resolved through the partition.[184]

The British Government introduced Montague-Chelmsford Reforms in 1919 which was said to be the culmination of Montague's August declaration of 1917.[185] This Act further expanded the separate electorate system and introduced dyarchy in provinces which was full of drawbacks. However, this Act has been defended by Moore like other imperial ideologues. He writes, "The Preambles' provision of this Act for advance by progressive successive stages was a logical approach to the problem of constitutional and social heterogeneity. Responsibility must be devolved gradually, for Britain was obliged to protect the Princes and the minorities, until they were prepared to entrust their interest to a self-governing dominion."[186] He also defends it by saying that it implemented in substance the Congress-League scheme of representation.[187] It should be noted here that Moore derives this conclusion from the Lucknow Pact signed between the Congress and the Muslim League in 1916. In this way, Moore's description of the Act is not impartial and objective, rather tilted towards the imperial ideology.

However, he has described the effects of this Act on the Indian polity in fairly objective manner. He is of the view that the later demands by the Muslims of a federal structure and more Muslim-majority provinces resulted when the Act of 1919 was implemented. He writes, "The Montford Reforms left the Central Government intact. However, the provinces were divided along communal line. Aided by separate electorate even in their majority provinces, Muslim parties ware able to enjoy ministerial power, most notably in the Punjab and Bengal. In so doing they soon realized the advantages to them of a federal form of constitutional development."[188] He further argues that the decentralisation, devolution and the right of the members brought power to Muslim politicians in the majority provinces. The lesson was clear : Muslims should press for further Muslims majority provinces being carved out of British India and for the steady devolution of central authority upon autonomous provinces.[189] Moore rising above his ideological affiliation projects the divisive nature of the Act of 1919.

As we know that the Congress decided not to cooperate with this Act and started the anti-colonial Non-cooperation Movement under the leadership of Gandhi. This first all-India Gandhian movement resulted into considerable erosion of colonial hegemony. Therefore, all British historians denounce this movement in different ways. Moore by citing the formation of Khilafat Swaraj Party and subsequent split in it, emphasized that the failure of the Congress to respond to the policy of devolution by stages had resulted into a series of fissures.[190] He does accept the strength of the Non-cooperation Movement but like classic imperialist ideologues, explains the 'Mopilah rebellion'[191] in a communal colour and generalised it as all Indian trend. He writes, "In August the bloody rising of the Muslim peasants (the Mopilahs) on the Malabar coast against their Hindu landlords brought latent communal animosities to the surface all over India."[192] In this way, Moore's approach to the Government of India Act 1919 and the Non-cooperation Movement is relatively less biased but by and large in line with the imperialist writings.

It should be noted here that the Khilafat Swaraj Party in combination with other parties, made the Montford Reforms unworkable. Therefore, the British Government had to appoint the Simon Commission in 1927, two years earlier of the scheduled date. However, Moore has negated the role of the Swarajist politics in the national movement. He further suggests that the Secretary of State's announcement regarding the appointment of Simon Commission was to sound the depth of the cleavages caused by the strains of a decade of devolution.[193] This conclusion is based on the hypothesis that Indian did not oppose the Commission unanimously. It is true that a section of the Muslim League and the Justice Party did not oppose it because of their vested interest. But generalising this exception and regarding it as divide in the nationalist rank is historically not wise.

The Indians' response to the challenge of the Secretary of State was the Nehru Report, prepared by All-Party Committee. Negating the known facts, Moore calls it essentially a plan by the nationalist Hindus. Therefore, it was rejected by the Muslims. But it should be pointed out here that this report could not be ratified due to fundamentalists, pressure from both the communities. Moore opines that the bargaining position of the Muslims and the Hindus left little room for communal agreement. The Jinnah-Jayakar debate at the All-Party Conference at Calcutta, marked a turning point in the Hindu-Muslim negotiations for an agreed solution to the communal problem.[194] Thus, through sheer generalisation, Moore is trying to impress that the Muslims in general rejected the Nehru Report. The main reason for this conflict and divergence, in his view, was the gradual devolution of power.[195] In this way, his description of the Simon Commission and its aftermath, is symptomatic of imperial mindset.

Irwin, the then Viceroy declared that the purpose of the Raj was to grant 'Dominion status'[196] and a conference would be organised to discuss the future course of constitutional reforms. Motilal Nehru called an all-Party meeting in Delhi and a manifesto was issued which offered cooperation with the British in framing the new constitution. This manifesto also interpreted Irwin's declaration to mean that the conference was to be convened not to discuss when the Dominion status was to be established but to frame a scheme of Dominion constitution for India. Moore writes, "This manifesto masked for a brief moment the division within the nationalists rank over the declaration."[197] Possibly it was this unity which compelled the British Government to deny the interpretation of Irwin's declaration put forward in the Delhi manifesto. But Moore's imperialist affiliation has persuaded him to refrain from this discussion.

The Congress under the guidance of Gandhi moved forward and changed its aim from the establishment of Dominion status to the attainment of *Purna Swaraj* (Complete independence) in the Lahore session in 1929. In the changed circumstances and with changed aim Gandhi decided to start the Civil Disobedience Movement by breaking Salt Law in 1930. This Gandhian repudiation of conference method and adoption of confrontation method have found sufficient echo in the writings of Moore too. He writes that Gandhi preserved substantial unity of the Congress by bowing to the younger Nehru, though older Congressmen, Moderates, Muslims, Hindu communalists and industrialists regarded the resolution (*Purna Swaraj*) a mistake.[198] Thus, Moore like his co-ideologues tries to impress that the Muslims in general did not take part in the Civil Disobedience Movement. But differing from his school, he blames the British Government for this state of affairs.[199] He opines that to save the Simon Report, Reading and others compelled Irwin to drop his plan.[200]

Obviously, therefore, the Congress decided not to attend the Round Table Conferences and concentrated on the movement. Moore supports the Gandhian decision of not attending the conference in that circumstances. He argues, "It is scarcely surprising that Gandhi refused to attend a conference in London without being assured of either Indian unity or Government support for Indian freedom."[201] Maintaining the tradition of Oxbridge group, Moore calls the Civil Disobedience an "experiment in anarchy"[202] but unlike his group he praises Gandhian leadership for obtaining unexpected massive support.[203] Thus, he concludes that Gandhi succeeded in achieving national unity during the conflict. But he asserts that Gandhi's main problem was to secure in peace, the unity achieved in conflict.[204]

It should be noted here that while the Congress was deeply involved in the anti-colonial movement, the first Round Table Conference was organised in London. Moore says that the Indian delegates remained divided over what was to be demanded. On the other hand, he writes that prior to the conference itself, it had been agreed that the British delegations would work as a single parliamentary team.[205] He even suggests that a common policy in advance had been formulated. Thus,

Moore has brought forth the secret game of the British Government during the Round Table Conference. He writes that All-India Federation was the dominant principle throughout the nine weeks of the first Round Table Conference. All of the major delegations subscribed to it. The Federal Structure Committee, chaired by Sankey, submitted its report on 15 January 1931. MacDonald declared the conference closed on 19 January with pledge of central responsibility with safeguards. Moore comments that it enabled Sapru and Liberals to go home with the claim that they had extracted a promise of Dominion status with safeguards. It left Irwin and Benn to reflect that a year of civil disorders might have been avoided if only Reading had been so liberal in 1929.[206] In this way, Moore has criticised the imperialist policy and policy-makers at this juncture.

Coming back to India, Sapru and Jayakar mediated between the Congress and colonial regime. It resulted into 'Gandhi-Irwin Pact'[207] signed in March 1931. Moore opines that the settlement was a truce rather than a peace, the suspension rather than the abandonment of the civil disobedience.[208] To ratify this pact Congress met at Karachi. The Nehru resolutions on Fundamental Rights and Economic Policy were accepted at this session. Moore is of the opinion that it alarmed Muslim elites and the Princes.[209] Moore concludes that the deepest of Indian division continued to be that of between the Hindus and the Muslims. As a result of the Gandhi-Irwin Pact, Gandhi attended the second Round Table Conference in 1931 but returned home after greater disappointment.

Moore tries to impress that the Muslims had crystallised their views on Muslim India by 1931. Their demand in relation to Hindu India was not unlike that of Gandhi in relation to Britain. They wanted partnership not subordination. Their strategy was first to destroy the unitary Raj and consolidate their strength in some of the fragments, then to enter into a voluntary partnership with the Hindu India fragments, always retaining the right to secession.[210] In this way, Moore tries to conceal the separatist nature of the Muslim League and its movement by equating it with the anti-colonial movement led by Gandhi and the Congress.

The second Round Table Conference failed to solve the communal problem mainly because of the communal and colonial connivance. But Moore blames the Muslims' attitude responsible for it. He writes, "The deadlock was the result of the Muslims having concerted a clear programme in advance and refusing to surrender any part of it."[211] He also blames minor minorities, Sikhs and Mahasabhites for it. It is clear that he does not refer to the British policy during this conference which emphasised the need of expansion of the separate electorate. Gandhiji opposed the expansion of separate electorate but in vain. The failure of the consultations at the second Round Table Conference placed the initiative with the imperial Government and more particularly with Tory Secretary of State. Samuel Hoare envisaged a plan which included almost all the demands of the Muslim and minor minorities. Moore writes, "Hindus sensed that the tide had turned. A Tory-bureaucratic-Muslim alliance was at hand."[212] Thus, it seems that he, too, is aware of the colonial-communal alliance working against the nationalist plan but accepts it by saying it Hindu feelings.

It should be noted here that after the collapse of the second Round Table Conference, the Home Government and the Government of India favoured the divisive forces in India. This trend has been clearly mentioned by Moore. He argues, "In 1931 when Gandhi's repudiation of the conference formula was added to the economic crisis, the 'Crescent card' became a trump in the hands of the Conservative and Unionist party."[213] To wean Muslims away from the civil disobedience, Hoare proposed two phased plan by postponing the federation for five or probably ten years and by giving early satisfaction to Muslims' claim of Provincial Autonomy.[214] Moore opines that this two-phase plan was symptomatic of a British concern for Muslims' support that grew at the possibility of reaching agreement with Gandhi.[215] In India Wellingdon, too, became solicitous of Muslim interest after the second Round Table Conference and assured the Muslims that the communal problem would be settled with an Award.[216] In this way, we see that in spite of his imperial affiliation, Moore has tried to assess the British policy very objectively during this period. Possibly, due to his aversion to Tory Government, he has been more objective here.

Coming back, Gandhiji tried to revive the civil disobedience but this time the colonial set-up suppressed it with heavy hands. Unlike the imperialist tradition, Moore recognised the success and strength of the civil disobedience. He argues that the preparation of such a heavy artillery from fear of the organised might of the Congress was in itself recognition of the success of Gandhi's experiment.[217] He further opines that the repressive policy was adopted from the need to reassure Muslim collaborators of the supremacy of the Raj and to prevent their desertion to the Congress as the presumed successor authority.[218]

In this way, the writings of Moore have shown emphatically that the sole aim of the Home Government and Government of India was to appease forces other than the Congress. Indeed, the tendency of the policy was to alienate rather than to reconcile the communities.[219] Moore suggests that in spite of opposition by Gandhi and liberals, Hoare and Wellingdon were convinced to appease the Muslims and minor minorities through the Communal Award.[220] This Communal Award, he argues, was a His Majesty's Government's attempt to vivisect and disrupt Hinduism but it was averted by Gandhi's opposition.[221] In spite of its failure, this Award succeeded in consolidating the Muslim loyalty to the Raj.[222] Thus, we see that Moore is critical to British Government's policy towards India during this period.

Even after the collapse of the second Round Table Conference, the British Government decided to convene the third and last Round Table Conference. Moore opines that essentially Conservative Government gave little away by agreeing to the third Round Table Conference. Yet it achieved impressive sectional support, from the commercial community, the liberals, the Muslim, the Hindu Moderates, the untouchables and leading Mahasabhites. The Congress was effectively isolated from the other British Indian parties.[223] This was a conference only in name. Hoare and Sankey had decided the agenda and the issues prior to it.[224] In this way, the conference achieved little by way of agreed solution to the outstanding constitutional problems. The conference closed the way for the measured series of stages necessary to parliamentary legislation.[225]

The result of the vigorous exercise of nearly a decade was the Government of India Act, 1935. This Act among many things provided for Provincial Autonomy and proposed an All India Federation. Moore has discussed this Act in detail and concluded that inherent weaknesses of this Act and policies and attitudes of the Congress, the Muslim League and Princes made the partition almost inevitable. He writes that the Muslims fared well. They obtained full provincial status for the North-West Frontier Province, the separation of Sind, a virtual statutory majority in the Punjab and an assured 48.6 per cent of the seats in Bengal. In short, they achieved power in four autonomous provinces. They also obtained separate electorate.[226] However, Moore tries to defend this collaborative imperial policy which disunited India and Indians and blames Congress for it. He writes, "In the absence of the Congress, the constitution that was made between 1930 and 1935 favoured the Princes and the Muslims. It seemed to take India a step closer to responsible self-government but it really contributed to disunity."[227]

In 1936-37, elections were held to implement the Provincial Autonomy. The Congress got over 50 per cent of the total votes cast. Moore, separating himself from his group, calls it the result of the Congress popularity mainly due to civil disobedience.[228] But like his colleagues, he, too, blames the working of the Provincial Congress Ministries for encouraging separatism in more than one way.[229] Finally, he, holds the Congress policy responsible for making the Muslim League more separatist. He argues that the grievances against the Congress Ministries developed through assault on the Muslim culture and religion and Urdu language. They culminated in fear that the Congress High Command would obtain dominance at the federal level, thereby reiterating the balance between Muslim and Hindu provinces. Alarm at the strength of the centralised Congress machinery and of Congress unitarianism, converted the League into a Muslim separatist organisation.[230]

The proposed federation has been discussed in its possible detail. While discussing the federal constitution and its final suspension in 1939, Moore argues that the collapse of the Paper Federation in 1939 precipitated a crisis of freedom.[231] He has assessed the role of the British Government, the Government of India, Linlithgow, the Congress, the League and the Princely States in the failure of the proposed federation. He seems to be more objective here.[232] He asserts that the proposed All India Federation failed due to inherent weaknesses.[233] However, he places major responsibility on Indians themselves. He argues that the States' accession was not simply a matter at issue between the Government of India and the Princes. It came to acquire a communal dimension. The activities of the Congress and the Muslim League were largely responsible for the failure of the Princes to accede.[234] In this way, we see that Moore, too, tries to defend the colonial policy.

It was in this situation that a world crisis came in the form of World War II. It further complicated the already complex Indian problem. India was declared on war without taking its consent. Different Indian parties and personalities differed over the next step to be taken. Therefore, the problem of freedom with unity could not be solved immediately. Moore holds the British Indian Government responsible for not solving Indian problems. He further argues, "In the absence of effective diplomacy during the first year of War, the gap between the British policy and the Congress demands became a gulf, the communal rift became a chasm and party resolutions hardened into ultimata."[235] For the ineffectiveness and insincerity, Moore criticises Linlithgow and says that the latter believed that he had the trump card. For as long as the Congress failed to secure the amity of the Muslims, it remained impossible to meet their demand for self-government. The existing discord between the communities could strengthen Britain's control in India for many years.[236] In this way, Moore occupies a unique place among the Oxbridge group because of his critical assessment of the British policy towards India especially during the War.

However, in the second year of the War, the British Government was in mood to break the constitutional deadlock. The Secretary of State, Zetland took several steps in this direction. He was even ready to provide a constitution-making body.[237] But it was refused by the Cabinet in December 1939.

He again tried the Cabinet to realise the need for action to prevent the Indian situation from reaching a stage of utter intractability. This time the Cabinet was ready to discuss it, but waited for Linlithgow's assessment of Indian situation. But before he could budge it, both the Congress (by claiming complete independence at Ramgarh on 20 March) and the Muslim League (by claiming Pakistan at Labore on 24 March) adopted unapproachable postures.[238] Moore locates this Pakistan Resolution in the logic of the Act of 1935. He writes, "The very creation of autonomous Muslim Provinces under the Act of 1935, encouraged and validated the demand for separate nationhood. The Muslim League's achievement was to convert the process of provincialisation into the process of separation. Defeated by the Congress in the politics of Indian unity, Muslims sought refuge through the politics of Partition."[239] Thus, he indicates that by 1940, the partition became almost a definite possibility due to the function of the colonial-communal and nationalist politics.

The new Secretary of State, Amery pressurised Linlithgow and the fall of France compelled Britain to enlist India's active cooperation. The result was the 8 August Offer of 1940. The original draft of Linlithgow, Moore says, had been revised by Churchill himself.[240] But on the other occasion, he himself asserts that Amery's draft finally appeared as Linlithgow's August Offer.[241] Whosoever had drafted this offer, it was rejected by all the Indian parties.[242] Moore has interpreted this slowness on the part of Linlithgow as a diplomatic failure, who could neither accept the Congress demand nor tried to allay Muslim apprehensions. Contrary to his ideological affiliation, he further argues that it is difficult to avoid the conclusion that Linlithgow was merely interested in preserving a policy to retain the support of the Muslims rather than in solving the problem of devising safeguards to accommodate the Muslims within a united India.[243]

In this way, we see that the colonial regime, too, has been held responsible for the Pakistan Resolution of the League. At the same time, Moore says that it was logical in that situation and relates it with the Congress policy. The communal dialectics that had become the dynamic force of the Indian politics between 1937 and 1939 meant that each Congress resolution provoked a Muslim reply. The Ramgarh demand for complete independence, the result of Britain's failure to treat with the Congress was quickly followed by the Lahore Resolution.[244] But this correlation is illogical and ahistorical because the Congress resolution was aimed at freeing the motherland from colonial yoke while that of the Muslim League proposed the division of India.

Thus, in Moore's scheme, 1940 was a decisive year in the history of India's freedom and partition. Perhaps the Ramgarh and Lahore Resolutions marked the beginning of the end of Indian unity or perhaps end should be dated from Churchill's frustration of Linlithgow's belated initiative.[245] No doubt, the year 1940 proved to be a turning point in the history of this subcontinent but Moore loses his impartiality in explaining it in detail.

It should be noted here that Churchill was not ready even to discuss the Indian situation and reforms and denied the applicability of the Atlantic Charter to India in September 1941.[246] Towards the end of 1941, opinion in London was becoming favourable to a new initiative. After the Pearl Harbour (6 December 1941) the Labour and American pressure on Churchill became irresistible. The British Government response was the Cripps Mission.[247] According to one provision of the Cripps proposals, the Muslim majority provinces might opt out of the new union, once the new constitution was framed and implemented. Moore is of the opinion that it marked a historic departure in British policy on the problem of freedom with unity.[248] Actually, it was for the first time that British conceded India's right to freedom without imposing the condition of unity. No longer was the accession of the States or the agreement of all provinces, made a prerequisite to Dominionhood. This departure of Cripps has been assigned to Amery's pressure. Moore writes, "Probably Cripps accepted this new departure for which Amery was responsible because of his first-hand acquaintance with the views of Jinnah and Liaqat Ali, together with their success since 1939 in making the Muslim League the mouthpiece of Muslim nationalism."[249] Last but not least, Moore even goes to the extent of saying that it also indicated the possibility of redistribution of provincial boundaries or partition to precede the transfer of power.[250]

Thus, Moore like a professional, impartial and objective historian has clarified the pros and cons of the imperial secret game.

The Cripps proposals were rejected by all parties but due to different reasons. But even then, the negotiation was going on for the Indianisation of the Executive Council. Moore opines that in this effort Cripps could have succeeded but in between, the Mission was sabotaged by Churchill-Amery-Linlithgow triumvirate on the pretext that Cripps was bypassing Linlithgow.[251] Moore praises Cripps because the latter did not blame this triumvirate and accepted his own defeat. Thus, he kept the inside story to himself.[252]

In fact, in Moore's opinion, the Cripps Mission was a clever propaganda exercise — a plan merely so devised as to range world opinion against India, just bluff to influence American opinion. Therefore, it was bound to be destroyed by Churchill's imperialism itself. Moore rising above his group affiliation writes that the repudiation of Cripps in 1942 was one of the many bricks that Churchill placed in the wall of partition.[253]

After the failure of the Cripps Mission, the Congress started the Quit India Movement which proved to be the climaxing of the anti-colonial movement. It definitely sealed the fate of colonial regime in the Indian subcontinent.[254] But Moore nowhere mentions the epic movement and its role in the Indian freedom. Henceforth, the Churchill Government did not make any effort to solve Indian problem and the colonial regime collaborated with those who were opposed to the Congress policy. This collaboration strengthened the collaborators including the Muslim League. Moore has indicated but defended this collaborative policy of the regime. He argues, "Once declaration was made or reforms were in progress, *satyagraha* simply led Britain to rely upon the non-Congress parties and Princes. As the Congress protest movements were largely an attempt to win a national mandate by direct action, it is scarcely surprising that Indians who could not subscribe to Congress policies sought British protection under the constitution."[255]

In this way, Moore would like to impress that during the War the Churchillian imperialism effectively isolated the Congress and provided opportunity and sufficient time to the

League to strengthen itself. He writes, "The India Committee under Churchill's guidance consistently rejected the proposal of Linlithgow's successor Wavell, to revive the Cripps Plan because he regarded the Hindu-Muslim division as strength of the Raj."[256] He further tries to show as to how Churchill helped the Muslim separatism though sometimes unwillingly. He argues, "Throughout the 1930s Churchill had fought to prevent the introduction of responsibility in the Central Government. In 1940, he had so watered the draft of August Offer that the Congress were bound to reject it. In 1944-45, he was to obstruct, Wavell's scheme for a conference that would set up an Interim National Government of the type that Cripps had wanted, finally allowing the new initiative only when he felt sure of its failure. His constant intervention gave the Muslim League precious time in which to substantiate its claim to separate nationhood."[257] Thus, we see that Moore is very critical towards the Conservatives, especially towards Churchill.

Wavell convened an all-party conference at Simla (25 June-14 July). His aim was to Indianise the Executive Council on the Hindu-Muslim parity. This conference collapsed.[258] Even after its failure, it has been interpreted correctly by Moore, as the second major victory for two-nation theory, the first being the August Offer.[259] He further writes, "By applying the theory (two-Nation theory) vigorously, Jinnah engineered the nationalisation of Muslim politics throughout the War. The theory's meaning was revealed more dramatically at Simla on 25 June, when Jinnah demanded not only Hindu-Muslim parity in the Viceroy's Executive but also that all the Muslim members must be League's nominees."[260] Thus, Jinnah and the Muslim League got veto on any constitutional scheme. It should be noted here that Jinnah could have been pressurised to accept the Plan or the Congress alone could have been invited as was done in the Cabinet Mission plan. But Moore does not have any word on this indecisiveness of Wavell.

The end of the War and coming of the Labour Government under the leadership of Clement Attlee, changed the British approach towards Indian problem. Moore says that Attlee's Government viewed Indian problem from post-imperial perspectives seeking a nationalist succession compatible with the British economic interest, the stability of the subcontinent and the security of the Indian Ocean area. In consequence, an overriding value was placed upon the cooperation of the Congress and maximising Indian unity.[261] The British Government appointed Cabinet Mission for solving the Indian constitutional deadlock. This was the last chance for preserving Indian unity. Though it rejected the League's demand for Pakistan, its grouping of provinces had the potentiality to create a sovereign Pakistan.[262] This grouping has been criticised by Moore, which is unique in imperialist historiography. He writes, "It offered either truncated Pakistan or group of provinces under a union. Its refusal by Jinnah led to the rejection of fully Independent Pakistan. But it proposed a powerful sub-national Pakistan."[263]

Moore argues that the League was ready to accept the Plan on the assumption that the grouping of the Muslim provinces into sections B and C was compulsory and the League would enjoy parity with the Congress in an Interim Government.[264] As we know that the League rejected the Plan in July 1946 and decided to start Direct Action from 16 August. Moore has criticised both the Congress and His Majesty's Government for compelling the League to a course of direct action.[265] He further asserts that the League's strategy was destroyed by the Congress refusal to contemplate parity in the Interim Government or the compulsory grouping of the provinces for the constitution making together with His Majesty's Government conviction that the Congress goodwill was vital for a peaceful transfer of power. Thus, the Labour's Cabinet Mission foundered on the Pakistan issue.[266]

It should be noted here that from 16 August 1946, the communal situation of India deteriorated very fast. The pressure from below was also increasing in India, thereby threatening the regime. The post-War Britain was not in a position to maintain the Indian subcontinent by force. In this way, the British Government had to quit India. In December 1946, Churchill affirmed in the debate in parliament that the Muslim India and the Princes should be accorded Commonwealth membership. In other words, the opposition leaders in Britain were demanding the division of India. The Labour Government responded to this situation and Attlee made a Declaration in the parliament on 20 February 1947.[267] Mountbatten replaced Wavell as the Viceroy to implement this Declaration.

In this way, Moore indicates a clear deviation from older British policy of freedom with unity. He writes that the circumstances in India that contributed to the policy shift and the change of Viceroy included : the steady run-down of administration which Wavell's breakdown plan emphasised, the communal change that followed Jinnah's rejection of constitutionalism, the emergence of para-military forces and the paralysis of Nehru's communally divided Interim Government. No doubt this explanation of Indian situation is almost objective but his conclusion that there was a shift in British policy of freedom with unity seems to be fallacious. In fact, there is a continuity in the British divisive policy.

Henceforth, Moore tries to emphasize the point that before Mountbatten arrived, the Congress had reconciled itself with the Pakistan demand.[268] This conclusion is based on the 'March Resolution of the Congress.'[269] Since the creation of Pakistan, in his words, had become inevitable, Mountbatten could have neither prevented nor sensibly delayed partition. He also defends the deadly speed at which Mountbatten worked.[270]

It should be noted here that Mountbatten had drafted a Plan Balkan[271] which was rejected by Nehru. After this, the discussion between Nehru and Mountbatten, Moore says, formed the basis of the 3 June Plan which aimed at averting the fragmentation of British India.[272] He further suggests that Mountbatten's meeting with India Committee between 19 and 28 May settled the terms for the final transfer of power in accordance with the deal with Nehru. Given the necessity of Pakistan, they enabled India to achieve freedom with the greatest possible unity. They were embodied in the 3 June statement policy, which formed the basis for the enactment of Indian independence and partition well before the end of 1947.[273] In this way, Moore would like to impress that Nehru was largely responsible for the 3 June Plan which provided for the partition and independence.

We know that on the basis of this plan, India was partitioned and freed on 15 August 1947. The Indian national movement played important role in the decolonisation of India. But Moore, like his colleagues, negates the role of India's national movement in its liberation and regards it a result of the process of devolution. He writes, "The process inaugurated in 1917 largely as a means of rallying support in War time was only completed thirty year latter when the Second World War had exposed the palpable inadequacy of British resources to sustain an empire."[274] At the same time he tries to show that the partition was also natural and the best solution to the problem of freedom with unity. He opines that the ultimate solution to the problem of freedom with unity involved the partition of British India between two dominions and the accession of Princely States to one or the other of them.[275]

Thus, objectively speaking, India was partitioned under the Labour Government of Mr. Attlee. But Moore tries to give a clean chit to the Labour Government on the assumption that had the transfer of power been under the Churchillian leadership India would have had to pay even costlier price. He asserts proudly, "Under the auspices of Churchill Government a post-War transfer of power would assuredly have sundered subcontinental unity by encouraging several successor states."[276]

In this way it becomes crystal clear that Moore has explained the partition in a unique way in the sense that in spite of representing the British historiographcal tradition his interpretations are very much objective on several occasions. Overall, his is a balanced discussion of the causes and effects of events and processes leading to partition. In macro-analysis, he seems to be an ideal representative of the imperialist tradition but in micro-analysis we find that he differs from his colleagues on several important and vital issues. He is not as hostile to the Congress and leaders like Gandhiji, Nehru and Patel as his school has been. To top it all, while assessing the role of Jinnah, he has not made the latter a superman.[277] He is very critical of the Conservatives and has held Churchill individually responsible for creating dangerous speed breakers in India's path to freedom with unity. His critical attitude towards the Conservatives and Churchill has made him to suspect an alliance between the Muslim separatism and the Conservatives. On the basis of parliamentary debates in 1948, he asserts half-heartedly, "It should be much to speak of a Conservative-Muslim League accord but after March 1946, when Attlee removed Dominionhood as a step prerequisite to freedom, both the Conservative leaders and Jinnah insisted upon the right of Muslim India or Pakistan to remain in the Commonwealth. Churchill and Templewood upheld that right, the right, in effect, ultimately to divide India."[278]

In a nutshell, it may be said that R.J. Moore, in spite of belonging to the imperialist school represents a new trend in this historiographical tradition. He has utilised almost whole gamut of primary and secondary sources related with partition. To top it all, methodologically, he seems to be sound. Therefore, he is less biased and more objective. He has successfully raised himself from group affiliation on several occasions.

NOTES AND REFERENCES

1. Penderal Moon has written and edited several books including *Strangers in India,* London, 1943; *Future of India,* London, 1945; *Divide and Quit,* London, 1951; *Warren Hastings and British India,* London, 1961; *Gandhi and Modern India,* London, 1969; *Wavell : The Viceroy Journal* (ed.), London, 1973; *Plain Tales of the Raj,* London, 1973; and *The British Conquest and Dominion of India,* London, 1989.
2. R.Coupland has been an important imperial ideologue. Being a participant in the colonial regime, he has tried his best to defend the colonial rule especially in its last phase. Some of his works are — *The Cripps Mission,* London, 1942; *The Future of India,* London, 1943; *Indian Politics, 1936-42,* London, 1943; and *India : Re-statement,* London, 1945.
3. P.N.S. Mansergh is another British historian who has written extensively on the partition of India. His writings related with the partition are — *Commonwealth and the Nations,* London, 1968; *Commonwealth Experience,* London, 1969; *Constitutional Relation between Britain and India,* London, 1970; *Name and the Nature of the Commonwealth,* Cambridge, 1955; and 'Some Reflections on the Transfer of Power in Plural Societies', in C.H. Philips and M.D. Wainwright (eds.), *The Partition of India, Policies and Perspectives, 1935-1947,* London, 1970.
4. The India Office documents on the transfer of power have been published in twelve vols. under the chief editorship of Mansergh entitled, *The Constitutional Relations between India and Britain, 1942-47; The Transfer of Power.*
5. After his resignation from Indian Civil Service (1943) he produced two books on the constitutional problem of India in 1943 and 1945.
6. His last work was published posthumously in 1989.
7. Penderal Moon, *Gandhi and Modern India,* p. 79.
8. *Ibid.,* p. 2.

9. Penderal Moon, *Future of India,* p. 23.
10. Penderal Moon, *Gandhi and Modern India,* p. 276.
11. *Ibid.*, p. 79.
12. The Morley-Minto Reforms 1909, introduced several changes having far reaching impact on Indian politics. The most notorious provision was that of the separate electorate system which provided for the election of Muslim candidates by Muslim voters. It was granted on the assumption that the interests of Indian Muslims differed from that of Hindus. Thus started the colonial policy of appeasement which culminated in imposition of the partition of India.
13. Penderal Moon, *Gandhi and Modern India,* p. 80.
14. *Ibid.*, p. 105.
15. *Ibid.*, p. 108.
16. *Ibid.*, p. 112.
17. *Ibid.*, p. 132.
18. *Ibid.*, p. 133.
19. *Ibid.*, p. 163.
20. The British policy of 'Divide and Rule' found another expression in the announcement of the Communal Award in August 1932. The Award allotted to each minority a number of seats in the legislatures to be elected on the basis of separate electorate.
21. Penderal Moon, *Gandhi and Modern India,* pp. 195-96.
22. *Ibid.*, pp. 196-97.
23. *Ibid.*, p. 197.
24. *Ibid.*, p. 198.
25. *Ibid.*, p. 206.
26. In March 1940, in its Lahore session the League asserted that Hinduism and Islam were not merely different religions but different social orders and hence India was not one nation but two. The so-called Pakistan Resolution was drafted by Sikandar Hyat Khan, moved by Fazlul Haq and seconded by Khaliquzzaman, demanded "that geographically contiguous units are demarcated into regions which should be so constituted with such territorial readjustment as may be necessary that the areas in which the Muslims are numerically in a majority as in the North-Western and Eastern zones of India should be grouped to constitute Independent States in which the constituent units shall he autonomous and sovereign." Sumit Sarkar, *Modern India 1885-1947,* Delhi, 1983, p. 379.
27. The Cripps Mission came to India in order to ensure India's full cooperation in the War efforts and to break the constitutional deadlock.

Among other things it included the demand for Pakistan for the first time in official documents and thereby extended support to the Muslim League.

28. Rajaji Formula enunciated a post-war commission to demarcate contiguous districts of North-West and North-East India where Muslims had an absolute majority; plebiscite of all inhabitants in such areas to decide whether they would prefer a separate Pakistan; mutual agreement in case of separation to run certain essential common services like defence or communication and implementation of the whole scheme only after full transfer of power by the British. See Sumit Sarkar, *op. cit.*, p. 415.
29. Penderal Moon, *Gandhi and Modern India*, p. 218.
30. *Ibid.*, p. 228.
31. *Ibid.*, p. 237.
32. In order to appease the League, the Cabinet Mission provided the grouping of British Indian provinces — Group A included Hindu majority provinces, Group B that of Muslim majority provinces of the North-West and Group C that of Muslim majority provinces of North-East India.
33. The Muslim League demanded that there should be Hindu-Muslim parity in the proposed Interim Government and the League should have the right to nominate all the Muslim members.
34. Penderal Moon, *Divide and Quit*, p. 54.
35. Penderal Moon, *Gandhi and Modern India*, p. 246.
36. *Ibid.*, p. 249.
37. *Ibid.*, p. 252.
38. Ramakant and Rajan Mahan (eds.), *India's Partition — Prelude and Legacies*, Jaipur, 1998, p. 22.
39. *Ibid.*, p. 23.
40. Penderal Moon, *Gandhi and Modern India*, p. 72.
41. Mahatma Gandhi has been named "Asian of the Century" by the *Asia Week Magazine*, quoted in *The Times of India*, New Delhi, 2 September 1999.
42. Penderal Moon, *Gandhi and Modern India*, p. 276.
43. *Ibid.*, p. 277.
44. In the twentieth century, the peasant movements, the trade union movements and the revolutionary movements had developed considerably and become part and parcel of the freedom movement. On the other hand, the social base of the Indian National Congress

and movement led by it had widened considerably which had been exhibited in the non-cooperation movement (1920-22).

45. The nationalist writings and the Gandhian techniques were definitely eroding the colonial hegemony by exposing its true nature before the literate group.
46. Simon Commission was appointed in 1927 according to provision of the Indian Council Act, 1919 two years prior to its scheduled date. Its work was to inquire into the working of the Act of 1919 and recommend for further constitutional reforms. Since it was an all-whitemen Commission it was opposed by Indians unitedly with few exceptions.
47. R. Coupland occupies a prominent place among the imperialist ideologues. His writings include *Britain and India, 1600-1941; Constitutional Problem in India; Cripps Mission; Future of India; Indian Politics 1936-1942; India and Indian Problem, 1833-1935.*
48. See Penderal Moon, *Divide and Quit.*
49. Penderal Moon, *Gandhi and Modern India.*
50. See P.N.S. Mansergh in Chapter 2.
51. See Penderal Moon, *The British Conquest and the Dominion of India.*
52. Penderal Moon, *Divide and Quit,* p. 11.
53. Penderal Moon, *Liberalism and Indian Politics,* p. 89.
54. Penderal Moon, *Future of India,* p. 23.
55. *Ibid.,* p. 22.
56. Penderal Moon, *Gandhi and Modern India,* p. 79.
57. Penderal Moon, *Future of India,* p. 23.
58. See the writings of Hindu and Muslim communal ideologues, referred to in the introduction.
59. Penderal Moon, *Liberalism and Indian Politics,* p. 89.
60. Moon says that between 1895 and 1905 some 10 per cent of the delegates to the annual session of the Congress and two of the Presidents were Muslims. But considering the level of consciousness among the Muslims in view of educational backwardness and the percentage of their population in India, it is not a small figure. Therefore, it does not reflect the Muslim attitude towards the Congress and the national movement.
61. Penderal Moon, *Gandhi and Modern India,* p. 79.
62. *Ibid.,* p. 77.
63. The Muslims were given the right to select their representatives for provincial legislatures on the basis of separate electorate. This had been provided on the hypothesis that the Muslims formed a distinct

community and their need and interests differed from other communities. This in practical words would mean state within state. This provided justification for the later 'two-nation theory' propounded by the Muslim separatists. Thereby, it sowed the seeds of Pakistan.

64. Penderal Moon, *Gandhi and Modern India,* p. 80.
65. Penderal Moon, *Liberalism and Indian Politics,* pp. 90-91.
66. *Ibid.*, p. 99.
67. *Ibid.*, p. 107.
68. *Ibid.*, pp. 108-09.
69. See Mridula Mukherjee, 'The Non-cooperation Movement 1920-22', in Bipan Chandra *et. al.* (eds.), *India's Struggle for Freedom,* p. 134.
70. Penderal Moon, *Gandhi and Modern India,* p. 105.
71. See K.N. Panikkar, *Against the Lord and State,* New Delhi, 1992.
72. Penderal Moon, *Gandhi and Modern India,* p. 108.
73. *Ibid.*, p. 112.
74. *Ibid.*, p. 132.
75. *Ibid.*, p. 133.
76. Penderal Moon, *Divide and Quit,* p. 11.
77. *Ibid.*, p. 12
78. *Ibid.*, p. 13.
79. See Sugata Bose and Ayesha Jalal, *op. cit.*
80. See Judith Brown, *op. cit.*
81. Penderal Moon, *Gandhi and Modern India,* p. 163.
82. Penderal Moon, *Divide and Quit,* p. 13.
83. *Ibid.*, p. 14.
84. *Ibid.*, p. 15.
85. Penderal Moon, *Future of India,* p. 25.
86. See in Bipan Chandra *et. al.* (eds.), *op. cit.*, pp. 356-74.
87. Penderal Moon, *Gandhi and Modern India,* pp. 195-96.
88. Penderal Moon, *Future of India,* p. 24.
89. Penderal Moon, *Gandhi and Modern India,* p. 199.
90. *Ibid.*, p. 198.
91. Penderal Moon, *Divide and Quit,* pp. 17-18.
92. *Ibid.*, p. 14.
93. *Ibid.*, p. 21.
94. Penderal Moon, *Gandhi and Modern India,* p. 208.

95. Penderal Moon, *Divide and Quit*, p. 31.
96. *Ibid.*, p. 24.
97. *Ibid.*, p. 25.
98. See Sumit Sarkar, *Modern India, 1885-1947.*
99. Penderal Moon, *Divide and Quit*, p. 23.
100. See Bipan Chandra, *Epic Struggle*, New Delhi, 1993.
101. Penderal Moon, *Gandhi and Modern India*, p. 215.
102. Panderal Moon, *Divide and Quit*, pp. 26-27.
103. *Ibid.*, p. 27.
104. Penderal Moon, *Gandhi and Modern India*, p. 215.
105. *Ibid.*, p. 217.
106. Penderal Moon, *Future of India*, p. 28.
107. See R.J. Moore, *Churchill, Cripps and India.*
108. Penderal Moon, *Divide and Quit*, p. 26.
109. Rajaji formula envisaged a plebiscite in contiguous Muslim majority districts in North-West and East India to decide on separation from India. This would be after the War and would follow League participation in an Interim Government and support to independence. Rajagopalachari believed that an understanding with Jinnah was necessary before the establishment of National Government.
110. Penderal Moon, *Gandhi and Modern India*, p. 218.
111. Penderal Moon, *Divide and Quit*, p. 28.
112. Penderal Moon, *Gandhi and Modern India*, p. 228.
113. *Ibid.*, pp. 234-35.
114. *Ibid.*, p. 237.
115. See Introduction to Moon edited *Wavell, The Viceroy Journal.*
116. See Penderal Moon, *Gandhi and Modern India*, p. 239, and *Divide and Quit*, p. 41.
117. *Ibid.*, p. 43.
118. Penderal Moon, *Gandhi and Modern India*, p. 240.
119. It should be noted here that in 1946 only six million Muslims had right to vote in the total of 71 million population.
120. Penderal Moon, *Divide and Quit*, p. 44.
121. Penderal Moon (ed.), *Wavell, The Viceroy Journal*, p. 450.
122. Penderal Moon, *Divide and Quit*, p. 63.
123. Penderal Moon (ed.) *Wavell, The Viceroy Journal*, p. 451.

124. *Ibid.*, p. 452.
125. Penderal Moon, *Gandhi and Indian Politics*, p. 121.
126. Penderal Moon, *Gandhi and Modern India*, p. 257.
127. *Ibid.*, p. 277.
128. Penderal Moon, *Divide and Quit*, pp. 63-64.
129. R.J. Moore, *The Crisis of Indian Unity, 1917-40*, Oxford, 1974; *Churchill, Cripps and India, 1939-45*, Oxford, 1979; *Escape from Empire : The Attlee Government and the Indian Problems*, New Delhi, 1981; *Endgames of Empire : Studies of Britain's Indian Problem*, New Delhi, 1988; 'The Making of India's Paper Federation, 1927-35,' in C.H. Philips and M.D. Wainwright (eds.), *The Partition of India — Policies and Perspectives, 1935-1947*, London, 1970; 'British Policies and Indian Problem, 1936-40', in C.H. Philips and M.D. Wainwright (eds.), *op. cit.*
130. R.J. Moore, *The Crisis of Indian Unity, 1917-1940*, p. 7.
131. R.J. Moore, *Endgames of Empire : Studies of Britain's Indian Problem*, p. 9.
132. R.J. Moore, *The Crisis of Indian Unity, 1917-1940*, p. 7.
133. *Ibid.*, p. 8.
134. The historians of the imperialist school argue that the Muslims remained separate as a distinct community. In order to help them maintain their identity, the colonial authority provided them separate electorate. However, this separate electorate system in the long run helped in the fulfilment of the Pakistan movement.
135. R.J. Moore, *The Crisis of Indian Unity, 1917-1940*, p. 19.
136. *Ibid.*, p. 21.
137. *Ibid.*, p. 21.
138. *Ibid.*, p. 21.
139. *Ibid.*, p. 21.
140. *Ibid.*, p. 25.
141. *Ibid.*, p. 34.
142. *Ibid.*, p. 35.
143. *Ibid.*, p. 34.
144. *Ibid.*, p. 36.
145. *Ibid.*, p. 38.
146. *Ibid.*, p. 40.
147. *Ibid.*, p. 102.
148. *Ibid.*, p. 107.

149. *Ibid.*, p. 287.
150. R.J. Moore, *Endgames of Empire : Studies of Britain's Indian Problem,* pp. 15-16.
151. R.J. Moore, *The Crisis of Indian Unity, 1917-1940,* p. 305.
152. *Ibid.*, p. 306.
153. R.J. Moore, *Endgames of Empire : Studies of Britain's Indian Problem,* p. 16.
154. R.J. Moore, *The Crisis of Indian Unity, 1917-1940,* p. 311.
155. R.J. Moore, *Endgames of Empire : Studies of Britain's Indian Problem,* p. 17.
156. R.J. Moore, *The Crisis of Indian Unity, 1917-1940,* p. 311.
157. R.J. Moore, *Endgames of Empire : Studies of Britain's Indian Problem,* p. 17.
158. C.H. Philips and M.D. Wainwright (eds.), *op. cit.*, p. 78.
159. *Ibid.*, p. 78.
160. *Ibid.*, p. 77.
161. *Ibid.*, p. 83.
162. *Ibid.*, pp. 79-80.
163. *Ibid.*, pp. 84-85.
164. *Ibid.*, p. 94.
165. The August Offer emphasised continuity with past policy as expressed in October 1939, that the future object was Dominion Status and that the present offer was enlargement of the Viceroy's Council to include party representatives and the establishment of a War Consultation Committee. It also emphasised that in the future constitutional changes, the minorities would be given due weightage.
166. The Cripps Mission was sent to India in order to obtain India's cooperation in War effort and to break the constitutional deadlock. For the first time, the League's demand for Pakistan was given a place in the official document though implicitly.
167. R.J. Moore, *Endgames of Empire : Studies of Britain's Indian Problem,* p. 33.
168. R.J. Moore, *Churchill, Cripps and India, 1939-45,* p. 146.
169. *Ibid.*, p. 145.
170. R.J. Moore, *Endgames of Empire : Studies of Britain's Indian Problem,* p. 105.
171. R.J. Moore, *Churchill, Cripps and India, 1939-45,* p. 146.
172. *Ibid.*, p. 146.

173. The British Labour Government intervening directly sent the Cabinet Mission in 1946. The aim was to seek agreement with Indian leaders on constitutional issues. Its recommendations proved to be the apple of discord because the Congress and the League took different postures. The Government sided with the League. But it has been deliberately omitted by Moore.

174. R.J. Moore, *Endgames of Empire : Studies of Britain's Indian Problem,* p. 130.

175. *Ibid.,* p. 131.

176. *Ibid.,* p. 135.

177. R.J. Moore, *Escape from Empire : The Attlee Government and the Indian Problem,* p. 287.

178. R.J. Moore, *The Crisis of Indian Unity, 1917-1940,* p. 316.

179. See reference no. 129 of Chapter 2.

180. R.J. Moore, 'British Policies and Indian Problem, 1936-40,' in C.H. Philips and M.D. Wainwright (eds.), *op. cit.,* pp. 79-80.

181. R. J. Moore, *Endgames of Empire : Studies of Britain's Indian Problem,* p. l.

182. R.J. Moore, *Crisis of Indian Unity,* 1917-1940, p. vii.

183. *Ibid.,* p. viii.

184. Secretary of State Montague declared in the House of Commons on 20 August 1917 that British policy in India henceforth have as its overall objective 'the gradual development of self governing institutions with a view to the progressive realisation of responsible government in India as an integral part of the British Empire.' Sumit Sarkar, *Modern India 1885-1947,* p. 165.

185. R.J. Moore, *Endgames of Empire : Studies of Britain's Indian Problem,* p. 14.

186. R.J. Moore, *Crisis of Indian Unity, 1917-1940,* p. 21.

187. R.J. Moore, *Endgames of Empire : Studies of Britain's Indian Problem,* p. 15.

188. R.J. Moore, *Crisis of Indian Unity, 1917-1940,* p. 21.

189. *Ibid.,* p. 19.

190. It was out and out agrarian and anti-colonial movement. See K.N. Panikkar, *Against the Lord and State, Religion and Peasant Uprisings in Malabar, 1836-1921,* Delhi, 1992.

191. R.J. Moore, *Crisis of Indian Unity,* p. 22.

192. *Ibid.,* p. 34.

193. *Ibid.,* p. 36.

194. *Ibid.*, p. 37.

195. *Ibid.*, p. 40.

196. Balfour had explicitly defined the Dominions in 1926 as autonomous communities within the British Empire, equal in status, in no way subordinate to another in any aspect of their domestic or external affairs, though united by a common allegiance to the Crown and freely associated as members of the British Commonwealth of Nations. See D.L. Keir, *The Constitutional History of Modern Britain, 1485-1937,* London, 1948, p. 543.

197. R.J. Moore, *Crisis of Indian Unity, 1917-1940,* p. 96.

198. *Ibid.*, p. 102.

199. *Ibid.*, p. 107.

200. *Ibid.*, pp. 111-12.

201. *Ibid.*, p. 102.

202. *Ibid.*, p. 167.

203. *Ibid.*, pp. 172-73.

204. *Ibid.*, p. 175.

205. *Ibid.*, p. 119.

206. *Ibid.*, p. 151.

207. The Pact was signed by Gandhiji on behalf of the Congress and by Irwin on behalf of the Government. The terms of the agreement included the immediate release of all political prisoners not convicted for violence, the remission of all fines not yet collected, the return of confiscated land not yet auctioned, and lenient treatment for those government employees who had resigned. The Congress agreed to suspend the Civil Disobedience Movement. See Mridula Mukherjee, 'Civil Disobedience, 1930-1932,' in Bipan Chandra, *et. al.* (eds.), *India's Struggle for Independence,* pp. 280-81.

208. R.J. Moore, *Crisis of Indian Unity, 1917-1940,* p. 183.

209. *Ibid.*, pp. 187-88.

210. *Ibid.*, p. 192.

211. *Ibid.*, pp. 222-23.

212. *Ibid.*, p. 69.

213. R.J. Moore, "The Making of India's Paper Federation 1927-35," in C.H. Philips and M.D. Wainwright (eds.), *op. cit.*, p. 68.

214. R.J. Moore, *Crisis of Indian Unity 1917-1940,* p. 261.

215. *Ibid.*, p. 69.

216. *Ibid.*, p. 70.

217. *Ibid.*, p. 207.

218. *Ibid.*, p. 261.

219. R.J. Moore, 'The Making of India's Paper Federation, 1927-35,' in C.H. Philips & M.D. Wainwright (eds.) *op. cit.*, p. 77.

220. R.J. Moore, *Crisis of Indian Unity, 1917-1940,* pp. 262-63.

221. MacDonald's Communal Award of August 1932 created separate electorates for Untouchables. Poona Pact was signed on 20 September 1932 between Gandhiji and B.R. Ambedkar. It modified the Award. The Hindu joint electorate was retained with reserved seats for Untouchables. See Sumit Sarkar, *Modern India*, p. 328.

222. R.J. Moore, *Crisis of Indian Unity, 1917-1940,* p. 265.

223. *Ibid.*, p. 770.

224. *Ibid.*, p. 284.

225. *Ibid.*, p. 288.

226. R.J. Moore, 'The Making of India's Paper Federation 1927-35,' in C.H. Philips and M.D. Wainwright (eds.), *op. cit.*, p. 77.

227. R.J. Moore, *Endgames of Empire : Studies of Britain's Indian Problem,* pp. 15-16.

228. R.J. Moore, *Crisis of Indian Unity, 1917-1940,* pp. 305-06.

229. R.J. Moore, British Policies and Indian Problem,' in C.H. Philips and M.D. Wainwright (eds.), *op. cit.*, p. 83; *Crisis of Indian Unity,* pp. 306-07; and *Endgames of Empire : Studies of Britain's Indian Problem,* pp. 16-17.

230. R.J. Moore, *Crisis of Indian Unity, 1917-1940,* p. 311.

231. R.J. Moore, *Endgames of Empire : Studies of Britain's Indian Problem,* p. 17.

232. See R.J. Moore, *Crisis of Indian Unity,* pp. 307-12; *Endgames of Empire : Studies of Britain's Indian Problem,* p. 16; 'The Making of India's Paper Federation,' p. 77; and 'British Policies and Indian Problem,' pp. 80-89, in C.H. Philips and M.D. Wainwright (eds.), *op. cit.*

233. R.J. Moore, 'The Making of India's Paper Federation,' in C.H. Philips and M.D. Wainwright (eds.), *op. cit.*, p. 78.

234. R.J. Moore, 'British Policies and Indian Problem,' in C.H. Philips and M.D. Wainwright (eds.), *op. cit.*, p. 82.

235. *Ibid.*, pp. 84-85.

236. *Ibid.*, p. 87.

237. *Ibid.*, p. 89.

238. R.J. Moore, *Endgames of Empire : Studies of Britain's Indian Problem,* p. 23.

239. R.J. Moore, *Crisis of Indian Unity*, p. 312.

240. R.J. Moore, *Endgames of Empire : Studies of Britain's Indian Problem*, p. 24.

241. R.J. Moore, 'British Policies and Indian Problem,' in C.H. Philips and M.D. Wainwright (eds.), *op. cit.*, p. 91.

242. The August Offer envisaged Indianisation of Executive Council and a War Advisory body for the present, full weightage to minorities in constitutional advance and Dominion Status in future. See R.J. Moore, 'British Policies and the Indian Problem,' in C.H. Philips and M.D. Wainwright (eds.), *op. cit.*, p. 91.

243. *Ibid.*, p. 93.

244. *Ibid.*

245. *Ibid.*, p. 94.

246. R.J. Moore, *Endgames of Empire : Studies of Britain's Indian Problem*, pp. 24-25.

247. For detail, see Bipan Chandra, 'The Crisis at Tripuri to the Cripps Mission,' in Bipan Chandra *et al.* (eds.), *op. cit.*, pp. 443-56.

248. R.J. Moore, *Endgames of Empire : Studies of Britain's Indian Problem*, p. 26.

249. *Ibid.*, pp. 27-28.

250. *Ibid.*, p. 27.

251. *Ibid.*, pp. 29-30.

252. *Ibid.*, p. 102.

253. *Ibid.*, p. 105.

254. For detail see Sumit Sarkar, *op. cit.*, pp. 388-99.

255. R.J. Moore, *Endgames of Empire : Studies of Britain's Indian Problem*, p. 33.

256. *Ibid.*, p. 31.

257. *Ibid.*, p. 105.

258. Sumit Sarkar, *op. cit.*, pp. 416-18.

259. R.J. Moore, *Endgames of Empire : Studies of Britain's Indian Problem*, p. 123.

260. *Ibid.*, p. 124.

261. *Ibid.*, p. 2.

262. See Sucheta Mahajan, 'Freedom and Partition,' in Bipan Chandra *et al.* (eds.), *op. cit.*, pp. 487-504.

263. R.J. Moore, *Endgames of Empire : Studies of Britain's Indian Problem*, p. 128.

264. *Ibid.*, p. 129.
265. *Ibid.*, p. 130.
266. *Ibid.*, p. 5.
267. *Ibid.*, p. 6.
268. *Ibid.*, p. 133.
269. *Ibid.*, p. 155.
270. *Ibid.*, p. 158.
271. Plan Balkan provided for self-determination by provinces and the partitioning of provinces which could be members of Hindustan or Pakistan or independent from both, prior to the concession of the Dominion status. *Ibid.*, p. 177.
272. *Ibid.*, p. 180.
273. *Ibid.*, p. 168.
274. *Ibid.*, p. 9.
275. *Ibid.*, p. 6.
276. *Ibid.*, p. 5.
277. *Ibid.*, pp. 132-33.
278. *Ibid.*, p. 5.

4

Main Points of Similarities and Differences

The historians of Oxbridge group have produced enormously rich but varied literature on India's partition. Due to their commitment to a long cherished common ideology, they have adopted by and large identical approach and arrived at almost similar conclusion. However, due to gap in generations and differences in personal background, these historians differ from each other on different issues related to partition. The British historiographical tradition on partition has been influenced by different factors. The works of earlier historians[1] reflect the indelineable impact of the classical imperialist ideology while later writings[2] may be regarded as counter-reactions to the nationalists' assertion. Finally, the recent trend is representative of the neo-imperial tradition.[3]

Broadly speaking, these historians' approach to the partition of India was shaped by different noticeable factors. Firstly, as we have discussed in previous chapters, with one exception, historians studied here had been associated with the colonial regime in one or another capacity. They had witnessed the climax and the decline of the Raj. They had also witnessed the gradual intensification of India's liberation movement and the gradual erosion of the colonial hegemony. Therefore, these scholars tried to restrengthen the ideological base of the regime and to defend the latter in post-colonial period. Secondly, communalism played a decisive role in the partition and this communalism was a direct product of the colonial regime. This ideology-turned-phenomenon affected the national movement adversely. Hence, it needed fresh theorisation by the imperial ideologues and authority, so that the catalytic role of the regime in its emergence and fulfilment could be denied.[4] Thirdly, in the post-World War II period the colonialism was losing its material base. Therefore, it needed ideological support. The support was needed to provide safety to the imperial interests in the post-colonial period as well. Last but not least, in the post-colonial phase Oxbridge scholars have been busy in defending the earlier imperial writings. The changing contexts have been playing important role in shaping the British writings on partition. Obviously, therefore, we find similarities as well as differences in the writings of the scholars studied here.

The historians studied here have traced the beginning of partition from different points of time in the Indian history. Percival Spear starts his discussion from A.D. 712 when the Arabs invaded and conquered Sind.[5] H.V. Hodson traces the beginning of partition from the eleventh century A.D. when the Turks invaded India. He opines, "The tale that ended in 1947 can be said to have had its beginning eight or nine centuries earlier. The transfer of power to two successor states was the end of the story, preface of which was the annexation of the Punjab by Mahmood Ghazni in A.D. 1018 and which began earnest with the defeat of Prithviraj by Muhammad Ghori in A.D. 1192."[6] Penderal Moon too locates the roots of partition in pre-colonial India. He does not specify any point of time. However, he asserts that the permanent divide and the cultural clash were the reasons for it. This divide, he further argues, was intensified due to the nature of the national movement. He opines, "Gandhian appeal to the mass feeling aroused communal passion that existed at mass level and thus thwarted his own aim of the Hindu-Muslim Unity."[7] Nicholas Mansergh does not give any specific date but by calling the partition natural in a pluralistic society, he too has emphasised its pre-colonial origin.[8] R.J. Moore has traced the origin of partition from 1917 and related it with the gradual devolutionary process adopted by the British Government and the nature of Indian society and the national movement.[9] A.C. Johnson has concentrated mainly on the events of 1946-47 but asserts that the disunity in India was natural and a pre-colonial legacy, while the unity had been the greatest legislative and administrative achievement of the Britishers.[10] But the latent disunity surfaced and manifested into partition. Thus, we see that these historians have tried to trace the origin of partition from different points of time. However, they regard it mainly a result of pre-colonial legacy.

Undoubtedly, the divide and rule policy played important role in the creation of the British Indian empire and gave sustenance to it. This policy took different shapes at different point of time. It was under this scheme that the colonial regime promoted communalism. Therefore, it is least surprising that the whole Oxbridge exercise has been concentrated at defending this long cherished policy of *divide et empera* with few exceptions.[11] The historians studied here variously deny the fact that the colonial regime promoted the policy of divide and rule. They also try to refute the charge that this policy culminated into the partition.

It was due to their blind and uncritical support to the colonial regime that they have tried to defend the separate electorate system.[12] Moon regards it an indispensable safeguard of the Muslim interests.[13] H.V. Hodson argues that aware of the risk that one class or community might by virtue of its superior numbers, wealth or education come to dominate India's nascent political life and the counsel of the Government, successive Viceroys supported the policy of separate communal or class representation.[14] Spear defends communalism on the basis that Muslims in India formed a separate and distinct community. Therefore, they needed separate treatment.[15] Unlike other scholars, R.J. Moore attacks the separate electorate system for its divisive role. He opines, "The separate electorate of Minto introduced at least in part, out of a respect for minority interest had been prepetuated by Montague and Chelmsford. The Communal Award embodied in the Act of 1935 wove together the strands of communalism and separatism by giving the Muslims virtually perpetual majorities in the legislatures of the Punjab, the North-West Frontier Province, Sind and Bengal."[16] In this way, we see that all the British historians but R.J. Moore, defend the separate electorate system in different ways.

It should be noted here that in the post-1857 period, the colonial regime promoted communalism as a counter-force to the nascent nationalism. This policy succeeded and the Muslim League was formed in 1906. Aware of the colonial regime's direct responsibility in it, most of the imperial ideologues are either silent over these issues or have attempted to trace their origins in the Indian milieu. H.V. Hodson interprets the communalism in terms of inter-community differences. He suggests, "Hindus and Muslims lived in a village separated not only by religious creed and rituals but by whole modes of life and attitudes of mind each a permanent hereditary group without inter-marriage or mutual absorption."[17] Penderal Moon relates communalism with the clash between Hinduism and Islam. He opines that of several differences, the most serious was the clash of Hinduism with Islam and these two groups constituted two distinct and often antagonistic communities.[18] It was this antagonism which manifested into communalism. Percival Spear occupies prominent place among the imperialist scholars, mainly because he has discussed communalism in quite detail. He has traced its origin from medieval period and related it with the evolution of Indian culture. He regards Hinduism and Islam as two mutually antagonistic religions having no meeting point. Therefore, he opines that communalism was the by-product of this clash between Hinduism and Islam.[19]

In a likewise manner, the imperialist historians defend the formation and role of the Muslim League. Knowing the fact that it was formed at the instance of the colonial regime and it played negative role, the imperialist ideologues are conscious to free the Britishers from their responsibility in the formation and fulfilment of the League's aim. Spear has tried to impress that the Indian National Congress had become a Hindu body. Therefore, the Muslims needed a separate organisation. Thus, they formed the Muslim League in 1906.[20] He also relates it with the Indian renaissance. He defends the Muslim League because of its collaborative nature. He opines that the Muslims collaborated with the English because of similarity between Islam and Christianity.[21] R.J. Moore has explained the sectarian and divisive role of the League but he, too, does not find anti-national trend in it. He opines that the aim of the Muslim League was to destroy the unitary Raj and consolidate their strength in a separate state.[22]

Thus, started two parallel movements — nationalism and sectarianism turned separatism. In this situation the colonial regime supported the latter in order to weaken the former.

This is the reason that the Indian National Congress, which was the consequence and the cause of the growth of nationalism, has been declared a Hindu organisation by the imperial ideologues unanimously. They have been trying to negate its role in India's liberation movement. Representing the classical imperialist mindset, Percival Spear opines that the Indian National Congress was both cultural and political voice of Hindu India.[23] In the same manner, Penderal Moon regards the Congress a Hindu body and blames mainly Gandhiji for it.[24] Their aim is to hold Congress responsible for the partition.

Thus, we see that almost all important Oxbridge scholars have been biased towards the Congress mainly because it was the most important anti-colonial organisation. This is the reason that they are critical towards all the movements led by the Congress, especially in the Gandhian era. As we have seen in the previous chapters, the Non-cooperation Movement, Anti-Simon Commission Movement, Civil Disobedience Movement and above all the Quit India Movement have either been bypassed or have been underestimated or have been distorted in the writings of the historians analysed here. Only R.J. Moore seems to have been objective towards these movements but he, too, sometimes has failed to free himself from the imperialist ideology. Unlike his group he asserts the strength and success of the Civil Disobedience Movement. He argues that the preparation of such a heavy artillery from fear of the organised might of the Congress was itself the recognition of the success of Gandhi's experiments.[25]

The Quit India Movement (1942-45) was the most intense and widest anti-colonial movement but it has found either small place in the imperialist writings or has been totally distorted and neglected. H.V. Hodson calls it an insurrection which led to serious disorders and disturbances.[26] In almost same voice, Moon has termed it a campaign of violence and sabotage which ultimately helped the Muslim League and Jinnah to strengthen their position.[27] Percival Spear seems to be more aggressive. He calls the Quit India Movement a rebellion and its failure in his opinion discredited the Congress. He opines, "The Congress had not only acted wrongly, they had made a mistake. They had backed wrong horse."[28] R.J. Moore has totally omitted it in his discussion. Thus, we see that these scholars have interpreted the Quit India Movement in its distorted form and held it responsible for the partition as well.

Thus, by underestimating the important events of the national movement, these scholars have tried to negate the role of the latter in India's liberation. They have tried to re-emphasize 'white man's burden theory.' Penderal Moon would like to impress that India could have won independence even without these movements. He writes, "Had Gandhi followed the constitutional path, independence would have been achieved earlier and with less disorders, perhaps even without the disaster of partition." Hodson writes that what India achieved on the night of 14-15 August 1947, was not the fulfilment of the national movement rather it was the culmination of Britain's long term policy of granting India self-rule, which had been promised by Montague in 1917. In a likewise manner, R.J. Moore regards the independence a result of the process of devolution which had started from 1917. He opines, "The process inaugurated in 1917 largely as a means of rallying support in War time, was only completed thirty years later when the Second World War had exposed the palpable inadequacy of Britain's resources to sustain an empire."[29] In this way, we see that they negate the role of national movement unanimously and try to show that the aim of the British rule was to impart Indians the training in self-rule. They also try to show that the anti-colonial movement produced strains which culminated into partition.

The historians studied here extend their full support to the colonial regime and its policies with few exceptions. Their sole aim is to absolve the Britishers of any responsibility in the partition. Thus, we find the commonality of aim. For this purpose, they have produced the distorted picture of events just preceding the partition. Among those scholars only P. Spear[30] and H.V. Hodson[31] have gone as far back as early medieval period of the Indian history. But they, too, concentrate on the events of the last few decades of the British rule. They have been biased towards the events of the twentieth century.

These historians extend their full support to the Indian Council Act, 1919. R.J. Moore opines that it gave Indian ministers power and privileges to extend patronage in important departments of state.[32] He further suggests that the Congress by deciding not to cooperate with this Act, created several cleavages. Spear, too, holds the Congress responsible for encouraging Muslim separatism by not cooperating with the Act of 1919. Hodson and Moon have bypassed it.

The imperialist scholars consider the post-Non-cooperation period as a turning point in the Indian history. The period between 1928 and 1932, they opines, was important to understand the partition. They opine unanimously that due to mistakes of the Congress and its leaders, Muslim separatism intensified and took definite shape. They support this hypothesis by explaining the Simon Commission and its boycott by Indians, the Nehru Report, the Lahore Session of the Congress, Civil Disobedience Movement and Round Table Conferences. Moore opines that the appointment of the Simon Commission sounded the depth of the cleavages caused by the strains of a decade of devolution.[33] The Indian response to the imperial challenge was the Nehru Report. But Moon says that it was the parting of ways between the League and the Congress.[34] Moore calls it essentially a plan by Hindu nationalists.[35] Above all, the rejection of the Nehru Report by the League has been generalised by Spear, Moon and Moore. They opine that it was rejected by the Muslims and it strengthened Jinnah.[36] Spear goes to the extent to suggest that due to the Congress policy, the Muslim separatism grew. He suggests that Sayyed Ahmad gave Indian Islam a sense of separate existence, Iqbal a sense of separate destiny. The British Government declaration to hold the Round Table Conference for constitutional reform have been praised but the Congress decision to boycott it has been denounced. These scholars unanimously opine that the absence of the Congress gave strength to separatist tendency. However, only Moore has criticised the British Government for encouraging separatism.[37]

The whole imperial exercise of late 1920s and early 1930s resulted into the Government of India Act, 1935 which has found sufficient place in the imperialist writings. Moore is of the view that this Act encouraged Muslim separatism in more than one way but mainly due to Indians' response especially due to Congress policy.[38] He defends it by saying that in the absence of the Congress, the constitution that was made between 1930 and 1935, favoured the Princes and the Muslims.[39] The making and working of the Provincial Autonomy provisions and the failure of the proposed federation are said to have given Muslim separatism a definite shape. They have over emphasized the Congress decision of not including the members of the League in Provincial ministries. They have also blamed the Congress Governments of working in a partisan manner. Moore writes that the grievances against the Congress ministries developed through assault on Muslim culture and religion and Urdu language. They culminated in fears that the Congress High Command would obtain dominance at the federal level, thereby reiterating the balance between Muslim and Hindu provinces. Alarmed at the strength of the centralised Congress machinery and of Congress unitarianism, converted the League into Muslim separatist organization.[40] Hodson opines that the Act of 1935 was a turning point in the history of the Indian National Congress and the Muslim League *vis-a-vis* Hindu-Muslim relation. The election in the Provinces to implement the Provincial Autonomy and its result left the League in wilderness in six provinces and thenceforward accepted the Congress as its mortal foe. In a likewise manner, Spear asserts that the political foundation of Pakistan was laid down in 1937, when the Congress failed to accept the League as a coalition partner in the United Provinces.[41] He further argues that this Act made the partition inevitable. Moon, too, argues that the Congress refusal to form a coalition Government in the United Provinces and the Congress Governments' policies made the Muslims apprehensive of the Congress Raj and this influenced the Muslim thinking. This feeling strengthened the League.[42] Mansergh, too, calls the decision of 1937 ill-advised.[43]

In the same way, the Federal section of the Act has been interpreted. Moore argues that the collapse of the Paper Federation in 1939 precipitated a crisis of freedom with unity.[44] However, unlike his group, Moore accepts that the proposed Federation failed due to inherent weaknesses[45] but blames mainly Indians for it. He writes, "The States' accession was not simply a matter at issue between the Government of India and the Princes. It came to acquire a communal dimension. The activities of the Congress and the Muslim League were largely responsible for the failure of the Princes to accede."[46] On the other hand, Mansergh does not regard the Federal scheme an ideal. He suggests, "Many of the plans for preserving, the framework of Indian unity within a federal system displayed at once, the greatest ingenuity and flexibility of federalism as an instrument of Government. But at a deeper level, however, it is hard to escape from the conclusion that the agreement for federalism in India was essentially defensive much indeed, as Diecy conceived them to be. In political terms it was a second best to the majority who preferred unity and also to the minority who preferred partition."[47] In a likewise manner, Hodson asserts that even the federation could not have averted the partition.

The period between 1939 and 1945 witnessed remarkable developments in the separatist as well as nationalist movements. The British Government had declared India on war without its consent. Therefore, the Congress decided not to cooperate with the regime. Hence, the latter collaborated with the Muslim League. The Churchill-Linlithgow combination promoted the divisive forces in India. This period has found prominence in the imperialist writings. The imperialist ideologues with few exceptions defend the colonial policies. On the other hand, as we have seen, they have denounced Congress policies especially the Quit India Movement.

The British Government made several attempts to obtain India's full cooperation in the war effort. The August Offer of 1940 was the first concrete effort of the regime. But it was rejected by the Indian parties. In 1942, Cripps Mission came to India with the same aim. But it, too, failed. Almost all the scholars of the Oxbridge group hold Indians responsible for its failure. They also opine that its failure was prelude to partition. Hodson says that in its effect the Cripps Mission widened the gulf between the Congress and the Government and created frustration among Congressmen.[48] Spear blames Indians for its failure and argues that the constitutional as well as communal deadlock was complete than ever.[49] He further argues that with the failure of the Cripps Mission, the golden moment passed and with it the last chance of establishing a united independent India. The rejection of the offer was the prelude to partition.[50] Moon, too, opines that the Cripps proposals provided golden opportunity which was not availed by the Congress under the Gandhian leadership.

However, R.J. Moore, unlike his school's opinion has described the Cripps Mission's aims and objectives and failure with higher degree of objectivity. He opines that it marked a historic departure in British policy on the problem of freedom with unity.[51] He further suggests that it also indicated the possibility of redistribution of provincial boundaries or partition to precede the transfer of power.[52] While dealing with its failure he has been very impartial. He argues that Cripps could have succeeded in his effort but in between the Mission was sabotaged by the Churchill-Amery-Linlithgow triumvirate on the pretext that Cripps was bypassing Linlithgow.[53] Thus, we see that different scholars have opined differently on the Cripps Mission's proposals and failure.

In this way, except Moore, all the historians studied here have fully supported the colonial policy and regime on the occasion of Cripps Mission. Moore is of the opinion that the Cripps Mission was a clever propaganda exercise — a plan merely devised so as to range world opinion against India, just bluff to influence American opinion. He also criticises Churchill individually for his role in the failure of the Mission. He writes that the repudiation of the Cripps Mission in 1942 was one of the many bricks that Churchill placed in the wall of partition.[54] He also criticises Linlithgow for slowness and ineffectiveness.[55]

It is known that after the failure of the Cripps Mission, the Congress started Quit India Movement. Subsequently, the colonial regime arrested all important leaders who were suspected to participate in the movement and the regime utilised unprecedented force to suppress the movement. Almost all the scholars, mentioned above, have opined that the Muslim League was strengthened during this period mainly due to absence of the Congress leaders from the scene. So much so, that by 1945, the former claimed to be the sole organization of the Muslims. Except Moore, other historians have tried to blame the Congress for indirectly strengthening the Muslim League.

Moore suggests that during the war, the Churchillian imperialism effectively isolated the Congress and provided opportunity and sufficient time to the League to strengthen itself. He opines, "The India Committee under Churchill's guidance consistently rejected the proposals of Linlithgow's successor Wavell to revive the Cripps Plan because he regarded the Hindu-Muslim division as strength of the Raj."[56] Moore also holds Churchill responsible for encouraging Muslim separatism on more than one occasion. He suggests, "Throughout the 1930s Churchill had fought to prevent the introduction of responsibility in the central government. In 1940, he had so watered the draft of August Offer that the Congress was bound to reject it. In 1944-45 he was to obstruct Wavell's scheme for a conference that would setup an Interim National Government of the type that Cripps had wanted, finally allowing the new initiative only when he felt sure of its failure. His constant intervention gave the Muslim League precious time in which to substantiate its claim to separate nationhood."[57]

In 1945, Wavell convened Simla Conference to break the deadlock but this Wavell Plan failed. Moon has praised this plan knowing the fact, that it gave veto to Jinnah and the League in the constitutional matters. Hodson calls the proposed council as politically representative. On its failure, however, he has criticised Wavell. He writes, "If the Viceroy had been adamant as Mr. Jinnah, the latter would have obliged himself to give in."[58] But in final discussion he turns towards the inevitability of the failure of the plan. He opines that all this may have been inevitable because the Muslim League's demand of Pakistan and the Congress demand of United India were incompatible.[59]

After the Simla Conference, Indian and world situation changed. The World War II ended and the Labour Government took over in Britain. In India, too, anti-colonial and anti-feudal movements re-emerged with new vigour. The Labour Government under the leadership of Mr. Attlee intervened directly to solve Indian problems and sent Cabinet Mission in 1946. The Cabinet Mission Plan and its aftermath have attracted the attention of scholars due to several factors. Broadly speaking, the imperialist historians have sided with this Plan. However, H.V. Hodson criticises the Labour Government for not enjoining the Commission to impose any solution.[60] Percival Spear opines that the Cabinet Mission Plan in operation extinguished the hope of a united independent India and made partition inevitable.[61] Johnson is of the opinion that the Cabinet Mission Plan was the last attempt to achieve a unitary system for India.[62] Penderal Moon has to tell the same story in a different way. He argues that the Cabinet Mission Plan had been accepted by the Congress and the League. But due to Gandhi's intervention, the Plan was rejected by the Congress Working Committee and subsequently by the Muslim League.[63] He concludes that the disorders that followed the 'Direct Action Day'[64] made the partition inevitable.[65] Moore explaining the Plan more objectively opines that it offered either truncated Pakistan or grouping of provinces under a union. Its refusal by Jinnah led to the rejection of fully independent Pakistan. But it proposed a powerful sub-national Pakistan.[66] "However, he, too, blames the Congress for compelling the League to a course of direct action.[67] Ultimately, he concludes that the Labour's Cabinet Mission foundered on the Pakistan issue.[68]

All the historians analysed here have shown that by the beginning of 1947, partition had become unavoidable due to several reasons. Johnson argues that by the time Mountbatten arrived in India, partition had become inevitable.[69] Mansergh opines that in the last phase of the transfer of power in all plural societies, the freedom of action declines. For the British in particular there was a progressively diminishing range of choice.[70] Moon emphasises that the transfer of power became certain after the Attlee's Declaration of 20 February 1947, but the Congress-League feud made it certain that partition was the only solution to the prolonged civil war. Hodson suggests that creation of Pakistan and transfer of power well before 1947, were implicitly but plainly written in the statement of 20 February 1947.[71] In fact, their aim is to absolve Mountbatten of any responsibility in the partition, hence the attempt to impress that, well before his arrival in India, the only choice was partition.

Mountbatten consulted the Indian leaders and prepared 3 June Plan. On the basis of this Plan, the Indian Independence Bill was passed and enacted which divided and freed India. Mountbatten has been praised by all the British scholars without any exception and reservations. Hodson opines that partition was the need of the hour when Mountbatten came to the stage.[72] Spear would like to impress that what Mountbatten implemented had been demanded by the Indians themselves. Moore has tried to show that Nehru was largely responsible for the 3 June Plan.[73] He concludes that the achievement of Mountbatten is that the elusive condition of a successful transfer of power, *i.e.*, the agreement between the Congress and the League, had at last been fulfilled.[74] Johnson has exaggerated Mountbatten. He writes that the situation in India was extremely grave and in this situation only Mountbatten could succeed.[75]

It should be noted here that Mountbatten worked at a deadly speed, which resulted into further disorders on unprecedented scale. But his working style has not only been defended but also admired by the imperialist scholars. Hodson regards the partition as panacea for all ills and justifies the speedy transfer of power. He writes, "The difficulties in governing India between the date of announcement and effective establishment of successor authorities rendered it advisable to make the transition period as short as possible."[76] Johnson tries to justify this haste on the ground that everybody was asking for speedy solution of the Indian problems. However, Moore does not agree with his school and calls this hastiness on the part of Mountbatten as 'indecent.'

The imperialist scholars mentioned here regard the partition natural and inevitable. The elements of determinism and inevitability are more prominent in the writings of H.V. Hodson. He opines that what happened in 1947 was merely a by-play that the die was cast much further back, when the Cabinet Mission persisted in seeking consent to compromise, rather than imposing compromise by arbitration or when Lord Wavell failed to secure a National Government at Simla Conference or when the Congress rejected Cripps Offer in 1942 or when the Muslim League adopted Pakistan as its goal or when they failed to admit the Muslim League ministers in 1937 or other dates perhaps earlier.[77] He further suggests that what happened in 1947 was bound to happen because Linlithgow and Wavell, Mountbatten and Cripps, Gandhi and Jinnah, Sikandar Hayat Khan and Jawaharlal Nehru and all the others were mere puppets moved by historical forces which they had no power to deflect.[78] Spear highlights the cultural evolution of India and opines that heterogenetic Indian culture produced strains and stresses which inevitably lead to territorial divisions like that of 1947. Further, in order to show that partition was natural and inevitable, he underlines the short gap between the coining of the term Pakistan and its fulfilment. He opines, "Clearly such a rapid growth leading to such a spectacular success must have sprung from roots deeper than purely political motives and stretching far beyond the twenties of the twentieth century."[79]

In a likewise manner, Penderal Moon has tried to show that the Indian society was a divided society having mutually antagonistic interests. He suggests, "Of the several differences, the most serious was the clash of Hinduism with Islam. And these two groups constituted two distinct and often antagonistic communities."[80] In a nutshell, he tries to impress that the divisions were pre-colonial and the partition was natural. Johnson, too, tries to impress upon that the legislative and administrative unity was the greatest achievement of the Britishers but by the time of transfer of power, the only alternatives were Pakistan or chaos.[81] Almost in a similar tone, Mansergh opines that it was the unity of India that was artificial and imposed; the divisions natural. That of course presupposed a transfer of power to two successor authorities.[82] However, R.J. Moore differs slightly from his school on this issue too. He does not regard the partition natural rather interprets it in terms of failure of different policies, parties and personalities. He opines that the separate electorate,[83] the process of devolution of power by stages,[84] failure of the Congress,[85] British Government policies[86] and Muslim League's policies collectively contributed to the partition.

In the imperialist writings on partition of India, personalities like Gandhiji, Jawaharlal Nehru, Mohammad Ali Jinnah and Mountbatten and organisations like the Indian National Congress and the Muslim League have found considerable space but with different reasons. Broadly speaking, Gandhiji has been the main target of Oxbridge group because the former was first among the important anti-colonial activists. Therefore, this attempt to malign his personality and ideologies. It should be noted here that partition was proposed by the colonial authorities and accepted by the Muslim League and the Congress. However, Gandhiji is held responsible for it. Moon's attitude towards Gandhian era and Gandhiji has been most critical and highly biased. Initially he tries to negate the role of Gandhiji in the Indian liberation movement.[87] Then he blames Gandhiji individually for the partition on the basis of the latter's policies and programmes.[88] He concludes that the disorders that followed the Direct Action Day made partition inevitable and holds Gandhiji personally responsible for the direct action started by the Muslim League.[89] Spear too blames Gandhian personality for the separatist tendency. He writes, "In post-Khilafat period of the Hindu majority personified in the enigmatic figure of Gandhi seemed to be the main threat to a separate Muslim existence."[90]

However, R.J. Moore, in spite of his affiliation with the imperialist ideology, has been soft and more objective while dealing with Gandhi and his role. Johnson praises Gandhiji for his role during the partition. He suggests that it was the miracle of Gandhi's moral influence that checked the communal violence in the east during the partition.[91]

The aforesaid historians have also blamed Jawaharlal Nehru for the partition. Almost unanimously, Nehru has been criticised for his role during the formation of ministries in provinces in 1937. Secondly, Nehru has been held individually responsible for the partition on the basis of his press statement of 10 July 1946.[92] This statement has been singled out as the *casus belli* of the League's call for the 'Direct Action' which could be stopped only with partition. R.J. Moore has tried to impress that the League was ready to accept the Cabinet Mission Plan but due to Nehru's statement rejected it and decided to start Direct Action from 16 August 1946.[93] The rejection of the plan and starting of the Direct Action are said to be the prelude to partition.

Broadly speaking, Mohammad Ali Jinnah has been raised to very high pedestal in comparison with other leaders. He has been credited solely for the creation of Pakistan and regarded as champion of the Muslim nationalism. While exaggerating him, Spear writes, "The differences of community and religion were elevated by the Qaid-i-Azam into the fundamental divisions of the country. As oil and water, so the Hindus and Muslims can never mix."[94] Hodson admires Jinnah on several occasions and concludes that it was he who strengthened the bargaining power of the Muslims and the Muslim League and created a separate nationhood. Johnson calls him the creator of a nation but has indicated his unpopularity though unwillingly. He writes, "I had never dreamt that the creator of a nation at the moment of reaching the promised land could when surrounded by his devoted followers, be at such a distance from them."[95] Mansergh too opines, "Mr. Jinnah as constant in saying no with a resolution as unyielding as that of Lord Craigavon was reaping the reward of a man of single-minded vision"[96] Contrary to his school, R.J. Moore has not overemphasized the role of individual in the making of history.[97] This overestimation of the role of Jinnah in the creation of Pakistan is aimed at absolving the colonial authority of its responsibility in the partition.

The personality and role of the last Viceroy, Mountbatten have found considerable space in the writings of the historians studied here. Without any exception, these scholars have praised the role of Mountbatten especially for ensuring 'peaceful' and 'speedy' transfer of power. As we have seen, Mountbatten was selected for implementation of the Attlee's Declaration. No doubt he worked hard but in a partisan manner and decided the issues arbitrarily. Therefore, the imperialist scholars have tried to defend him and absolve him of any responsibility in the partition. Hodson opines that partition was the need of the hour, when Mountbatten came to the stage. He further suggests, "Whatever other criticism may be made of Lord Mountbatten's Plan for the transfer of power, it certainly can't be said that it was imposed without the fullest consultation with India's political leaders or that it was contrary to the ultimate consensus of their views. It may certainly be said that it was not he but the Indians who divided India."[98] Johnson exaggerates Mountbatten and defends him on all occasions. He suggests that the 3 June Plan was prepared and Indian leaders accepted it only because of Mountbatten's personality.[99] Moon admires the lightning speed at which Mountbatten worked and proposed the 3 June Plan. Further, he would like to impress that Mountbatten proposed to divide and quit India in the interests of its inhabitants. Although Moore does not exaggerate him but in simple words tries to free Mountbatten from any responsibility in the 3 June Plan and partition.[100] Spear, too, would like us to believe that what Mountbatten proposed and implemented was the demand of Indians themselves.

Finally, while explaining the partition, the imperialist scholars differ over the main factors which led to the division of India. Though their aims and objectives are common but difference in generations and approaches have led to differences in centrality of the theme. However, one thing is common. All these scholars have exploited the plurality of the Indian society in some form or the other to explain the partition. Mansergh has explained the partition in terms of the plurality of Indian social milieu. He writes, "In the last phase of transfer of power chiefly because of the constricting and in this case triangular relationship implicit in all plural societies, the freedom of action of all parties declined. For the British in particular, there was a progressively diminishing range of choice."[101] Spear locates the roots of partition in medieval period and suggests that in the process of cultural interaction, strains and stresses were created, which was partly resolved by the partition. He has tried to highlight the point that Muslims in India had succeeded in maintaining their separate identity and were sufficiently different from their Hindu neighbour. So much so, that they considered themselves a separate nation.[102] Hodson with a typical imperialist mindset has adopted determinist approach. He goes back to eleventh century to support his hypothesis. He has overemphasized inter-community differences and sidelined the similarities.[103] His conclusion is the climax of the element of inevitability. He says that what happened in 1947 was bound to happen.

However, R.J. Moore has been by and large more objective. His main emphasis is on the constitutionalism. He argues that the policy of gradual constitutional reform was the reason of the division of India. He opines that each instalment of constitutional reform created further division in India, which culminated in the partition. His uniqueness lies in the fact that he has tried for equitable distribution of responsibility among all the parties involved in the partition. However, he has not maintained his objectivity and impartiality throughout his discussion. Contrary to Moore, Moon has tried to locate the reasons for partition among Indians and Indian situation. He opines that the working of the Congress and the nature of

Gandhian leadership acted to disunite Indians which culminated into partition. He concludes, "The inevitable consequences of the Gandhian personality was the Hinduisation of the Congress and the national movement which was injurious and ultimately fatal to the Hindu-Muslim unity."[104]

However, Johnson does not involve himself in explaining the background of the partition in detail and refrains from assigning any specific reason. He asserts that the definite objective of the British Government was to obtain a unitary Government for British India and Indian States.[105] But in an answer as to why the British Government decided to divide and quit, he suggests that under the Viceroyalty of Mountbatten the situation had fallen beyond control. He writes, "We have inherited inter alia communal rioting which is spreading as though by chain reactions, the key provinces of the Punjab with its threefold Hindu-Muslim and Sikh communal problem. So, in short, we have the people rioting, the Princes falling out among themselves, the entire Indian Civil Service and police running down and the British who are left sceptical and full of foreboding."[106]

In this way, we see that though the aim of the Oxbridge group has been common and still unaltered, they differ among themselves on several counts. The reasons for similarities and startling differences are obvious. Their unquestionable commitment to a common ideology has induced them to maintain a common tradition with the element of continuity. Therefore, we find a set model of expression and by and large same conclusion. Thus, following different paths they have tried to reach a common destination. However, differences are many and at times more prominent mainly due to personal background of the historian concerned, changes in the theory and practice of history and shift in the context and point of emphasis.

NOTES AND REFERENCES

1. See the writings of H.V. Hodson, Percival Spear and Penderal Moon.
2. See the works of Allen Campbell Johnson.
3. See the writings of R.J. Moore, analysed in Chapter 3.
4. See the writings of Spear, Hodson and Moon.

5. Percival Spear, 'A Third Force in India 1920-47 : A Study in Political Analysis,' in C.H. Philips and M.P. Wainwright (eds.), *op. cit.*, p. 495.
6. H.V. Hodson, *The Great Divide — Britain, India and Pakistan*, p. 181.
7. Penderal Moon, *Gandhi and Modern India*, p. 72.
8. P.N.S. Mansergh, 'Some Reflections on the Transfer of Power in Plural Societies,' in C.H. Philips and M.D. Wainwright (eds.), *op. cit.*, p. 43.
9. R.J. Moore, *Crisis of Indian Unity, 1917-1940.*
10. A.C. Johnson, *Mission with Mountbatten*, p. 354.
11. We have seen in the previous sections that among the historians studied here, only P. Moon and R.J. Moore have discussed the British policy of divide and rule. However, they have not crossed the limit of the school they belong. At best Moore goes to the extent of criticising the Conservatives especially Churchill's attitude towards India. But he rolls back again and blames the Indian leaders and the milieu for the division.
12. It should be noted here that the colonial regime encouraged Muslim separatism when the national movement was taking definite shape. The separatist tendency was institutionalised through the Morley-Minto Reforms in 1909 which provided separate electorate for the Muslims. This was based on the irrational hypothesis that the interests of Muslims were different from those of other Indians. Thus, the foundation of a state within state was laid down which partially fulfilled in 1947, when India was partitioned ostensibly on religious line.
13. Penderal Moon, *op. cit.*, p. 80.
14. H.V. Hodson, *op. cit.*, p. 13.
15. Percival Spear, *India, Pakistan and West*, p. 77.
16. R.J. Moore, 'British Policies and the Indian Problem, 1936-40,' in C.H. Philips and M.D. Wainwright (eds.), *op. cit.*, p. 79.
17. H.V. Hodson, *op. cit.*, p. 10.
18. Penderal Moon, *op. cit.*, p. 79.
19. Percival Spear, *The Oxford History of Modern India*, p. 354; *India, Pakistan and West*, p. 90 and 'A Third Force in India, 1920-47 : A Study in Political Analysis', in C.H. Philips and M.D. Wainwright (eds.), *op. cit.*, pp. 496-97.
20. Percival Spear, *The Oxford History of Modern India*, p. 462.
21. *Ibid.*, p. 360.
22. R.J. Moore, *The Crisis of Indian Unity*, p. 192.
23. Percival Spear, *India, Pakistan and West*, p. 206.
24. See Penderal Moon, *Gandhi and Modern India.*

25. R.J. Moore, *The Crisis of Indian Unity*, p. 207.
26. H.V. Hodson, *op. cit.*, p. 107.
27. Penderal Moon, *op. cit.*, p. 228.
28. Percival Spear, *The Oxford History of Modern India*, p. 384.
29. R.J. Moore, *Endgames of Empire : Studies of Britain's Indian Problem*, p. 9.
30. Percival Spear starts from A.D. 712.
31. H.V. Hodson starts from eleventh century A.D.
32. R.J. Moore, *The Crisis of Indian Unity*, p. 21.
33. *Ibid.*, p. 34.
34. Penderal Moon, *op. cit.*, p. 133.
35. R.J. Moore, *The Crisis of Indian Unity*, pp. 36-37; Penderal Moon, *op. cit.*, pp. 133-34 and Percival Spear, *The Oxford History of India*, pp. 356-64.
36. Percival Spear, *The Oxford History of Modern India*, p. 362.
37. R.J. Moore, *The Crisis of Indian Unity*, pp. 262-65.
38. See R.J. Moore, *The Crisis of Indian Unity*; and 'The Making of India's Paper Federation' and 'The British Policy and Indian Problem,' in C.H. Philips and M.D. Wainwright (eds.), *op. cit.*
39. R.J. Moore, *Endgames of Empire : Studies of Britain's Indian Problem*, pp. 15-16.
40. R.J. Moore, *The Crisis of Indian Unity*, p. 311.
41. Percival Spear, *The Oxford History of Modern India*, p. 375.
42. Penderal Moon, *op. cit.*, pp. 195-96.
43. P.N.S. Mansergh, *op. cit.*, p. 47.
44. R.J. Moore, *Endgames of Empire : Studies of Britain's Indian Problem*, p. 17.
45. R.J. Moore, 'The Making of India's Paper Federation,' in C.H. Philips and M.D. Wainwright (eds.), *op. cit.*, p.78.
46. R.J. Moore, 'The British Policy and Indian Problem,' in C.H. Philips and M.D. Wainwright (eds.), *op. cit.*, p. 82.
47. P.N.S. Mansergh, *op. cit.*, p. 46.
48. H.V. Hodson, *op. cit.*, p. 105.
49. Percival Spear, *The Oxford History of Modern India*, p. 382.
50. *Ibíd.*, pp. 303-84.
51. R.J. Moore, *Endgames of Empire : Studies of Britain's Indian Problems*, p. 26.

52. *Ibid.*, p. 27.
53. *Ibid.*, pp. 29-30.
54. *Ibid.*, p. 105.
55. R.J. Moore, 'British Policies and Indian Problem,' in C.H. Philips and M.D. Wainwright (eds.), *op. cit.*, p. 93.
56. R.J. Moore, *Endgames of Empire : Studies of Britain's Indian Problem*, p. 31.
57. *Ibid.*, p. 105.
58. H.V. Hodson, *op. cit.*, p. 125.
59. *Ibid.*, p. 128.
60. *Ibid.*, p. 133.
61. Percival Spear, *The Oxford History of Modern India*, p. 388.
62. A.C. Johnson, *op. cit.*, p. 354.
63. Penderal Moon, *op. cit.*, p. 54.
64. The confusion that followed over the Cabinet Mission led to its rejection by the Congress and the Muslim League. The Congress adopted the path of constitutionalism while the League selected the confrontationist policy and celebrated Direct Action Day on 16 August 1946. This resulted into widespread organised communal violence, which engulfed almost whole northern India.
65. Penderal Moon, *op. cit.*, p. 246.
66. R.J. Moore, *Endgames of Empire : Studies of Britain's Indian Problem*, p. 128.
67. *Ibid.*, p. 130.
68. *Ibid.*, p. 5.
69. A.C. Johnson, *op. cit.*, p. 354.
70. P.N.S. Mansergh, *op. cit.*, p. 50.
71. H.V. Hodson, *op. cit.*, p. 203.
72. *Ibid.*, p. 247.
73. R.J. Moore, *Endgames of Empire : Studies of Britain's Indian Problem*, p. 168.
74. R.J. Moore, *Escape from Empire : The Attlee Government and the Indian Problem*, p. 207.
75. A.C. Johnson, *op. cit.*, pp. 40-44.
76. H.V. Hodson, *op. cit.*, p. 319.
77. *Ibid.*, p. 181.
78. *Ibid.*, p. 12.

79. Percival Spear, *The Oxford History of Modern India*, p. 355.
80. Penderal Moon, *op. cit.*, p. 79.
81. A.C. Johnson, *op. cit.*, p. 354.
82. P.N.S. Mansergh, *op. cit.*, p. 50.
83. R.J. Moore, 'British Policies and Indian Problem,' in C.H. Philips and M.D. Wainwright (eds.), *op. cit.*, pp. 78-80.
84. R.J. Moore, *Endgames of Empire : Studies of Britain's Indian Problem*, p. 1.
85. R.J. Moore, *The Crisis of Indian Unity*, p. 311.
86. R.J. Moore, *Endgames of Empire : Studies of Britain's Indian Problem*, pp. 31 and 105.
87. Penderal Moon, *op. cit.*, p. 276.
88. Penderal Moon, *Future of India*, p. 23.
89. Panderal Moon, *Gandhi and Modern India*, p. 249.
90. Percival Spear, *The Oxford History of Modern India*, p. 361.
91. A.C. Johnson, *op. cit.*, p. 357.
92. See Anita Inder Singh, *The Origins of Partition of India*, p. 177.
93. R.J. Moore, *Endgames of Empire : Studies of Britain's Indian Problem*, pp. 132-33.
94. Percival Spear, *The Communal Harmony*, p. 6.
95. A.C. Johnson, *op. cit.*, p. 155.
96. P.N.S. Mansergh, *Commonwealth and the Nations*, p. 131.
97. R.J. Moore, *Endgames of Empire : Studies of Britain's Indian Problem*, pp. 132-33.
98. H.V. Hodson, *op. cit.*, p. 247.
99. A.C. Johnson, *op. cit.*, p. 117.
100. R.J. Moore, *Endgames of Empire : Studies of Britain's Indian Problem*, p. 168.
101. P.N.S. Mansergh, 'Some Reflections of the Transfer of Power in Plural Societies,' in C.H. Philips and M.D. Wainwright (eds.), *op. cit.*, pp. 43-53.
102. Percival Spear, *India, Pakistan and West*, p. 79.
103. H.V. Hodson, *op. cit.*, p. 10.
104. Penderal Moon, Gandhi and Modern India, p. 276.
105. A.C. Johnson, *op. cit.*, p. 31.
106. *Ibid.*, p. 40.

5

Conclusion

To conclude, the British historians writings on the different issues of partition of India reveal a characteristic duality and in view of this ambivalence demonstrate a commonality of purpose as well as heterogeneity in both the approaches and frameworks adopted for enquiry by different historians. As has been seen, all the historians studied here evince a common concern as well as praise, which is in some cases tinged with nostalgia for their colonial possession which at one time happened to be the "brightest jewel" of the British Crown.

The earlier historians were mainly administrator-turned historians. They were under the influence of preceding schools of British historiography — the Orientalist, the Utilitarians and the Evangelicals. They tried their best to defend the colonial policy and its policy-makers by tracing the origins of partition in pre-colonial India and by roundly blaming Indian National Congress and its leaders for it. Such an attempt on the part of British scholars naturally resulted in distortion and subjective biases. Evidently, however, the course of British historiography underwent a process of evoluation and change and this got reflected in the subsequent writings by British historians on partition. This change becomes clearly noticeable in the writings of British historians after the partition and independence of India. Apart from the fact that now both the partition and independence of India were translated into realities, there were other factors also which accounted for the change.

In the late 1960s, the British Government decided to publish the archival materials related to the transfer of power. These documents made the vast primary sources publicly available and this naturally brought into focus many issues which had been hitherto either neglected or ignored. It was this realization which impelled a group of scholars in England, India and Pakistan to think of organising a seminar on issues related to partition. This seminar became a reality which took place in London in 1969. The seminar papers published under the title the *Partition of India : Policy and Perspectives, 1935-1947* in 1970, highlighted the process of evoluation of partition historiography in three nations. The way some of the issues were discussed and the variety of approaches and perspectives underlined the need for further inquires on fresh lines. Moreover, the independence of East Pakistan as a new nation-state of Bangladesh in 1972, compelled the scholars to review most of the earlier hypotheses, especially, the religion-based two-nation theory. No wonder then that as the time passed, the scholars became more sober and sophisticated.

Coming to the earlier group of prominent British scholars on partition, H.V. Hodson appears to be a model of typical determinist historian. He tried to trace the origin of the partition from the Arab invasion and highlighted inter-community differences and neglected the similarities. Bypassing the colonial encouragement given to Muslim separatism, he asserts that the Congress policy especially after 1935 strengthened the Muslim separatism. However, in final discussion he opines that what happened in 1947 was bound to happen. It could not have been averted or avoided. He has also defended Mountbatten in all possible ways.

In a similar fashion, Percival Spear also underlines the decisive role of communalism responsible for partition. He has traced it in pre-colonial period. He has relied heavily on the Orientalist views that Hindus and Muslims in India form a separate, distinct and often mutually antagonistic communities, having no meeting point. When this compartmentalised society came under Western influence the responses and products were different. He opines that Hindus organised into the Indian National Congress while Muslims formed the All India Muslim League. These two organisations fought for different purposes. He blames the Congress policies for making the Muslims apprehensive of the Hindu Raj. Therefore, they demanded a separate nation-state. This communal deadlock could not be resolved due to Congress confrontationist policy. Therefore, the only option remained was partition which partially resolved this communal deadlock. Thus, Spear denies any role of the regime in the partition.

In the foregoing pages, we have seen that by March 1947, partition had become inevitable. Allen Campbell Johnson starts his discussion from this point of time and refrains from discussing the reason for the partition. He tries to impress that by the time Mountbatten arrived in India, both the Congress and the League had reconciled with the partition in some form or the other. The law and order situation had deteriorated to its lowest point. In this grim situation, he opines, only Mountbatten could succeed. He devised an agreed solution of the problem in the form of the 3 June Plan. And since this Plan was accepted by the Indian National Congress and the League, he generalised it as the acceptance by Indians. Thus, India, in his view, was partitioned with the agreement of Indians which has been presented as natural and obvious.

In spite of the fact that the 1970s witnessed a shift in the British historiography, Mansergh has tried to revive the classical imperialist hypotheses. He has denied simply that the British had promoted the policy of divide and rule which led to the partition. He opines that the Indian society was typical pluralistic society. Therefore, when Britishers decided to transfer the power they had to consider different successors. Thus, he asserted that although the British tried to have a united India, yet it was not possible due to natural plurality and the Congress policy. The other alternatives closed down and partition was the sole option. He also suggests that the Muslim League won Pakistan due to its concentration on this only option. In other words, Mansergh suggested that Britishers did not have any responsibility in the partition.

With the passage of time, the British scholars have realised that the negative role of the Raj especially towards its end could not be overlooked. Therefore, they have started by and large objective assessment of the role of the Raj and the British Government in the events leading to the partition. This trend got first prominent reflection in the writings of Penderal Moon. He has criticised the regime and the His Majesty's Government on several occasions. However, in final discussion, he comes very close to the traditional school of British historians. He blames the Congress in general and Gandhiji in particular for the division of India. He opines that Gandhi Hinduised the national movement. Therefore, the Muslim separatism grew. Thus, the pre-colonial gulf between two communities widened which could not be bridged. Hence, India was partitioned and the largest responsibility for this falls on the Congress and the least on the regime.

The British historiography of India's partition has taken a new shape in the writings of R.J. Moore. He has taken note of all the trends and utilised a vast range of official and private papers. He has traced the history of partition from the second decade of the twentieth century and discussed along with the British Government's policy of devolution of power by stages. He has discussed the role of the Congress, the League and the regime and different personalities. He has attempted to impress that the process of gradual devolution of power created several cleavages in the Indian society. This rifts widened gradually into unbridgeable gulfs. He blames the Congress as well as the British Conservative Government for intensifying the Muslim separatism. Thus, Moore has accepted the divisive impact of the British policy. But he does not equate it with the policy of divide and rule, rather he calls it a policy of collaboration in order to facilitate devolution. Thus, Moore has been by and large more objective and representative of the new trend within the broader framwork of the British historiography.

On the basis of foregoing discussion, it may he said that the British historians approached the theme of partition with a set goal and interpreted it on the basis of predetermined model. Therefore, they were in perfect agreement on several issues. They unanimously declare that the Indian society had been divided in mutually antagonistic blocks. They refute the charge that the colonial regime adopted and promoted the policy of divide and rule. They support the theme of civilising mission and the notion of white man's burden. They regard the Congress as a Hindu body and the Muslim League a nationalist organisation representing the Muslim nationalism. They completely negate the role of national movement in India's liberation. Although the neo-imperial trend is at times distinctly critical to the British policies in the last years of the Raj, the nostalgia for the Raj and its defence, by and large, runs as a common theme in the whole gamut of British writings on the partition. However, in the light of new researches and in view of the opening up of vast range of primary sources, the British historiography in recent times has been showing signs of a shift in a new and more pragmatic direction.

Bibliography

(A) PRIMARY SOURCES

Hodson, H.V., *The Great Divide : Britain, India and Pakistan,* London, 1969.

——, *Twentieth Century Empire,* London, 1966.

——, 'The Role of Lord Mountbatten,' in C.H. Philips and M.D. Wainwright (eds.), *The partition of India : Politics and Perspectives, 1935-47,* London, 1970.

Johnson, Allen Campbell, *The Mission with Mountbatten,* London, 1951.

——, *Growing Opinion,* London, 1935.

——, *Peace Offerings,* London, 1936.

——, *Anthony, Eden — A Biography,* London, 1938.

——, *Viscount Halifax — A Biography,* London, 1941.

Mansergh, P.N.S., *The Name and Nature of Commonwealth,* Cambridge, 1955.

——, *Commonwealth and the Nations,* London. 1968.

——, *Commonwealth Experience,* London, 1969.

——, *Prelude to Partition : Concepts and Aims in Ireland and India,* Cambridge, 1978.

——, 'Some Reflections on the Transfer of Power in Plural Societies,' in C.H. Philips and M.D. Wainwright (eds.), *op. cit.*

——, *The Constitutional Relation between Britain and India, 1942-1947, The Transfer of Power,* 12 Volumes, London, 1970-1983 (Editor-in-Chief).

Moon, Penderal, *Strangers in India,* London, 1943.

——, *Future of India,* London, 1945.

——, *Divide and Quit,* London, 1961.

——, *Warren Hastings and British India,* London, 1961.

——, *Gandhi and Modern India,* London, 1968.

——, 'May God be with you Always,' *The Round Table,* July 1971.

——, *Plain Tales from the Raj,* London, 1973 (ed.).

——, *Wavell* : *The Viceroy's Journal,* London, 1973.

——, *The British Conquest and Dominion of India,* London, 1989.

Moore, R.J., *Liberalism and Indian Politics, 1872-1922,* London, 1966.

——, *Crisis of Indian Unity,* Oxford, 1974.

——, *Churchill, Cripps and India 1939-45,* Oxford, 1979.

——, *Endgames of Empire* : *Studies of Britain's Indian Problem,* Oxford, 1988.

——, *Escape from Empire* : *The Attlee Government and the Indian Problem,* Oxford, 1983.

——, (ed.) *Tradition and Politics in South Asia,* New Delhi, 1979.

——, *Making of the New Commonwealth,* Oxford, 1987.

——, 'The Mystery of Cripps Mission,' *Journal of Commonwealth Political Studies,* XI (03) November 1973.

——, 'Recent Historical Writings on the Modern British Empire and Commonwealth, Later Imperial India,' *Journal of Imperial and Commonwealth History,* 4(1) October, 1975.

——, 'Mountbatten, India and Commonwealth,' *Journal of Commonwealth and Comparative Politics,* 19(1) March 1981.

——, 'Towards Partition and Independence in India,' *Journal of Commonwealth and Comparative Politics,* 20(2) July 1982.

——, 'The Mountbatten Viceroyalty,' *Journal of Commonwealth and Comparative Politics,* 22(2), 1984.

Spear, Percival, *Delhi* : *A Historical Sketch,* London, 1937.

——, *Communal Harmony,* London, 1940.

——, *India, Pakistan and West,* London, 1952.

——, *Delhi* : *Its Monuments and History,* London, 1945.

——, *Nabobs,* Karachi, 1955.

——, *India* : *A Modern History,* Michigan, 1961.

——, *Master of Bengal : Clive and His India,* London, 1975.

——, *The Oxford History of Modern India, 1740-1975,* Oxford, 1978.

——, (ed.) with S.M. Ikram, *Cultural Heritage of Pakistan,* Karachi, 1955; and with Spear Margaret, *India Remembered,* New Delhi, 1961.

(B) SECONDARY SOURCES ON THE PARTITION

Alexander, H.G., *India since Cripps,* London, 1944.

Adhikari, G.M., *Pakistan and Indian National Unity,* London, 1943.

——, *Pakistan and National Unity : The Communal Solution,* Bombay, 1942.

——, *The Imperiaslist Alternatives : Cripps Conspiracy for the Communal Award,* Bombay, 1945.

Agrawalla, N., *The Hindu-Muslim Question,* Calcutta, 1951.

Ahmad, A., *Islamic Modernism in India and Pakistan, 1857-1964,* London 1967.

Ahmad, Bashir, *Why Pakistan,* Lahore, 1978.

Ahmad, Jamiluddin, *Final Phase of Struggle for Pakistan,* Karachi, 1964.

——, *Muslim India and its Goal,* Aligarh, 1940.

——, *Through Pakistan to Freedom,* Lahore, 1944.

Ahmad, K.A., *The Foundation of Pakistan through Trial to Triumph,* Cambridge, 1942.

Ahmad, N., *The Basis of Pakistan,* Calcutta, 1977.

Ahmad, Qadeeneddin, *Pakistan Facts and Fallacies,* Karachi, 1979.

Ahmad, Qaidsaid-ud-din, *The Communal Pattern of India,* Lahore, 1945.

Ahmad, Saley, *The All India Muslim League,* Bahawalpur, 1989.

Ahmad, Sir S.S., *A Treaty between India and the United Kingdom,* New Delhi, 1945.

Ahmad, Rafiuddin, *The Bengal Muslims, 1871-1906, A Quest for Identity,* Delhi, 1981.

Ahmad, T., *Responsible Government and the Solution of the Hindu-Muslim Problem,* London, 1928.

Aiyar, H.R., *Why Pakistan?*, Tiruvanantpuram, 1945.

Akbar Pasha, M., *Pakistan Achieved,* Madras, 1947.

Albiruni, A.H., *Makers of Pakistan and Modern Muslim India,* Lahore, 1950.

Ali, Chaudhari Muhammed, *The Emergence of Pakistan,* New York, 1967.

Ali, Mohamed, *My Life : A Fragment,* London, 1942.

Ali, Tariq, *Can Pakistan Survive?* Hammondsworth, 1983.

Aman, Akhatar, *Pakistan and the Challenge of History,* Lahore, 1975.

Amery, L.S., *My Political Life,* 4 Vols., London, 1953-55.

Ambedkar, B.R., *Thoughts on Pakistan,* Bombay, 1943.

——, *Pakistan or the Partition of India,* (3rd edn.), Bombay, 1946.

——, *Ranade, Gandhi and Jinnah,* Bombay, 1943.

Ansari, S., *Pakistan : The Problem of India,* Lahore, 1944.

Asar, Harvani, *Before and After Freedom,* Delhi, 1989.

Ashe, G., *Gandhi : A Study in Revolution,* London, 1968.

Ashraf, K.M., *Pakistan Forward,* Delhi, 1940.

Aslam, A., *Pakistan Explained,* Delhi, 1940.

Attlee, C.R., *As It Happened,* London, 1954.

Azad, A.K., *India's Choice,* London, 1940.

——, *India Wins Freedom,* Bombay, 1959.

Aziz, K.K., *Britain and Indian Muslims, 1857-1947,* London, 1963.

——, *The Making of Pakistan : A Study in Nationalism,* London, 1967.

Bahadur, L., *The Muslim League, its History, Activities and Achievements,* Agra, 1954.

Bakshi, S.R., *Congresss, Muslim League and Problem of India,* Delhi, 1991.

Balabushevich, V.V. and Dyakov A.M. (eds.), *Contemporary History of India,* New Delhi, 1964.

Balitho, H., *Jinnah : Creator of Pakistan,* London, 1954.

Bandhopadhaya, *Caste and Communal Politics in South Asia,* Delhi, 1993.

Banerjee, D.N., *Partition or Freedom,* London, 1931.

Banerjee, S.N., *Psychotherapy of Indian Riots : A Study of the Causes, the Consequences and the Remedies of the Communal Riots in India,* Calcutta, 1941.

Bapat, N.S., *Nationalism versus Communalism — An Eassay on Hindu-Muslim Unity,* Poona, 1943.

Bayly, C.A., *Rulers, Townsmen and Bazars : North Indian Society in the Age of British Expansion 1770-1870,* Cambridge, 1983.

——, *Indian Society and the Making of the British Empire,* Cambridge, 1988.

Bhagat, K.P., *A Decade of Indo-British Relations, 1937-47,* Bombay, 1959.

Bhalla, Alok, *Stories about the Partition of India,* 3 Vols., Delhi, 1993.

Bhasin, Avtar Singh, *Some called it Partition, Some called Freedom, Last 75 Days of the Raj,* Delhi, 1998.

Bhasin, Kamla and Meron Ritu, *Borders and Boundaries : Women in India's Partition,* New Delhi, 1998.

Bhatt, S.C., *The Great Divide : Muslim Separatism and Partition,* New Delhi, 1998.

Bhide, A.S., *From Quit India to Split India,* Poona, 1945.

Birla, G.D., *In the Shadow of Mahatma : A Personal Memoir,* Bombay, 1953.

Bose, N.K., *My Days with Gandhi,* Calcutta, 1953.

——, *Studies in Gandhism,* Calcutta, 1967.

Bose, S.C., *The Indian Struggle,* London, 1935.

Bose, Sarat Chandra, *I Warned my countrymen,* Calcutta, 1968.

Bose, Sugata and Jalal, Ayesha, *Modern South Asia, History Culture, Political Economy,* Delhi, 1999.

Brittain, Vera, *Pathick Lawrence : A Portrait,* London, 1963.

Brown, Judith, *Gandhi : Prisoner of Hope,* London, 1990.

Callard, K., *Pakistan : A Political Study,* London, 1957.

Carritt, Michael, *A Mole in the Crown,* Calcutta, 1986.

Casey, R.G., *An Australian in India,* London, 1947.

Chakravarti, A., *Hindus and Musalmans of India,* Calcutta, 1940.

Chand, Duri, *The Ulster of India,* Lahore, 1936.

Chandra, Bipan, *Nationalism and Colonialism in Modern India,* New Delhi, 1979.

——, *The Indian Left : Critical Appraisal,* New Delhi, 1983.

——, *Communalism in Modern India,* New Delhi, 1984.

——, *Indian National Movement : Long-Term Dynamics,* New Delhi, 1988.

Chandra, Prabodh, *Rape of Rawalpindi,* Lahore, 1947.

Chatterji, A., *Constitutional Development in India : 1937-47,* Calcutta, 1958.

Chatterji, Joya, *Bengal Divided — Hindu Communalism and Partition, 1932-47,* Delhi, 1994.

Chaudhari, B.M., *Muslim Politics in India,* Calcutta, 1946.

Chaudhari, G.W., *Pakistan's Relations with India, 1945-66,* Lahore, 1968.

Chaudhari, N.C., *An Autobiography of an Unknown Indian,* London, 1951.

Chaudhary, Sandhya, *Gandhi and Partition of India,* New Delhi, 1984.

Chaudhary, Zahid, *Pakistan Ki Siyasi Tarikh — Pakistan Kaise Bana,* 4 Volumes, Lahore, 1989-90.

Cohn, Bernard, *Colonialism and its Forms of Knowledge : The British India,* Delhi, 1996.

Collins, Larry and Lapeirre, Daminique, *Freedom at Midnight,* New York, 1975.

——, *Mountbatten and Partition of India,* New Delhi, 1982.

Colonel, J., *Auchinleck,* London, 1959.

Cooke, C., *Life of Richard Stafford Cripps,* London, 1957.

Dalal, M.N., *Whither Minorities?,* Bombay, 1940.

Dalal, Sir A.R., *An Alternative to Pakistan,* New Delhi, 1945.

Damodaran, Vinita, *Broken Promises : Congress Party in Bihar, 1935-46,* Delhi, 1992.

Dani, Ahmad Hasan, *Founding Father of Pakistan,* Islamabad, 1981.

Danis, K., 'India and Pakistan : The Demography of Pakistan,' *in Pacific Affairs,* xxii, Sept. 1949.

Dar, B.A., *Why Pakistan?,* Lahore, 1946.

Darling, M.L., *The Punjab Peasants in Prosperity and Debt,* London, 1947.

Das, M.N., *The Political Philosophy of Jawaharlal Nehru,* London, 1961.

Das, Manath Nath, *Partition and Independence of India,* Delhi, 1982.

Das, Suranjan, *Communal Riots in Bengal, 1905-47,* Delhi, 1993.

Das, Veena, *Mirror of Violence,* Delhi, 1990.

Datta, V.N. and others, *A Nationalist Muslim and Indian Politics,* Delhi, 1974.

Desai, A.R. (ed.), *Peasant Struggle in India,* Bombay, 1979.

Desai, M., *Maulana Abul Kalam Azad,* Agra, 1948.

Deva, Narendra, *Socialism and National Revolution,* Bombay, 1979.

Durrani, F.K.K, *The Making of Pakistan,* Lahore, 1944.

——, *The Future of Islam in India,* Lahore, 1946.

Dutta, B.C., *Mutiny of the Innocents,* Bombay, 1971.

Dutta, R.P., *A Guide to the Problem of India,* London, 1942.

——, *Freedom for India : The Truth about the Cabinet Mission's Visit,* London, 1946.

——, *A New Chapter in Divide and Rule,* Bombay, 1946.

——, *India Today,* London, 1940.

Dwarkadas, K., *India's Fight for Freedom,* Bombay, 1966.

Edwards, M., *The Last Years of British India,* London, 1963.

E.L. Hamza, *Pakistan : A Nation,* Lahore, 1946.

Embree, A.T., *Religion and Nationalism in Modern India,* Oxford, 1992.

Epstein, Simon, *The Earthly Soil — Bombay Peasants and the Indian National Movement, 1919-47,* Delhi, 1988.

Evans, Hubert, *Looking Back on India,* London, 1988.

Farooqui, M., *India's Freedom Struggle and the Communist Party of India,* New Delhi, 1974.

Faruqui, Z., *The Deoband School and Demand for Pakistan,* London, 1963.

Fazl-ul-Haq, A.K., *Muslim Suffering under Congress Rule,* Calcutta, 1939.

Fischer, Louis, *The Life of Mahatma Gandhi,* New York, 1956.

Fotimizi, S.Q., *Pakistan Movement and Kemalist Movement,* Lahore, 1977.

Francis, Tucker, *India's Partition and Human Debasement,* Vols. I and II, New Delhi, 1974.

Fraser, T.G., *Partition of Ireland, India and Palestine,* London, 1985.

Freitag, B., *Collective Action and Community, Public Arenas and the Emergence of Communalism in North India,* Delhi, 1990.

French, Patrick, *Liberty or Death, India's Journey to Independence and Division,* London, 1997.

Furnivall, J.S., *Colonial Policy and Practice,* Cambridge, 1998.

Gandhi, M.K., *An Autobiography or the Story of My Experiments with Truth,* Ahmedabad, 1940.

——, *Delhi Diary,* Ahmedabad, 1940.

——, *Communal Unity,* Ahmedabad, 1949.

——, *To the Protagonist of Pakistan,* Karachi, 1947.

Gauba, K.G., *The Assassination of Mahatma Gandhi,* Bombay, 1969.

Gauba, K.L., *The Consequences of Pakistan,* Lahore, 1946.

Gautam, Meena, *Communalism and Indian Politics,* Delhi, 1993.

Gehlet, N.S., *The Congress Party in India,* New Delhi, 1991.

Gellner, Ernest, *Post-Modernism, Reason and Religion,* New York, 1992.

Ghai, Premwati, *The Partition of Punjab, 1847-1947,* Delhi, 1986.

Ghosh, S., *Gandhi's Emissary,* London, 1967.

Golwalker, M.S., *We or our Nationhood Defined,* Nagpur, 1947.

Gopal, R., *Indian Muslims : A Political History,* Bombay, 1959.

Gopal, Ram, *How India Struggled for Freedom,* Bombay, 1967.

Gopal, S., *The Viceroyalty of Lord Irwin, 1926-31,* Oxford, 1957.

Gopal, S., *Jawaharlal Nehru : A Biography,* Vol. I 1889-1947, New Delhi, 1976.

——, *Jawaharlal Nehru : An Anthology,* Delhi, 1980.

——, *Selected Works,* New Delhi, 1980.

Gopalan, A.K., *In the Causes of the People,* New Delhi, 1978.

Gordon, Leonard A., *Brother against the Raj,* Oxford, 1990.

Graham, G.F.I., *The Life and Work of Syed Ahmad Khan,* Edinburgh, 1885.

Griffith, P.J., *The British Impact on India,* London, 1965.

——, *Modern India,* London, 1957.

——, *The British in India,* London, 1946.

Grover, Verinder (ed.), *B.R. Ambedkar,* New Delhi, 1993.

——, *Abul Kalam Azad,* New Delhi, 1993.

Gupta, A.K. (ed.), *Myth and Reality : The Struggle for Freedom in India, 1945-47,* Delhi, 1987.

Gupta, N.L., *Nehru on Communalism,* Delhi, 1965.

Gupta, Partha Sarthi, *Imperialism and British Labour Movement,* 1914-64, London, 1974.

Halide, Edib, *Inside India,* London, 1937.

Halifax, Lord, *Fulness of Days,* London, 1947.

Hamid, A., *A Brief Survey of Muslim Separatism in India,* Delhi, 1968.

Hamid, Shahid, *Disastrous Twilight : A Personal Record of the Partition of India,* London, 1986.

Hamza, E.L., *Pakistan, A Nation,* Lahore, 1941.

Haq, Ch. A., *Pakistan and Untouchability,* Lahore, 1941.

Haq, Jalalul, *Nation and Nation Worship in India,* Delhi, 1992.

Haq, M., *Muslims in India,* Delhi, 1964.

Hardy, P., *The Muslims of British India,* London, 1972.

Hasan, K. Sarwar, *The Transfer of Power,* Karachi, 1968.

Hasan, Mushirul, *Communal and Pan-Islamic Trends in Colonial India,* Delhi, 1981.

——, *India's Partition,* Delhi, 1993.

——, *Muslims and the Congress,* Delhi, 1979.

——, *Adjustment and Accommodation : Indian Muslims after Partition,* New Delhi, 1990.

——, *Congress Muslims and Indian Nationalism : Dilemma and Decline 1928-34,* New Delhi, 1985.

——, *In Search of Integration and Identity : Indian Muslims since Independence,* New Delhi, 1988.

——, *Legacy of a Divided Nation : India's Muslims since Independence,* New Delhi, 1997.

——, *Mohammad Ali : Ideology and Politics,* New Delhi, 1981.

——, *Muslim Mass Contact Campaign : An Attempt at Political Mobilisation,* New Delhi, 1984.

——, *Nationalism and Communal Politics in India, 1885-1930,* New Delhi, 1991.

——, *India's Partition Problems, Strategy and Mobilisation,* Delhi, 1993.

——, *India's Partition : The Other Face of Freedom,* 2 Vols., New Delhi, 1995.

——, *Islam, Communities and the Nations : Muslim Identities in South Asia and Beyond,* New Delhi, 1998.

Hasan, Qamrul, *Birth of Pakistan Step by Step,* Lahore, 1984.

Hough, Richard, *Mountbatten — Hero of our Time,* London, 1980.

Hunter, W.W., *Indian Musalmans,* Calcutta, 1945.

Hussain, A., *Sir Fazl-i-Hussain : A Political Biography,* Bombay, 1965.

Hussain, M, *et al.* (eds.), *A History of the Freedom Movement, 1909-47,* 4 Vols., Karachi, 1957-61.

Ikram, S.M., *History of Muslim Civilisation in India and Pakistan,* Lahore, 1961.

Iqbal, M., *Stray Reflections,* Lahore, 1961.

Ismail, Sir M., *My Public Life,* Lahore, 1954.

Ismay, Lord, *Memoirs,* London, 1960.

Ispahani, M.A.H., *Qaid-i-Azam Jinnah, As I knew Him,* Karachi, 1966.

Jain, A.P., *Rafi Ahmad Kidwai,* New Delhi, 1965.

Jalal, Ayesha, *The Sole Spokesman : Jinnah, The Muslim League and the Demand for Pakistan,* Cambridge, 1985.

Jamiluddin (ed), *M.A. Jinnah : Speeches and Writings,* 2 vols., Lahore.

Jaspal, J.I., *Jinnah and the Creation of Pakistan,* Delhi, 1983.

Jaya Prasad, K., *Rashtriya Swayam Sewak Sangh and Hindu Nationalism,* Delhi, 1991.

Jayakar, M.R., *The Story of My Life,* 2 Vols., Bombay, 1958-9.

Jeffries, C., *The Transfer of Power,* London, 1960.

Johnston, J., *Hindu Domination in India : An Examination of the Origins, Objectives and Results of the Government Proposals,* Southand, 1935.

——, *Can the Hindu Rule India?,* London, 1935.

Josh, Bhagwan, *Communist Movement in Punjab,* Delhi, 1979.

Joshi, P.C., *They Must Meet Again,* Bombay, 1944.

Kabir, H., *Muslim Politics, 1906-42,* Calcutta, 1943.

Karim, R., *For India and Islam,* Calcutta, 1937.

——, *Pakistan Examined, with Partition Schemes of Dr. Latif by Sikandar Hyat Khan and Others,* Calcutta, 1941.

——, *Muslims and the Congress,* Calcutta, 1941.

Kaushik, B.G., *The House that Jinnah Built,* Bombay, 1944.

Kidwai, M.H., *Pan-Islamism and Bolshevism,* London, 1937.

Khaliquzzaman, C., *Pathway to Pakistan,* Lahore, 1961.

Khan, A.M., *The Communalism in India, its Origin and Growth,* Lahore, 1944.

Khan, M., *Muslim Demand for Pakistan,* Lahore, 1942.

——, *Pakistan : A Hindu View,* Lahore, 1942.

Khan, M.H., *The Case for Pakistan,* Lahore, 1941.

Khan, Rasheeduddin, *Bewildered India : Identity, Pluralism, Discord,* Delhi, 1974.

Khan, Shafique Ali, *Separate Electorates as the Genesis of Pakistan,* Hyderabad, 1976.

——, *Two-Nation Theory : As a Concept, Strategy and Ideology,* Karachi, 1973.

——, *Iqbal's Concept of a Separate North-West Muslim State,* Karachi, 1987.

Khan, S. Shaukat-Hyat, *The Nation that Lost its Soul,* London, 1985.

Khan, Sir S.A., *What are the Rights of the Muslim Minority in India?*, Allahabad, 1928.

Khosla, G.D., *Stern Reckoning : A Survey of Events Leading up to and Following the Partition of India,* New Delhi, 1949.

Kripalani, J.B., *Fateful Year,* Bombay, 1948.

——, *Gandhi – His Life and Thought,* New Delhi, 1970.

Kripalani, Sucheta, *An Unfinished Autobiography,* (ed.) K.N. Vaswani, New Delhi, 1978.

Krishna, J.B., *The Problem of Minorities,* London, 1939.

Kulasrestha, M. and Mathur, R., *Writings on India's Partition,* Delhi, 1976.

Kulkarni, V.B., *Is Pakistan Necessary?,* Bombay, 1944.

Kumarappa, *Can India be United?,* 1945.

Kumar, Pramod, *Towards Understanding Communalism,* Delhi, 1992.

Kuwajima, Shao, *Muslims, Nationalism and the Partition : 1946 Provincial Elections in India,* Delhi, 1998.

Laclau, E. (ed.), *The Making of Political Identities,* New York, 1994.

Lahoi, Kumar Pradip, *Bengali Muslim Thought, 1918-47,* Calcutta, 1991.

Latif, S.A., *The Muslim Problem of India,* Bombay, 1939.

——, *The Great Leader,* Lahore, 1947.

Limaye, Madhu, *Mahatma Gandhi and Jawaharlal Nehru,* 4 Vols., New Delhi, 1989.

Linlithgow, *Speeches and Statements, 1936-43,* New Delhi, 1975.

Lohiya, Ram Manohar, *Guilty Man of Partition,* Allahabad, 1960.

Louis, W. Roger, *Imperialism at Bay : The United States and the Decolonisation of the British Empire, 1941-45,* New York, 1978.

Low, D.A. (ed.), *Congress and the Raj : Facets of the India Struggle, 1917-47,* London, 1977.

——, *The Indian National Congress, Centenary Hindsight,* Delhi, 1988.

——, *The Political Inheritance of Pakistan,* London, 1991.

Lumbey, E.W.R., *The Transfer of Power in India, 1945-47,* London, 1954.

Madhok, Balraj, *Hindustan on Crossroad,* Lahore, 1946.

——, *Dr. Shyama Prasad Mukherjee : A Biography,* New Delhi, 1954.

Mahajan, M.C., *Looking Back,* Bombay, 1963.

Mahajan, Sucheta, *Independence and Partition, Erosion of colonial Hegemony,* New Delhi, 2000.

Mahmood, *Founder of Pakistan,* Delhi, 1988.

Majumdar, A.K., *Advent of Independence,* Bombay, 1963.

Majumdar, R.C., *History of Freedom Movement,* Calcutta, 1962.

Majumdar, S.K., *Jinnah and Gandhi : Their Role in India's Quest for Freedom,* Calcutta, 1966.

Malik, H., *Moslem Nationalism in India and Pakistan,* Washington, 1963.

Malik, H., *Iqbal : Poet-Philosopher of Pakistan,* New York, 1971.

Manshardt, C., *The Hindu-Muslim Problem in India,* London, 1936.

Masani, R.P., *Britain in India,* London, 1960.

Masselos, J. (ed.), *India : Creating a Modern Nation,* New York, 1990.

Maudooi, A.A., *Nationalism and India,* Pathankot, 1947.

Mehta, A. *et al., The Communal Triangle in India,* Allahabad, 1942.

Meherally, Y., *A Trip to Pakistan,* 1943.

Mellor, A., *India since Partition,* New York, 1951.

Menon, V.P., *The Transfer of Power in India,* London, 1957.

Michel, A.A., *The Indus River : A Study of the Effects of Partition,* Newhaven, 1967.

Mishra, B.B., *The Unification and Division of India,* New Delhi, 1990.

Mitra, Ashok, *Towards Independence,* Bombay, 1991.

Mohammad Manawar, *Dimension of Pakistan Movement,* Lahore, 1987.

Mookerji, R.K., *A New Approach to Communal Problem,* Bombay, 1943.

Mosley, L., *The Last Days of the British Raj,* London, 1961.

Moulvi, Niamat U., *The Ideology of Pakistan,* Lahore, 1970.

Mountbatten, Lord, *Time only to Look Forward,* London, 1950.

Mujahid, Sharif al, *Quaid-i-Azam Jinnah : Studies in Interpretation,* Karachi, 1981.

Mujeeb, H., *The Indian Muslims,* London, 1967.

Mukherjee, Hiren, *Gandhijee : A Study,* Delhi, 1979.

Mukherjee, R., *The Economist Looks at Pakistan,* Bombay, 1944.

Mukherjee, S., *Communalism in Muslim Politics,* Calcutta, 1947.

Munshi, K.M., *Pilgrimage to Freedom,* Bombay, 1967.

——, *I Follow the Mahatma,* Bombay, 1940.

——, *Akhand Hindustan,* Bombay, 1942.

——, *Indian Deadlock,* Allahabad, 1945.

——, *The Changing Shape of Indian Politics,* Poona, 1946.

——, *The End of an Era,* Bombay, 1957.

Murphy, G., *In the Minds of Men,* New York, 1953.

Nagarkar, V.V., *Genesis of Pakistan,* New Delhi, 1975.

Naim, C.M., *Iqbal, Jinnah and Pakistan : The Vision and the Reality,* New Delhi, 1979.

Namboodaripad, E.M.S, *A History of Indian Freedom Struggle,* Trivendrum, 1986.

Nanda, B.R., *Mahatma Gandhi : A Biography,* London, 1958.

——, *Gandhi and His critics,* New Delhi, 1985.

——, *The Nehrus, Motilal and Jawaharlal,* London, 1962.

Naqvi, Mustaq, *Partition : The Real Story,* Delhi, 1995.

Narayan, J.P., *Towards, Struggle,* Bombay, 1946.

Nehru, Jawaharlal, *India and the World,* London, 1936.

——, *The Question of Language,* Allahabad, 1937.

——, *Where Are We?*, Allahabad, 1938.

——, *The Discovery of India,* London, 1946.

——, *An Autobiography,* London, 1936.

Nicholas, B., *Verdict on India,* Bombay, 1944.

Nicholas, M., *The Self-Government and the Communal Problem,* London, 1948.

Nirmal Kumar, *Rajendra Prasad and the Indian Freedom Struggle (1917-47)*, Delhi, 1991.

Nizami, K.A., *Maulana Azad,* Delhi, 1990.

Norman, M., *Muslim India : Rise and Growth of the All India Muslim League,* Allahabad, 1942.

——, *Our Struggle, 1857-1947, A Pictorial Record of the Pakistan Movement,* Karachi, 1947.

Noronha, R.P., *A Tale Told by an Idiot,* New Delhi, 1976.

Ovendale, Ritchie, *The English Speaking Alliance : Britain, the United States, the Dominions and the Cold War, 1945-51,* London, 1985.

Overstreet, Gene D. and Windmiller Marshall, *Communism in India,* Los Angeles, 1959.

Page, David, *Prelude to Parititition,* Oxford, 1982.

Pandey, Deepak, *The Role of Muslim League in National Politics,* Delhi, 1991.

Pandey, Gyanendra (ed.), *Indian Nation in 1942,* Calcutta, 1988.

Panjabi, K.L., *The Indomitable Sardar,* Bombay, 1962.

Panikkar, K.N., *Communalism in India,* Delhi, 1991.

Parekh, Bhikku, *Colonialism, Tradition and Reform : An Analysis of Gandhi's Political Discourse,* New Delhi, 1989.

Parikh, N.D., *Sardar Vallabhbhai Patel,* Ahmedabad, 1953.

Philips, C.H., *The Partition of India, 1947,* Leeds, 1967.

——, *The Evolution of India and Pakistan,* London, 1967.

Philips, C.H. and Wainwright, M.D. (eds.), *The Partition of India, Politics and Prespectives, 1935-47,* London, 1970.

Pirzada, S.S., *The Evolution of Pakistan,* Lahore, 1963.

——, *Some Aspects of Qaid-i-Azam's Life,* Islamabad, 1978.

——, *Foundation of Pakistan : All India Muslim League Documents, 1906-1947,* 2 Vols. Karachi, 1969-70.

Potter David and Stockwell, A.J., *British Imperial Policy and Decolonisation,* Vol. I, *1938-51,* Handsmills, 1987.

Prakash, I., *A Review of the History and Work of the Hindu Mahasabha,* New Delhi, 1953.

Prakash, Sri., *Pakistan Birth and Early Days,* Meerut, 1965.

Prasad, Bimal, *Gandhi, Nehru and Jayaprakash : Studies in Leadership,* Delhi, 1985.

Prasad, Rajendra, *Autobiography,* Bombay, 1957.

——, *India Divided,* Bombay, 1947.

Pyarelal, U.N., *Mahatma Gandhi : The Last Phase,* 2 Vols., Ahmedabad, 1956-58.

Qadri, Shamim Hussain, *Creation of Pakistan,* Rawalpindi, 1982.

Qureshi, I.H., *The Muslim Community of the Indo-Pakistan Subcontinent,* Is-Gravenhage, 1962.

Qureshi, A.I., *Economic Basis of Pakistan,* Lahore, 1947.

Qureshi, Fazal Haque, *Early Days with the Qaid-i-Azam,* Karachi, 1976.

Qureshi, S.M.M., *The Politics of Jinnah,* Karachi, 1988.

Rahmat Ali, C., *What Does Pakistan National Movement Stand for?,* Cambridge, 1933.

——, *Pakistan, the Fatherland of the Pakistan Nation,* Cambridge, 1947.

Rai, G., *Pakistan X-rayed,* Lahore, 1946.

Raja, S. Hasim, *Mountbatten and the Partition of India,* Delhi, 1989.

Rajput, A.B., *Muslim League Yesterday and Today,* London, 1948.

Raman, T.A., *What does Gandhi Want?,* New York, 1945.

Ranga, N.G., *Fight for Freedom,* New Delhi, 1968.

Rav, G.V. Subha, *The Partition of India,* Amlapuram, 1958.

Ravi, Vijay Shankar, *The Last Phase of the Transfer of Power in India,* Delhi, 1990.

Ravoof, A.A., *Meet Mr. Jinnah,* Lahore, 1944.

Rizvi, Begum F., *Pakistan Defined,* Lahore, 1945.

Reed, S., *The India I Knew, 1897-1947,* London, 1952.

Rizvi, S.S. Hussain, *Partition : End Product of the Trend,* Patna, 1998.

Robinson, F., *Separatism among Indian Muslims,* Delhi, 1993.

Russell, W.W., *Indian Summer,* Bombay, 1951.

Sahni, Bhisham, *Tamas,* New Delhi, 1984.

Saiyed, M.H., *Mohammed Ali Jinnah,* Lahore, 1953.

Saksena, R.N., *Refugees : A Study in Changing Attitudes,* New Delhi, 1961.

Sapru, T.B., *Welding a Nation,* edited by K.N. Raina, Bombay, 1974.

Sarkar, Sumit, *Modern India, 1885-1947,* New Delhi, 1983.

Savarkar, V.D., *Hindu Rashtra Darshan, A Collection of the Presidential Speeches,* Bombay, 1949.

Sayeed, K.B., *Pakistan : The Formative Phase, 1857-1948,* London, 1968.

Sen, D., *The Problem of Minorities,* Calcutta, 1940.

Sen, Sachin, *Birth of Pakistan,* Lahore, 1978.

Sen, Shila, *Muslim Politics in Bengal, 1937-1947,* New Delhi, 1976.

Sen, Sunil, *Agrarian Struggle in Bengal, 1946-47,* New Delhi, 1972.

Shervani, Latif Ahmad, *The Partition of India and Mountbatten,* Karachi, 1986.

Setalvad, C., *Recollections and Reflections,* Bombay, 1946.

Seth, L.H., *The Khaksar Movement under Searchlight and the Story of its Leader Allama Mushriqi,* Lahore, 1943.

Shafi, M.M., *Some Important Indian Problems,* Lahore, 1930.

Shah, I.A., *Pakistan : A Plan for India,* London, 1944.

Shah, K.T., *Why Pakistan? and Why not?,* Bombay, 1944.

Shahi, Shyamanandan, *Lala Lajpat Rai : The Life and Thought,* New Delhi, 1986.

Shaikh, Farzana, *Community and Consensus in Islam : Muslim Representation in Colonial India, 1860-1947,* London, 1989.

Shakir Moin, *India's March towards Freedom, 1935-47,* New Delhi, 1981.

Singh, Anita Inder, *The Origins of the Partition of India, 1936-1947,* New Delhi, 1987.

Singh, Braj Kishore, *The Indian National Congress and the Partition of India, 1937-47,* Delhi, 1990.

——, *The INC and the Partition Case,* Delhi, 1989.

Singh, Kirpal (ed.), *Selected Documents on Partition of Punjab, 1947, India and Pakistan,* Delhi, 1991.

Singh, Khushwant, *The Sikhs,* London, 1953.

——, *Train to Pakistan,* New Delhi, 1961.

Sinha, Sachchidananda, *Iqbal : The Poet and His Message,* Allahabad, 1947.

Singh, Tara, *Why We must Avoid a Civil War in India,* Lahore, 1946.

Sinha, R.K., *Communal Problem : A Fresh Approach,* Lucknow, 1946.

Smith, R.A., *Divided India,* New York, 1947.

Smith, W.C., *Modern Islam in India,* London, 1954.

——, *Islam in Modern History,* London, 1957.

Smith, W.R., *Nationalism and Reform in India,* New Haven, 1938.

Stephens, I., *Pakistan,* London, 1963.

——, *Monsoon Morning,* London, 1966.

Suleri, Z.A., *The Road to Peace and Pakistan,* Lahore, 1977.

——, *My Leader,* Lahore, 1946.

Sur, Atul, *Will the Two Bengals be one?,* Calcutta, 1989.

Symouds, R., *The Making of Pakistan,* London, 1950.

Tarachand, *History of Freedom Movement in India,* Vol. 4, New Delhi, 1972.

Templewood, *Nine Troubled Years,* London, 1954.

Tendulkar, D.G., *Mahatma : Life of Mohandas Karamchand Gandhi,* 8 Vols., Bombay, 1960-63.

Terraive, John, *The Life and Times of Lord Mountbatten,* London, 1980.

Tinker, H.R., *Experiment with Freedom : India and Pakistan 1947,* London, 1967.

Tirmizi, S.A.I. (ed.), *The Paradoxes of Partition, 1937-47,* 2 Vols., New Delhi, 1998.

Tomlinson. B.R., *The Political Economy of the Raj 1914-47,* New Delhi, 1979.

——, *The Indian National Congress and the Raj, 1929-42 : The Penultimate Phase,* London, 1976.

Toosy, Md. Sharif, *Pakistan and Muslim India,* Sind, 1992.

Trumbull, R., *India since Partition,* New York, 1954.

Tuker, Sir F., *While Memory Serves,* London, 1950.

Tyabji, H.B., *Why Musalmans should Oppose Pakistan?* Bombay, 1946.

Vairanapillai, M.S., *Are We Two Nations?, Nationalism in Indian Politics : Scientific and Non-Partition Approach,* Lahore, 1946.

Vakil, C.N., *Economic Cousequences of Divided India : A Study of the Economics of India and Pakistan,* Bombay, 1950.

Vivekanandan, V., *Shrinking Circle : The Commonwealth in British Foreign Policy, 1945-74,* Bombay, 1974.

Waheed, Khan A., *India wins Freedom, The Other Side,* Karachi, 1961.

Waheed-uz-zaman, *Towards Pakistan,* Lahore, 1964.

——, *Qaid-i-Azam Mohammad Ali Jinnah : Myth and Reality,* Lahore, 1985.

Wakefield, Edward, *Past Imperative : My Life in India, 1927-44,* London, 1966.

Williams, L.F. Rushhrook, *The State of Pakistan,* London, 1966.

Wingate, Ronald, *Lord Ismay : A Biography,* London, 1970.

Winterton, Earl, *Orders of the Day,* London, 1953.

——, *Fifty Tumultous Years,* London, 1955.

Wolpert, Stanlay, *Jinnah of Pakistan,* New York, 1984.

Woodruff, P., *The Men who Ruled India,* Vol. II, *The Guardians,* London, 1954.

Zahur, S., *A Case for Congress-League Unity,* Bombay, 1944.

Zaidi, A.M.(ed.), *Evolution of Muslim Political Thought in India,* Vol. 6; *Freedom at Last,* New Delhi, 1979; idem (ed.), *Encyclopaedia of the Indian National Congress,* Vols. 12 and 13, New Delhi, 1981.

Zaidi, Z.H. (ed.), *Introduction to M.A. Jinnah-Ispahani Correspondence, 1936-48,* Karachi, 1976.

(C) GENERAL WORKS ON HISTORIOGRAPHY

Achinstein, Peter, *The Nature of Explanation,* New York, 1983.

Ali, B. Sheik, *History : Its Theory and Method,* Madras, 1978.

Althusser, Louis, *For Marx,* London, 1969.

Anisuzzam, and Melek, Anwar Abdul, *Culture and Thought,* London, 1983.

Ankersmit, F.R., *Narrative Logic,* The Hague, 1983.

Aronson, J.L., *Realist Philosophy of Science,* London, 1984.

Atkinson, R.F., *Knowledge and Eplanation in History,* London 1978.

Ayer, A.J. and Winch, P., *British Empirical Philosophers,* London, 1965.

Ayer, A.J., *Philosophy in Twentieth Century,* London, 1982.

Baker, G.P. and Hacker, P.M.S., *Scepticism, Rules and Language,* Oxford, 1984.

Banga, Indu (ed.), *Causation in History,* 1989.

Bannet, E.T., *Structuralism and the Logic of Dissent,* London, 1989.

Bateson, Nicholas, *Data Construction in Social Surveys,* London, 1976.

Baumamn, Zygmunt, *Hemeneutics and Social Science,* London, 1978.

Berbshkina, Z, *et al., What is Historical Materialism*?, Moscow, 1985.

Berger, P.L. and Luckman, T., *Social Construction in Reality; A Treatise in the Sociology of Knowledge,* Harmondsworth, 1976.

Berlim, Isaiah, *Vico and Herder,* London, 1976.

Bernstein, Richard, *The Restructuring of Social and Political Theory,* London, 1979.

——, *Beyond Objectivism and Relativism,* Oxford, 1985.

——, *Philosophical Profiles,* Cambridge, 1986.

Bleicher, Josef, *Contemporary Hermeneutics, Hermeneutics as Method, Philosophy and Critique,* London, 1980.

Bloc, Marc, *The Historian's Craft,* New York, 1953.

Braudel, Fernand, *On History* (Trans. by Sarah Matthews), Chicago, 1980.

Brodbek, May (ed.), *Readings in the Philosophy of Social Science,* New York, 1968.

Brown, R.H. and Lyman, S.M. (eds.), *Structure, Consciousness and History,* Cambridge, 1978.

Brown, S.C. (ed), *Philosophers of Enlightenment,* Sussex, 1979.

Brown, S., J. Fauvel and Finnegan, R. (eds.), *Conceptions of Inquiry,* New York, 1981.

Bulhof, I.N., *Wilhelm Dilthey : A Hermeneutic Approach to the Study of History and Culture,* The Hague, 1981.

Burckhardt, Jakab, *Reflections on History,* London, 1950.

Burke, E.T., *The Philosophy of Proper,* Oxford, 1983.

Butterfield, Herbert, *Man on his Past : A Study of the History of Historical Scholarship,* Cambridge, 1969.

Butts, R.E. and Hentikka, I. (eds.), *Historical and Philosophical Dimension of Logic, Methodology and Philosophy of Science,* Dordrecht, 1977.

Carr, E.H., *What is History?* Harmondworth, 1971.

Cassirer, Ernest, *The Problem of Knowledge,* New Haven, 1950.

——, *The Philosophy of Enlightenment,* Boston, 1955.

——, *The Logic of Humanities,* New Haven, 1961.

——, *An Essay on Man; An Introduction to a Philosophy of Human Culture,* New Haven, 1962.

Chandra, Satish, *Historiography, Religion and State in Medieval India,* New Delhi, 1976.

Chaturvedi, Jayati, *Indian National Movement; A Critical Study of Five Schools,* Agra, 1990.

Cohen, M.R. and Nagal, E., *Introduction to Logic and Scientific Method,* London, 1957.

Cohn, Bernand S., *Colonialism and its Forms of Knowledge,* Delhi, 1997.

Collin, Fain, *Theory and Understanding,* Oxford, 1985.

Collingwood, R.G., *Essays in the Philosophy of History,* Austin,1965.

——, *The Idea of History,* New York, 1976.

Connerton, P. (ed.), *Critical Sociology,* Harmondworth, 1976.

Croce, Benedett, *Philosophy, Poetry and History : An Anthology of Essays,* London, 1966.

Dallmayr, F. and Carthy, T.Mc. (eds.), *Understanding and Social Inquiry,* Notre Dame, 1977.

Danto, A.C., *Narration and Knowledge,* New York, 1985.

Derrida, J., *Of grammatology* (trans. by G.C. Spivak), Maryland, 1976.

——, *Margins of Philosophy* (trans. by Alan Bats), Chicago, 1982.

Devahuti (ed.), *Problems of Indian Historiography,* Delhi, 1979.

Dilthey, Wilhelm, *Selected Writings* (trans. and ed. by H.P. Rickman), Combridge, 1976.

——, *Introduction to the Human Science* (trans. and ed. by R.J. Betanzos), London, 1988.

Dintalen, F.J. Van, *Contemporary German Philosophy and its Background,* Bonn, 1978.

Dovering, Folke, *History as Social Science : An Essay on the Nature and Purpose of Historical Studies,* The Hague, 1960.

Dray, W.H. *Laws and Explanation in History,* Oxford, 1970.

——, *Perspectives in History,* London, 1980.

Dreyfus, H.L. and Rabinow, P., *Michel Foucault : Beyond Structuralism and Hermeneutics,* Chicago, 1982.

Dussen, W.J., *History as a Science : The Philosophy of R.G. Collingwood,* The Hague, 1981.

Elton, G.R., *The Practice of History,* London, 1967.

Ermarth, Michael, *Wilhelm Dilthey; The Critique of Historical Reason,* Chicago, 1978.

Fain, Harkell, *Between Philosophy and History,* New Jersey, 1970.

Frank, P.C. (ed.), *The Validation of Scientific Theories,* New York, 1961.

Gadamer, H.G., *Truth and Method* (trans. by W. Glen Doepel), London, 1979.

Gallie, W.B., *Philosophy and the Historical Understanding,* London, 1964.

Gardiner, Patrick (ed.), *Theories of History,* New York, 1959.

——, *The Nature of Historical Explanation,* Oxford, 1961.

Geertz, Clifford, *Interpretation of Cultures : Selected Essays,* New York, 1973.

Genette, Gerard, *Narrative Discourse,* Oxford, 1980.

Gibbon, M.T. (ed.), *Interpreting Politics,* Oxford, 1987.

Goff, J. Le and Nova, P., *Constructing the Past,* Cambridge, 1985.

Goldstein, L.J., *Historical Knowing,* Illinois, 1976.

Gooch, G.P., *History and Historians of Nineteenth Century,* London, 1967.

Gottschalk, L., *Understanding History,* New York, 1969.

Guha, Ranajit, *An Indian Histotriography of India : A Nineteenth Century Agenda and its Implications,* Calcutta, 1987.

Habermas, Jurgen, *Knowledge and Human Interest* (Trans. by J.J. Schapiro), London, 1978.

——, *The Theory of Communicative Action,* Vol. I (trans. by T. McCarthy), Boston, 1984.

——, *The Theory of Communicative Action,* Vol. II (trans. by T. McCarthy), Boston, 1989.

Habib, Irfan, *Interpreting Indian History,* 1993.

Haddock, B.A., *An Introduction to Historical Thought,* London, 1973.

Hanson, N.R. *Observation and Explanation,* London, 1972.

Hart, H.L.A. and Honore, A.M., *Causation in Law,* Oxford, 1973.

Harvey, D., *The Condition of Postmodernity,* Oxford, 1989.

Hegel, G.W.F., *Logic : Being Part One of the Encyclopaedia of the Philosophical Sciences* (trans. by J. Findlay), Oxford, 1978.

Heller, A. and Feher, F., *The Postmodern Political Condition*, Cambridge, 1988.

Hellevick, Ottar, *Introduction to Causal Analysis*, London, 1984.

Hisse, Mary, *Revolutions and Reconstructions in the Philosophy of Science*, Sussex, 1980.

Hexter, J.H., *The History Primer*, New York, 1981.

Hiddens, Anthony, *New Rules of Sociological Method*, London, 1977.

Hinders, Barry, *Philosophy and Methodology in the Social Science*, Hassocks, 1977.

Hodges, H.A., *Wilhelm Dilthey — An Introduction*, London, 1949.

Hollinger, Robert (ed.), *Hermeneutics and Praxis*, Indiana, 1985.

Hollis, M. and Lukes, S. (eds.), *Rationality and Relativism*, London, 1982.

Holub, R.C., *Jurgen Habermas : Critic in the Public Sphere*, London, 1991.

Hook, Sidney (ed.), *Philosophy and History : A Symposium*, New York, 1963.

Hookway, C. and Pettit, P. (eds.), *Action and Interpretation*, Cambridge, 1977.

Hoy, D.C., *The Critical Circle, Literature, History and Philosophy Hermeneutics*, Los Angeles, 1978.

Husserl, Edamund, *Phenomenology and the Crisis of Philosophy* (trans. by Q. Lauer), New York, 1965.

Iggers, G.G. and Parker, H.T., *International Handbook of Historical Studies*, London, 1979.

Jameson, F., *Postmodernism or the Cultural Logic of Late Capitalism*, London, 1991.

Jenkins, Keith, *Re-Thinking History*, London, 1991.

Kant, Iammanuel, *Critique of Pure Reason* (trans. by Norman K. Smith), London, 1973.

Keat, R. and Urry, J., Social Theory as Science, London, 1982.

Kuhn, T.S., *The Structure of Scientific Revolution,* Chicago, 1970.

Lacapra, D., *History and Criticism,* Ithaca, 1985.

Laclau, E., *New Reflections on the Revolution of Our Time,* London, 1990.

Lakatos, I. and Musgrave, A. (eds.), *Criticism and the Growth of Knowledge,* Cambridge, 1978.

Langlois, Ch. V. and Ch. Seignobos, *Introduction to the Study of History,* New York, 1966.

Levy, David, *Realism : An Essay in Interpretation and Social Reality,* Manchester, 1981.

Lewis, David, *Philosophic Papers,* New York, 1983.

Lloyd, Christopher, *Explanation in Social History,* Oxford, 1986.

Louch, A.R., *Explanation and Human Action,* Berkeley, 1966.

Lyotard, J.F., *The Postmodern Condition : A Report on Knowledge* (trans. by Bennington and B. Massumi, Manchester, 1987.

——, *The Different Phases in Dispute* (trans. by G. van der Abbele), Minneapolis, 1988.

MacIntyre, Alasdair, *Whose Justice? Which Rationality?* London, 1988.

Mackie, J.L., *The Cement of Universe — A Study of Causation,* London, 1980.

Mahajan, Gurpreet, *Explanation and Understanding in the Human Science,* New Delhi, 1992.

Majumdar, R.K. and Srivastava, A.N., *Historiography : Method of History,* New Delhi, 1996.

Mandalbaum, Maurice, *The Problem of Historical Knowledge,* New York, 1998.

——, *An Anatomy of Historical Knowledge,* Baltimore, 1977.

——, *Philosophy, History and the Science,* Baltimore, 1984.

Marsak, Leonard M., *The Nature of Historical Inquiry,* New York, 1970.

Martin, Raymond, *The Part within Us : An Empirical Approach to the Philosophy of History,* New Jeresy, 1989.

Marwick, Arthur, *Nature of History,* London, 1970.

Marx, Engels, Lenin, *On Dilectical Materialism,* Moscow, 1977.

McCullagh, C.B., *Justifying Historical Description,* Cambridge, 1984.

——, *The Truth of History,* London, 1998.

McMurin, S.M. (ed.), *The Tanners Lectures on Human Values,* Cambridge, 1980.

Meiland, J.W., *Scepticism and Historical Knowledge,* New York, 1965.

Meinecke, Friedrich, *Historicism : The Rise of New Historical Outlook* (trans. by J.E. Anderson), London, 1972.

Merquior, J.G., *Rousseau and Weber,* London, 1980.

Milligan, David, *Reasoning and the Explanation of Action,* New Jeresy, 1980.

Mokrzycki, Edmund, *Philosophy of Science and Sociology : From Methodological Doctrine to Research Practice,* London, 1983.

Morick, Harold (ed.), *Challenge to Empricism,* London, 1980.

Mukherjee, R.K., *The Philosophy of Social Science,* London, 1960.

Munslow, Alun, *Deconstructing History,* London, 1997.

Murphy, John W. (ed.), *Postmodernism,* Meerut, 1989.

Nagel, Ernest, *The Structure of Science,* London, 1991.

Nandy, Ashis, *Tradition, Tyranny and Utopias,* Delhi, 1987.

Natanson, Maurice (ed.), *Philosophy of Sciences : A Reader,* New York, 1963.

O'Neill, John, *On Critical Theory,* London, 1976.

Oakeshatt, Michael, *On History and other Essays,* Oxford, 1983.

Ortega, Y. and Gasset, J., *Concord and Liberty* (trans. by Helena Weyl), New York, 1963.

Pandit, G.L., *The Structure and Growth of Scientific Knowledge,* Holland, 1983.

Papineau, David, *For Science in the Social Science,* London, 1978.

Pompa, L. and W.H. Dray (eds.), *Substance and Form in History,* Edinburgh, 1981.

Ponty, M.M., *Phenomenology, Language and Sociology,* (trans. by J. O'Nill), London, 1974.

Popper, Karl, *On Society and its Enemies,* Vol. I, London, 1966.

——, *The Logic of Scientific Discovery,* London, 1968.

——, *Objective Knowledge,* London, 1975.

Porter, D.H., *The Emergence of the Past,* Chicago, 1981.

Rabinows, P. and W.H. Sullivan, *Interpreting Social Science,* Berkeley, 1979.

Rayan, Alen (ed.), *The Philosophy of Social Explanation,* Oxford, 1973.

Recouer, Paul, *The Conflict of Interpretations : Essays in Hermenentics* (ed. by Don Ihde), Evanston, 1974.

——, *Hermeneutics and the Human Science* (trans. by J.B. Thompson), New York, 1981.

Reill, P.H., *The German Enlightenment and the Rise of Historicism,* Berkeley, 1975.

Rex, Martin, *Historical Explanation,* Ithaca, 1975.

Ricket, Heinrich, *Science and History* (ed. by A. Goddard and trans. by G. Reisman), New York, 1962.

Rickman, H.P., *Wilhelm Dilthey : Pioneer of the Human Studies,* London, 1979.

Rorty, Richard, *Philosophy and the Mirror of Nature,* Oxford, 1980.

Runciman, W.G. (ed.), *Max Weber,* Cambridge, 1978.

Ruthrof, H., *The Reader's Construction of the Narrative,* London, 1981.

Ryle, Gilbert, *The Concept of Mind,* Harmondsworth, 1980.

Sarkar, J.N., *Historiography Then and Now : Medieval Bihar,* Patna, 1989.

Sayer, Andrew, *Method in Social Science,* London, 1984.

Schlegel, Friedrichvon, *The Philosophy of History,* New York, 1979.

Schobs, R. and R. Kellogg, *The Nature of the Narrative,* Oxford, 1975.

Schutz, Alfred, *Collected Papers,* Vols. I and II, The Hague, 1967.

Searle, J.R., *Intentionality,* New York, 1983.

Sellitz, C. *et al., Research Method in Social Research,* London, 1965.

Sharma, T., *The Concept of History,* Delhi, 1987.

Silverman, H.J. and U. Ihde (eds.), *Hermeneutics and Deconstruction,* New York, 1985.

Silverman, H.J. (ed.), *Derrida and Deconstruction,* London, 1989.

Simmed, G., *Essays on Interpretation in Social Science,* Manchester, 1980.

Simon, J.L., *Basic Research Method in Social Science,* New York, 1969.

Skinner, Quentin, *The Return of Grand Theory in the Human Sciences,* Cambridge, 1985.

Sosa, Ernest (ed.), *Causation and Conditionals,* London, 1975.

Stanford, Michael, *The Nature of Historical Knowledge,* Oxford, 1987.

Stegmuller, Walter, *The Main Currents in Contemporary German, British and American Philosophy,* Holland, 1969.

Stephens, L.B., *Probing the past,* Boston, 1974.

Suppe, predrich (ed.), *The Structure of Scientific Theory,* Urbana, 1977.

Synder, P.L. (ed.), *The Detachment and the Writing of History : Essays and Letters of C.L. Becker,* Westport, 1972.

Taylor, Charles, *The Explanation of Behaviour,* Oxford, 1980.

Thakur, Vijay K., *Historiography of Indian Feudalism,* Patna, 1989.

Thapar, Romila, *The Past and Prejudice,* New Delhi, 1975.

Thompson, E.P., *Poverty of Theory and other Essays,* New York, 1978.

Thompson, J.B., *Critical Hermeneutics,* New York, 1981.

Thompson, J.B. and D. Held (eds.), *Habermas : Critical Debates,* London, 1982.

Tosh, John, *The Pursuit of History,* London, 1984.

Toulmin, Stephen, *The Philosophy of Science,* London, 1953.

Trigg, Roger, *Understanding Social Science,* Oxford, 1985.

Tuttle, H.N., *Wilhelm Dilthey's Philosophy of Historical Understanding : A Critical Analysis,* London, 1985.

Varma, L.B., *Understanding History,* Allahabad, 1995.

Venugopalan, T.R. (ed.), *History and Theory,* Thrissur, 1997.

Veyne, P., *Writing History : Essays on Epistemology,* Manchester, 1984.

Wallace, W.A., *Casualty and Scientific Explanation,* Vol. I, Michigan, 1972.

Walsh, W.H., *Introduction to Philosophy of History,* London, 1967.

Warnke, Gorgia Gadamer, *Hermeneutics, Tradition and Reason,* Cambridge, 1987.

Weber, Max, *The Methodology of Social Sciences* (ed. by Shils and Finch), New York, 1968.

Wedgewood, C.V., *History and Hope, The Collected Essays,* Glasgow, 1987.

Wells, G.A., *Herder and After,* Gravenhage, 1959.

White, Haydeny, *Metahistory, The Historical Imagination in Nineteenth Century Europe,* London, 1975.

Willer, D. and J. Willer, *Systematic Empiricism,* Jeresy, 1973.

Wilson, B.R. (ed.), *Rationality,* Oxford, 1970.

Winch, Peter, *Idea of a Social Science and its Relations to Philosophy,* London, 1973.

Wittgenstein, Ludwing, *Tractatus,* Oxford, 1981.

——, *Philosophical Investigation,* Oxford, 1983.

Important Date and Events (1935-1947)

1935

2 August	Government of India Act received royal assent.
6 August	Marquess of Linlithgow appointed to succeed Lord Willingdon as Viceroy from April 1936.
5 September	Nehru released from prison : flew to Europe to his wife.
17-18 October	All-India Congress Committee meeting at Madras resolved not to come to any decision on question of acceptance of office.

1936

16 February	All-India Muslim Conference met in New Delhi, Aga Khan in the chair. Question of amalgamating with Muslim League left over for decision by Muslims elected to new provincial legislatures.
12 March	Nehru returned to India.
21-24 March	Congress Working Committee met in Delhi.
1 April	Inauguration of new province of Sind.
6 April	Inauguration of Orissa province.
6-7 April	Congress Working Committee met in Allahabad.
9-15 April	All-India Congress Committee met at Lucknow : Nehru took over presidentship. New Working Committee appointed.
11-12 April	24th Session of the All-India Muslim League meeting in Bombay attacked federal scheme in new Act but decided

	to work provincial scheme. Central parliamentary board formed to contest coming elections, Jinnah President was authorized to organize provincial parliamentary boards.
12-14 April	49th Session of Indian National Congress at Lucknow rejected new constitution and demanded constituent assembly, but decided to take part in elections to provincial legislatures. Committee appointed to consider mass contact.
18 April	Marquess of Linlithgow installed as Viceroy.
27-29 April	New Congress Working Committee met at Wardha. Parliamentary Committee constituted to organize elections.
28 May	Nehru began tour in Delhi and Punjab.
11 June	Election manifesto of Muslim League issued from Lahore.
12 June	Muslim League declared that they would use new constitution to further their objective of full and complete home rule for India.
29 June–1 July	Congress Working Committee met at Wardha.
1–2 July	Congress Parliamentary Committee met at Wardha.
9 July	Death of Fazl-i-Husain.
13 July	Executive Council of Bengal United Moslem party invited Jinnah to visit Calcutta in connection with elections.
18-26 July	Nehru toured Sind.
27 July–5 August	Nehru visited Punjab.
18-23 August	Congress Parliamentary Committee, Working Committee, and A.I.C.C. met at Bombay. Election manifesto adopted.

19 September	Meeting of Muslim League Central Parliamentary Board at Simla. Jinnah announced that strong provincial boards had been established in U.P., Madras, Bombay and Assam; situation in Punjab not satisfactory; no progress in Frontier, Sind, Bihar and Orissa.
3 October	First Session of Bihar United Muslim Conference held at Patna.
24 October	Conference of C.P. Muslims considered formation of Muslim League parliamentary board in province.
24-25 October	C.P. Muslim Political Conference at Nagpur called on Muslims to unite under banner of Muslim League and Jinnah. Provincial branch of League formed.
30-31 October	Joint Conference of Indian princes and their ministers held in Bombay to consider federation : committee appointed to examine provisions of the Act.
2 November	Fazlul Haq leader of the Praja Socialist Party in Bengal removed from membership of Muslim League central parliamentary board.
9–11 December	Congress Working Committee met in Bombay. Nehru re-elected President of Congress : Working Committee passed resolution reiterating determination of Congress to reject new constitution.
23-29 December	Congress Working Committee, A.I.C.C., and Congress met at Faizpur.
27-28 December	50th Session of Congress at Faizpur reiterated its rejection of Act, but decided to contest elections to provincial legislatures.
December	Electioneering in full swing.

1937

January–February	Elections held for provincial assemblies (electorate, 37,000,000).
2 January	Viceroy's representative discussed with large number of princes in Calcutta, question of their accession to the Indian federation.
3 January	Jinnah spoke at Calcutta : warned Congress not to interfere in Muslim affairs. He then toured Bengal on behalf of League candidates.
17 January	Polling began in Calcutta for Bengal legislative assembly.
18 January	Polling in Calcutta for general seats in Bengal assembly.
21 January	Elections in Punjab, accompanied by rowdy incidents.
25 January	Constitution committee of chamber of princes met in Delhi to consider All-India federation.
27 January	Khwaja Sir Nazimuddin, member of Bengal executive council, defeated by Fazlul Haq, Praja party leader.
3 February	Fazlul Haq outlined his party's programme at Munshiganj.
15 February	Executive committee of Praja party ratified agreement reached between leaders of the party and Muslim League for purpose of working new constitution.
17 February	Sir Sikandar Hayat Khan invited to form ministry in Punjab.
	Constitution committee of chamber of princes submitted its first recommendations.
24-25 February	14th Session of the chamber of princes in Delhi.
27 February-1 March	Meeting of Congress Working Committee at Wardha. 'The Congress has entered

	the legislatures not to co-operate... but to combat the Act....' 'The objective of the Congress is...complete independence....' 'The immediate objective of the Congress in the Legislatures is to fight the new constitution....'
6 March	Fazlul Haq agreed to form ministry in Bengal.
16 March	Congress Working Committee passed resolution recommending conditional acceptance of office.
18 March	All-India Congress Committee meeting at Delhi passed resolution authorizing conditional acceptance of office in provinces.
1 April	Provincial responsible government came into force.
8 April	Lord Zetland in house of lords, and R.A. Butler in House of Commons defined H.M.G.'s attitude to political impasse.
10 April	Gandhi made statement in reply to Lord Zetland.
19 April	Jinnah criticized Congress attempt to divide Muslim ranks.
26 April	R.A. Butler made statement on political impasse.
	Nehru announced Muslim mass-contact programme.
	Nehru and Jinnah issued counter-statements on Congress bid to capture Muslim support.
28 April	Resolution of Congress Working Committee on political deadlock.
May	Nehru visited Burma and Malaya.
	Neville Chamberlain succeeded Stanley Baldwin as Prime Minister. Zetland remained India Secretary.

8 May	Statement by Lord Zetland on constitutional impasse.
21 June	Viceroy, Lord Linlithgow, issued statement interpreting constitution on special powers of Governors.
5–8 July	Congress Working Committee met at Wardha and resolved to accept office.
July	Congress ministries formed in Bihar, Orissa, C.P., U.P., Bombay and Madras.
25 July	Jinnah issued statement urging Hindu-Muslim unity. Called on Muslims to consolidate their strength for coming struggle.
14–17 August	Congress Working Committee met at Wardha and discussed general policy to be followed by Congress ministers.
15–18 October	25th Session of All-India Muslim League at Lucknow. Premiers of Punjab and Bengal joined League; resolution passed opposing introduction of federation. League decided to frame comprehensive social, economic and educational programme to win support of Muslim masses.
22-23 October	Wardha Educational Conference.
29-31 October	All-India Congress Committee met at Calcutta.
22 November	Congress membership 3,134,249.
27-28 December	First Session of All-India Muslim Students Federation held in Calcutta : Jinnah President.

1938

1 January	National Liberal federation of India meeting in Calcutta resolved to support federation scheme in new constitution.
	Hindu Mahasabha at its concluding Session urged government to expedite introduction of federation.

2-4 January	Congress Working Committee met in Bombay.
5 January	Jinnah speaking at Allahabad urged settlement of minorities problem.
18 January	Subhas Chandra Bose elected President of the Congress.
3 February	Congress Working Committee met at Wardha. Premiers of seven Congress provinces had been invited to attend : C. Rajagopalachari from Madras and N.B. Khare from C.P. did so.
4 February	Congress Working Committee passed resolution reiterating opposition to federation.
5 February	Gandhi and Nehru wrote to Jinnah asking for definite statement of League's demands.
6 February	Congress Working Committee decided not to set up Congress organizations in Indian states.
15 February	Bihar and U.P. ministries resigned over question of release of political prisoners.
19-21 February	51st Session of Indian National Congress at Haripura in Gujarat.
25 February	Constitutional crisis in U.P. ended.
26 February	Bihar cabinet withdrew resignation.
12 March	Congress Ministry formed in Assam.
21 March	Sind Ministry resigned. Leader of United party formed new ministry in coalition with Hindu Independent party.
10 April	Subhas Chandra Bose urged mass contact with Muslims and Scheduled Castes.
14 April	Subhas Chandra Bose appealed to Muslims to join Congress.
17–18 April	Special Session of Muslim League at Calcutta. Jinnah reported on success of League in organizing Muslims since Last Session in October 1937. Appealed to

	both communities to realize their moral obligations to each other.
21 April	Death of Sir Muhammad Iqbal.
24 April	Bengal Hindu Mahasabha in Calcutta appealed to Gandhi not to conclude his negotiations with Jinnah without consulting non-Congress political organizations.
28 April	Gandhi had interview with Jinnah in Bombay on communal question : sequel to correspondence between Jinnah, Nehru and Gandhi which had gone on for some months past. Joint statement issued.
1-8 May	Gandhi carried out an extensive tour in Frontier province.
11-12 May	Subhas Chandra Bose, Congress President, had discussions with Jinnah in Bombay on communal question.
12-14 May	Conference of premiers of seven Congress provinces and members of Congress parliamentary sub-committee in Bombay. Conference called by President of Congress to consider general questions of co-ordination and co-operation among Congress provinces. Among other matters it was decided to introduce Wardha education scheme in the seven provinces.
14 May	Congress leaders drafted memorandum in reply to Jinnah's point in connection with communal talks — taken to Jinnah by Subhas Chandra Bose when talks resumed.
20 May	Gandhi had talk with Jinnah in Bombay.
26 May	Talks between Jinnah and Subhas Chandra Bose continued.
2 June	Under-Secretary of State for India stated in House of Commons that no date had

	yet been fixed for inauguration of federation.
2 June	Nehru left Bombay for Europe. Returned in November.
4 June	Council of the Muslim League discussed Congress memorandum on communal peace terms and authorized Jinnah to send reply to Congress President.
11 June	Reorganization Committee of Chamber of Princes decided to constitute a committee to deal with matters of common interest to Indian states as regarded federation.
15 June	Full text of Gandhi-Jinnah and Jinnah-Nehru correspondence released.
20 June	Vallabhbhai Patel and Subhas Chandra Bose called at Wardha to decide on reply to Jinnah's letter.
	Sheriff of Bombay disputed Jinnah's claim to be sole representative of Muslims.
22 June	Fazlul Haq resigned and then formed new ministry.
24 June	Subhas Chandra Bose and other leaders discussed Congress-League negotiations with Gandhi at Wardha.
25 June	Viceroy left Bombay for England. Lord Brabourne acting Viceroy.
1 July	Nehru had long interview with Lord Halifax in London.
7 July	Two Muslim Organizations opposed to League established in Bihar, *viz.* Jamiat-ul-ulema and Momin Jamiat.
23-27 July	Congress Working Committee met at Wardha.
25 July	Gandhi dictated letter to be sent to Jinnah on communal problem. Congress unable to accept Jinnah's claim that

	League should be recognized as sole representative of Muslim population.
31 July	League Working Committee replied to Congress President's letter on communal settlement and criticized attitude adopted by Congress.
16 August	Subhas Chandra Bose, with Jinnah's permission, released correspondence between himself and Jinnah about Hindu-Muslim settlement.
24-26 September	A.I.C.C. met at Delhi. Resolution condemning negotiations with Jinnah defeated.
2 October	All-India Muslim Educational Conference rejected Wardha scheme.
5 October	Gandhi began Frontier Province tour which continued throughout October.
8-15 October	Sind Muslim League Conference at Karachi. Jinnah strongly criticized Congress attitude to Muslim interests and accused Congress executive of wanting to divide Muslims.
9 October	Bengal and Punjab premiers speaking at Sind Muslim League Conference challenged claim of Congress to represent Indian nation.
10 October	Sind Muslim League Conference discussed resolution urging that India be divided into two federations, one for Muslims and the other for non-Muslim groups.
12 October	Negotiations for League ministry in Sind broke down.
24 October	Viceroy returned to India.
17 November	Nehru returned to India.
28 November-1 December	Informal Conference of rulers and their ministers held in Bombay.
11-16 December	Congress Working Committee met at Wardha and passed resolution declaring

	Hindu Mahasabha and Muslim League communal organization (15 December). Hindu-Muslim question discussed. Correspondence of President of Congress with Jinnah closed.
18 December	Liaqat Ali Khan, Secretary of Muslim League, said at Nagpur that no agreement with Congress was possible so long as Congress was not prepared to recognize League as only representative organization of Indian Muslims.
19 December	Viceroy made statement on prospects of federation at opening of annual meeting of Associated Chambers of Commerce in Calcutta.
20 December	Jinnah issued statement on Viceroy's appeal to give federal scheme a trial. Criticized working of provincial autonomy in provinces.
26-29 December	26th Session of Muslim League held at Patna. Jinnah attacked Gandhi for giving to Congress Hindu outlook and Hindu ideals. Resolution passed favouring launching of civil disobedience in Bihar, U.P. and C.P. League established committee of enquiry into alleged Congress persecution of Muslims.
30 December	Hindu Mahasabha at Nagpur passed resolution accepting federation.
31 December	Speakers at National Liberal federation criticized Congress executive for interfering in administration of ministries in the provinces.

1939

End January	Princes received from viceroy draft instrument of accession.

30 January	Subhas Chandra Bose re-elected Congress President. Members of Working Committee resigned.
9 March	At Annual Session of Congress at Tripuri, C.P., Subhas Chandra Bose resigned and Rajendra Prasad elected President in his stead.
13 March	Viceroy Inaugurated Session of chamber of princes in Delhi.
April	Council of Muslim League meeting in Delhi passed resolution objecting to intensive propaganda of Congress in efforts to establish Hindu hegemony all over India.
June	Princes and their ministers meeting in Bombay pronounced terms in instrument of accession unacceptable. Time limit for replies extended to 1 September.
3 September	Viceroy announced that India was at war with Germany.
4 September	Viceroy saw Gandhi, Jinnah and chancellor of the chamber of princes.
8-14 September	Congress Working Committee met at Wardha in emergency session.
10 September	Nehru returned to India from China.
11 September	Negotiations with princes over 1935 Act suspended and federation postponed.
14 September	Resolution of Congress Working Committee on War crisis and India required declaration of War aims from British government.
18 September	Resolution of League Working Committee on war crisis.
26 September	Viceroy had meeting of over three hours with Gandhi.
2 October	Viceroy interviewed Rajendra Prasad and Nehru.

October	Viceroy had series of interviews with leaders of other political parties, including Jinnah.
10 October	A.I.C.C. Passed Resolution dealing with situation arising out of the War, endorsing working committee's statement of 14 September and requesting declaration from British government of its War aims.
18 October	Viceroy made statement on War aims and War effort.
22-23 October	Congress Working Committee met at Wardha and issued manifesto calling on Congress ministries to resign.
22 October	Manifesto by Muslim League asking for further discussion and clarification.
By end October	Ministries in all Congress provinces had resigned. Governors assumed control under Section 93 of Government of India Act, except in Assam where coalition ministry formed under Sir Mohamed Saadullah. Bengal, Punjab and Sind continued as before.
1 November	Gandhi, Rajendra Prasad and Jinnah had interviews with Viceroy to discuss proposal for expanding executive council.
5 November	Viceroy made statement on correspondence with Prasad, Gandhi and Jinnah, and published correspondence.
19-23 November	Meeting of Congress Working Committee passed Resolution demanding constituent assembly.
22 December	Observed as 'Deliverance Day' by followers of Muslim League throughout India.
1939	During this year partition schemes were put forward by Dr. Syed Abdul Latif, Sir Sikandar Hyat Khan and Professor

	Syed Zafarul Hasan, and Dr. Muhammad Afzal Husain Qadri.

1940

6 January	Viceroy in speech at Nagpur regretted interruption, because of resignation of Congress Ministries, in orderly progress of India towards goal of dominion status.
7 January	Jinnah released correspondence between himself and Nehru on Congress-League differences.
	Jinnah reiterated League demand for recognition as authoritative and representative organization of Muslims in India. Nehru stated that Congress did not recognize League as sole representative of Muslims. Negotiations discontinued.
10 January	Nehru at Ghaziabad said that there could be no question of settlement with government or of return of Congress Ministries to office until question of India's freedom finally settled.
13 January	Viceroy saw Jinnah and Bhulabhai Desai in Bombay.
17 January	Viceroy at Baroda stated that federation had been suspended not abandoned.
19-21 January	Congress Working Committee met at Wardha. Gandhi authorized to seek from Viceroy clarification of certain points in his speech of 10 January.
25 January	Viceroy saw Sir Sikandar Hyat Khan.
3 February	Viceroy saw premiers of Punjab and Bengal — Sir Sikandar Hyat Khan and Fazlul Haq — together.
3-6 February	League Working Committee met in New Delhi. Jinnah stated that Western democracy was unsuited for India.

4 February	Fazlul Haq, in New Delhi, suggested setting up of coalition governments in provinces for duration of War.
5 February	Viceroy saw Gandhi in attempt to break political deadlock. Gandhi issued statement to press next day.
6 February	Viceroy saw Jinnah.
11 February	Lord Zetland in interview in *Sunday Times* made appeal to leaders of Congress to 'escape from the tyranny of phrases.'
16 February	Abul Kalam Azad elected President of Congress.
25 February	Council of Muslim League met at New Delhi.
28 February	Congress Working Committee met in Patna to decide on Resolution to be put forward at forthcoming Congress Session at Ramgarh.
1 March	Congress Working Committee at Patna passed resolution declaring determination of party to resort to civil disobedience as soon as organization fit enough.
13 March	Viceroy saw Jinnah.
	Sir Michael O'Dwyer shot dead, and Lord Zetland wounded, at meeting of East India Association at Caxton Hall in London.
15 March	Congress Working Committee met at Ramgarh.
19-20 March	53rd Session of Congress held at Ramgarh. Patna Resolution of Working Committee carried by large majority. Complete independence and constituent assembly demanded.
22-24 March	27th Session of Muslim League held at Lahore.

22 March	Jinnah suggested division of India into two autonomous nation states.
23 March	'Lahore Resolution' of Muslim League.
31 March	Jinnah issued statement from New Delhi appealing to Hindus and Sikhs to give serious consideration to League scheme of partition.
3 April	Lord Zetland broadcast on Britain's policy towards India.
8 April	Vallabhbhai Patel in Ahmedabad stated a fight inevitable : question was when to start the fight.
10 April	White Paper on 'India and the War' issued : sought approval of Parliament for continuance of Section 93 proclamations in the seven provinces (approved 18 April).
15 April	Congress Working Committee met at Wardha.
	Master Tara Singh, presiding at first U.P. Sikh Conference at Lucknow, said 'If the Moslem League want to establish "Pakistan" they will have to pass through an ocean of 'Sikh blood'.
18 April	Lord Zetland reviewed in House of Lords position of India.
27 April-1 May	Azad Muslim Conference, Allah Baksh, premier of Sind, President, met in Delhi. Disputed claim of Muslim League to be only representative of Muslims and condemned demand for partition.
6 May	Nehru in Poona said that neither Mahasabha nor League had positive programme. Characterized Pakistan scheme as foolish and said that it would not last 24 hours.
10 May	Winston Churchill replaced Neville Chamberlain as Prime Minister.

	L.S. Amery succeeded Lord Zetland as Secretary of state (19 May).
10 May	German armies invaded Holland and Belgium.
19 May	Hindu Mahasabha condemned Pakistan scheme as 'anti-Hindu and therefore anti-national'.
23 May	Amery in commons stated that attainment by India of full and equal partnership in Commonwealth was goal of British policy.
27 May–3 June	British army evacuated from Dunkirk.
10 June	Italy declared war on allies.
16 June	League Working Committee endorsed Jinnah's policy and authorized him to continue his negotiations with Viceroy.
17 June	Fall of France.
17-21 June	Congress Working Committee met at Wardha and announced (21 June) that it could not accept Gandhi's extreme stand on non-violence.
27 June	Parliament passed India and Burma (Emergency Provisions) Act providing 'in the event of a complete breakdown of communications with the United Kingdom' for transfer to Governor-General of powers normally exercised by Secretary of state.
	Viceroy interviewed Jinnah.
29 June	Viceroy saw Gandhi at Simla.
1 July	Subhas Chandra Bose arrested.
3 July	Gandhi issued appeal 'To Every Briton' to accept method of non-violence and lay down his arms.
3-7 July	Emergency meeting of Congress Working Committee in Delhi renewed demand for immediate declaration of full independence for India, with provisional

	national government constituted at centre.
July	A.I.C.C. meeting at Poona ratified resolution of Working Committee.
7 August	Viceroy made statement on India's Constitutional Development — the 'August Offer' — and announced that executive council would be expanded and war advisory council established.
8 August	Viceroy's statement read in commons by Secretary of state.
11&13 August	Viceroy saw Jinnah.
13 August	V.D. Savarkar saw Viceroy and later accepted August Offer on behalf of Hindu Mahasabha, as did Sikhs, Scheduled Castes and other organizations.
18-22 August	Congress Working Committee met at Wardha and sent reply to Viceroy (20 August) rejecting August Offer.
23 August	Rajagopalachari made his 'sporting offer' to promote agreement with League.
29 August	Correspondence between Viceroy and Azad released for publication.
31 August-2 September	League Working Committee met in Bombay to consider viceroy's offer and passed Resolution stating that League's full co-operation in war effort would be conditional on Viceroy clearing certain points with Jinnah.
15 September	A.I.C.C. met in Bombay and rejected August Offer. Gandhi assumed active leadership of Congress.
24 September	Viceroy had long discussion with Jinnah.
27 September	Viceroy saw Gandhi.
28 September	Working Committee of League met in New Delhi and rejected August Offer.
29 September	Council of League passed Resolution rejecting August Offer.

13 October	Congress Working Committee at Wardha approved Gandhi's plan of individual civil disobedience. Vinoba Bhave selected to inaugurate movement.
17 October	Individual civil disobedience movement started by Vinoba Bhave.
21 October	Vinoba Bhave arrested. Nehru chosen to follow him.
31 October	Nehru arrested and sentenced to four years' imprisonment.
Mid-November	Second stage of civil disobedience movement began.
17 November	Sardar Patel arrested.
20 November	Viceroy announced that he would not proceed with enlargement of executive council or establishment of war advisory council as major political parties had rejected August Offer.
21 November	Secretary of State in London appealed to Indians to study afresh constitutional problem of India.
5 December	Subhas Chandra Bose released.
8 December	Fazlul Haq appealed to Jinnah to reopen negotiations with Congress.
31 December	Abul Kalam Azad arrested.
1941	
5 January	Third stage of civil disobedience campaign began.
27 January	Subhas Chandra Bose escaped to Germany.
22 February	League Working Committee re-affirmed basic principles laid down in Lahore Resolution of 1940.
11 March	Sir Sikandar Hyat Khan, premier of Punjab, explained his attitude to Pakistan in debate in Punjab legislative assembly.

13-14 March	Non-party Conference in Bombay, Tej Bahadur Sapru President, proposed reconstruction of Viceroy's executive council.
April	Fourth stage of civil disobedience campaign began.
22 April	Amery commented in commons on non-party scheme and civil disobedience campaign.
May	Statement by Jinnah on Sapru proposals.
1 July	Wavell appointed Commander-in-Chief of India.
21 July	Governor-General's council reconstituted to consist of 8 Indians, 3 Britons, Governor-General and Commander-in-Chief. National defence council of 30 members set up.
22 July	Both Gandhi and Jinnah reacted unfavourably to Simla announcement on expansion of Viceroy's executive council.
26-27 July	Non-party political leaders conference, Sapru President, met at Poona.
30 July	Jinnah threatened disciplinary action against members of Muslim League who joined viceroy's executive council and National defence council.
19 August	Provincial Prime Ministers invited by Viceroy to join National defence council. They accepted.
24 August	League Working Committee ordered three League premiers of Punjab, Bengal and Assam to resign from National defence council. Fazlul Haq resigned from Working Committee and council of League in protest. Sir Sultan Ahmed refused to resign from Executive Council and Begum Shah Nawaz from National defence council; both expelled from League.

August	Atlantic Charter : Joint declaration by Roosevelt and Churchill.
9 September	Churchill in House of Commons said Atlantic Charter did not qualify in any way various statements of policy relating to India.
10 September	Fazlul Haq resigned from National defence council.
6 October	First Session of National defence council held at Simla.
26 October	*Dawn* began publication from Delhi (weekly).
By mid-October	Expansion of Viceroy's executive council completed.
	Many Congressmen who had taken part in individual civil disobedience had been released. Section of Congress suggested that Congress should take back power in provinces : Gandhi refused to yield.
26 October	Council of Muslim League endorsed decisions made by Working Committee in August.
23 November	Ministry sworn in in Orissa and proclamation under Section 93 revoked.
1 December	Fazlul Haq's ministry resigned, but he returned as head of coalition cabinet of 9 members (5 Muslims, 4 Hindus) on 11 December.
3 December	Civil disobedience prisoners, including Nehru and Azad, set free.
6 December	Japanese destroyed American fleet at Pearl Harbour.
11 December	Fazlul Haq expelled from League.
13 December	Saadullah's ministry fell in Assam and was followed by Governor's rule (until August 1942).
23 December	Congress Working Committee met at Bardoli. Gandhi retired from leadership of Congress.

1942

January	A.I.C.C. met at Wardha.
1 February	Gandhi inaugurated All-India Goseva Sangh Conference at Wardha.
15 February	Fall of Singapore.
8 March	Fall of Rangoon.
11 March	Statement by Prime Minister in House of Commons announcing decision to send Cripps Mission to India.
22 March	Cripps arrived in Delhi and began series of conversations with leaders of all political parties.
29 March	Cripps held Press Conference on his draft declaration.
30 March	Draft declaration for discussion with Indian leaders published.
2 April	Congress Working Committee passed Resolution rejecting proposals put forward by Cripps Mission.
	League Working Committee passed Resolution rejecting proposal put forward by Cripps Mission.
3 April	Colonel Louis Johnson, President Roosevelt's personal envoy, arrived in Delhi.
4 April	Gandhi left Delhi after advising Cripps to take first plane home.
	Indian leaders saw commander-in-chief.
7 April	Cripps wrote to Azad and Jinnah on question of Indian defence member.
8 April	Cripps finalized his formula.
9 April	Azad and Nehru approached Cripps on question of Cabinet Government.
10 April	Azad wrote to Cripps demanding Cabinet Government. Cripps replied on same day taking Azad's letter as rejection by Congress Working Committee of draft declaration. Negotiations terminated.

11 April	Resolutions of Congress Working Committee and of League rejecting the proposals were published. Cripps held Press Conference and later broadcast on breakdown of discussions.
12 April	Cripps left India for England.
23 April	Rajagopalachari got Resolution passed by Congress members in Madras legislature recommending to A.I.C.C. that Congress should acknowledge Muslim League's claim for separation and start negotiations with League.
26 April	In the *Harijan* Gandhi pleaded for British withdrawal from India, and in following issues explained and elaborated his 'Quit India' programme.
28 April	Amery made statement in House of Commons on failure of Cripps Mission.
29 April– 2 May	A.I.C.C. met at Allahabad. Rajagopalachari's Madras Resolution rejected by large majority, and counter-Resolution on 'unity of India' passed. Resolution calling for non-co-operation and non-violent resistance to invader passed.
10 May	Gandhi in Bombay called on Britain to 'Leave India to God. If that is too much, then leave her to anarchy.'
11 May	Gandhi wrote an appeal 'To Every Briton' to retire from every Asian and African possession, at least from India.
18 May	Gandhi answered questions at Press Conference on his demand for British withdrawal from India and on Congress-League stalemate.
May-June	Rajagopalachari campaigned in Madras for forging of National front, establishment of National government and mobilization of country for defence.

2 July	Viceroy's executive council expanded from 12 to 15 members : 11 non-official Indian, 1 non-official European, and 3 European officials (including the Commander-in-chief).
6-14 July	Congress Working Committee met at Wardha and passed Resolution demanding withdrawal of British rule from India and determining on mass civil disobedience campaign under Gandhi's leadership if demand not complied with.
July	Jinnah, Hindu Mahasabha, Liberals, Communists, and other leaders dissented from Congress appeal for civil disobedience.
15 July	Rajagopalachari resigned from Congress.
27 July	Amery in House of Commons and Cripps in broadcast to America denounced Congress demand.
7 August	A.I.C.C. met in Bombay.
8 August	A.I.C.C. endorsed Working Committee's Resolution demanding withdrawal of British power from India and sanctioned beginning of mass struggle under Gandhi's leadership.
9 August	Gandhi and members of Congress Working Committee arrested, followed by arrest of all important Congress leaders. Congress Committee declared unlawful associations.
August-September	Disturbances throughout India continued until end of September.
16–20 August	League Working Committee met at Bombay and deplored decision of A.I.C.C. to launch open rebellion. Muslims called upon to abstain from participation.

August	Sir Mohamed Saadullah took office in Assam.
10 October	Allah Bakhsh, premier of Sind, dismissed by the Governor, Sir Hugh Dow. Sir Ghulam Hussain Hidayatullah took office with support of Muslim League.
Early November	Rajagopalachari had talks with Jinnah.
7 November	Anglo-American forces landed in French North Africa.
12 November	Rajagopalachari saw Viceroy and asked for permission to see Gandhi. Permission refused.
December	Council of Muslim League passed Resolution stating that Muslims were entitled to homelands in North-West and North-East of India where they were in majority.
Late December	Death of Sir Sikandar Hyat Khan.
31 December-8 February	Correspondence between Gandhi and Viceroy.
1943	
29 January	Gandhi informed Viceroy of his intention to fast.
8 February	Government of India offered to release Gandhi for duration of fast : offer refused.
9 February-3 March	Gandhi's fast.
10 February	Government issued statement on fast and events leading up to it.
17 February	Three members of Viceroy's executive council resigned over Gandhi's fast.
19 February	Non-party Conference, Sapru Chairman, met in Delhi, and urged Gandhi's immediate release. Jinnah refused to attend.
22 February	Government issued paper on Congress responsibility for disturbances in 1942.

March	Rajagopalachari's formula approved by Gandhi during fast.
28 March	Fazlul Haq forced to resign as premier of Bengal. Governor's rule continued until April 24.
24 April	Sir Nazimuddin formed mainly Muslim League Ministry in Bengal.
End April	At Annual Session of Muslim League announced that all Muslim majority provinces were now under control of League ministries.
May	Allah Bakhsh, ex-premier of Sind, murdered.
	Muslim League Ministry took office in N.W.F.P. under Aurangzeb Khan.
August-November	Bengal famine.
20 October	Lord Wavell succeeded Lord Linlithgow as Viceroy of India.
December	Muslim League meeting at Karachi resolved to establish committee of action to organize Muslims all over India to resist imposition of unitary constitution and to prepare for coming struggle for achievement of Pakistan.

1944

17 February	Wavell addressing Joint Session of central legislature stated Cripps offer still open. Said India a natural unit.
February	Wavell visited famine-afflicted areas.
March	Japanese advanced into Assam assisted by I.N.A.
8 April	Rajagopalachari's formula communicated to Jinnah, followed by discussions and correspondence. Jinnah agreed to place formula before League.
April	Jinnah went to Lahore to talk with Khizr Hyat Khan, Chief Minister of Punjab.

April-May	Non-party Conference at Lucknow authorized its President, Sapru, to prepare memorandum to be submitted to Viceroy.
6 May	Gandhi released unconditionally on medical grounds.
17 June	Gandhi wrote to Viceroy requesting permission to interview members of Congress Working Committee and asking for meeting with Viceroy. Permission refused.
20 June	Government published correspondence which had passed between Linlithgow, Wavell, Government of India, and Gandhi during his detention.
10 July	Rajagopalachari's formula made public for first time.
12 July	Gandhi at Press Conference gave authentic version of his interview with Stewart Gelder published in *Times of India,* previous day. He would be satisfied with National government in full control of civil administration; Viceroy and Commander-in-chief to have complete control of military operations.
15 July	Gandhi wrote to Wavell asking to see members of Working Committee and for an interview with Viceroy.
17 July	Gandhi wrote to Jinnah suggesting meeting. Jinnah replied that he would be glad to receive Gandhi at his house in Bombay on his return from Kashmir.
27 July	Gandhi in letter to Wavell made proposals to bring about a Congress-Government understanding. Prepared to renounce civil disobedience and give full co-operation to war effort if declaration of immediate Indian

	independence was made and national government formed.
28 July	In House of Commons Secretary of state said Gandhi's proposals did not even form starting-point for profitable discussion.
30 July	League Working Committee meeting at Lahore gave Jinnah full authority to negotiate with Gandhi. Jinnah dismissed Rajagopalachari formula.
15 August	Wavell replied to Gandhi that it was impossible to alter Constitution during War.
August	Wavell at Conference of Governors stated that after the War, promises made to India would have to be redeemed. Governors advised that positive move essential.
9-27 September	Gandhi-Jinnah talks. Correspondence released on 27 September.
October	Wavell sent proposals to Churchill and Secretary of State.
19 November	Standing Committee of non-party Conference decided to appoint Committee to examine communal and minorities question : members not to be actively associated with any recognized party.
3 December	Sapru announced names of members of committee. Jinnah refused to recognize committee or to meet Sapru.
1945	
20 January	Bhulabhai Desai saw Viceroy and told him of Desai-Liaqat Ali pact, approved by Gandhi. (Jinnah disclaimed all knowledge of pact.)
February	Governor of Bombay saw Jinnah about Desai proposals. Jinnah said they had been made without any authority from League.

February	League Ministry in Sind, led by Sir Ghulam Hussain Hidayatullah, defeated. Proposal to form coalition ministry upset by Jinnah.
12 March	Muslim League ministry in N.W.F.P. defeated. Dr. Khan Sahib, leader of Congress party, invited to form new government.
14 March	Sir Ghulam Hussain Hidayatullah formed new ministry in Sind.
23 March	Wavell went to London, accompanied by V.P. Menon and Sir Evan Jenkins, for discussions with Secretary of State and India committee.
28 March	Nazimuddin's ministry defeated in Bengal : Governor took over administration of province under section 93.
March	In Assam Sir Mohamed Saadullah formed coalition cabinet with Gopinath Bardolai, Congress leader.
3 May	British forces entered Rangoon.
7 May	Germany surrendered.
23 May	Caretaker government formed in London.
4 June	Wavell returned to Delhi.
14 June	Wavell broadcast his proposals to advance India towards full self-government, and announced Conference to be held at Simla. Amery announced in Commons that Viceroy had been empowered to make proposals on composition of interim government in India.
June	Viceroy sent invitations to all political leaders, and carried on correspondence with Gandhi, who issued various press statements.

15 June	Nehru and other Congress leaders released from prison.
24 June	Viceroy had separate interviews with Azad, Gandhi and Jinnah.
25 June-14 July	Simla Conference.
3-6 July	Congress Working Committee selected panel of names to submit to Viceroy.
6 July	League Working Committee met.
7 July	Jinnah wrote to viceroy.
8 July	Viceroy had prolonged discussions with Jinnah.
9 July	Viceroy sent Jinnah written reply.
11 July	Viceroy saw Jinnah. Conference failed. Viceroy saw Gandhi and told him that Conference had failed.
14 July	Fifth and Last Session of Conference. Wavell announced failure of Conference because League claimed right to nominate all Muslim members of executive council.
26 July	Labour government came into power in Britain, C.R. Attlee Prime Minister, Lord Pethick-Lawrence Secretary of State for India.
6 August	Jinnah demanded fresh elections.
10 August	Wavell convened meeting of Governors at which it was agreed that elections would be held as soon as possible.
14 August	Japanese surrendered.
21 August	Wavell summoned to London for discussions. Announced that general elections would be held in winter.
24 August	Wavell left for London, accompanied by V.P. Menon and Sir Evan Jenkins, for discussions with Secretary of state and India committee.

Late August	Azad approached Gandhi with plan for communal settlement.
16 September	Wavell returned to India.
19 September	Wavell made statement on elections and his plans for summoning constitution-making body.
21 September	A.I.C.C. meeting at Bombay passed resolution characterizing Wavell's proposal as 'vague and inadequate and unsatisfactory'.
24 November	I.N.A. trials began in Red Fort, Delhi.
4 December	Secretary of State in House of Lords announced that Parliamentary delegation would be visiting India.
7 December	Congress Working Committee meeting in Calcutta re-affirmed its faith in Non-violence.
Late December	Results of elections to Central Legislative Assembly announced.

1946

5 January	Parliamentary delegation, led by Professor Robert Richards, arrived in India.
11 January	Day celebrated by Muslim League as day of victory.
28 January	Viceroy addressed newly-elected central legislature.
January	Royal Air Force strike.
11-15 February	Riots in Calcutta.
18-23 February	Royal Indian Navy mutiny.
19 February	Secretary of State announced that Cabinet mission was to visit India.
16 March	Debate in House of Commons on Cabinet Mission's visit to India.
25 March	Cabinet Mission arrived in Delhi.
3-17 April	Cabinet Mission saw Indian leaders. Congress case put to Mission by Azad.

	Gandhi interviewed immediately afterwards (3 April).
	Mission interviewed Jinnah (4 April).
	Mission interviewed representatives of Sikhs, Scheduled Castes, Depressed Classes, Hindu Mahasabha and Liberals.
10 April	Jinnah called together in Delhi convention of over 400 members of various legislatures recently elected on Muslim League ticket. Resolution passed calling for independent Pakistan.
16 April	Mission saw Jinnah again.
17 April	Mission saw Azad again.
17-23 April	Mission went to Kashmir to rest.
24 April	Cabinet Mission scheme put before Jinnah and rejected. Rejected also by Congress leaders.
26 April	Cripps saw Azad who raised question of three-tier constitution. Cripps also saw Jinnah.
27 April	Letters sent by Secretary of State to Presidents of Congress and League inviting them each to send four negotiators to meet Mission.
5–12 May	Second Simla Conference between Cabinet Mission and Azad, Nehru, Patel, Abdul Ghaffar Khan and Jinnah, Muhammad Ismail Khan, Liaqat Ali Khan, Abdur Rab Nishtar. Conference failed.
16 May	Cabinet Mission put out statement in which it presented its own scheme.
	Broadcast by Secretary of State and statement by Cripps at Press Conference.
17 May	Broadcast by Cripps and Viceroy.
	Cabinet Mission held Press Conference on its plan.
22 May	Jinnah made statement on Cabinet Mission statement of 16 May.

24 May	Congress Working Committee adopted Resolution raising various points in regard to cabinet mission plan and putting its own interpretation on paragraph 15.
25 May	Cabinet mission and Viceroy issued statement saying that Congress interpretation of paragraph 15 was not in accordance with mission's intentions.
	Azad wrote to Viceroy asking for written confirmation that interim government would have same powers as a dominion cabinet. Viceroy denied ever having said that it would.
6 June	Council of Muslim League passed resolution accepting cabinet mission's scheme of 16 May.
10 June	Representative conference of Sikhs at Amritsar rejected cabinet mission's proposals and appointed committee of action under ex-I.N.A. officer to fight plan.
12 June	Viceroy saw Nehru. Meeting followed by meetings and correspondence over composition of interim government with Jinnah, etc. Deadlock continued.
16 June	Cabinet mission presented its own scheme for formation of interim government at centre.
18 June	Sikhs rejected interim proposals and refused to agree to any Sikh representative joining executive council.
19 June	Jinnah wrote to viceroy asking for clarification of points in statement of 16 June. Viceroy replied. Gist of correspondence communicated to Azad.
22 June	Viceroy wrote to Jinnah saying that he and cabinet mission could not accept Congress request for Muslim of their

	choice to be included in interim government.
25 June	Congress Working Committee meeting in Delhi passed resolution rejecting proposals for interim government but decided that Congress should join proposed constituent assembly.
	League Working Committee passed resolution agreeing to join interim government on basis of statement of 16 June.
	Azad in communicating Congress Resolution to Viceroy stated that Congress accepted proposals in 16 May statement but adhered to own interpretation.
	Cabinet mission saw Jinnah and informed him that scheme of 16 June had fallen through, but since Congress and League had both accepted 16 May statement it was proposed to set up coalition government.
26 June	Last meeting between cabinet mission and party leaders. Negotiations for interim government had failed.
29 June	Cabinet mission left India.
6 July	A.I.C.C. meeting in Bombay ratified resolution of Working Committee accepting cabinet mission plan. Nehru took over Congress Presidentship from Azad.
	Nehru made statement in which he said 'We are not bound by a single thing except that we have decided for the moment to go to the Constituent Assembly.' Jinnah characterized Nehru's statement as 'a complete repudiation of the basic form upon which the long-term scheme rests...'.

18 July	Pethick-Lawrence in Lords and Cripps in Commons reaffirmed cabinet mission plan denying Congress interpretation.
22 July	Viceroy wrote to Presidents of Congress and League putting forth proposals for interim coalition government.
23 July	Nehru replied that he was unable to co-operate in formation of government on lines suggested by Viceroy.
27 July	At meeting of council of Muslim League in Bombay Jinnah accused cabinet mission of bad faith and condemned Congress. League had no alternative but to adhere once more to national goal of Pakistan.
29 July	Council of League passed Resolution retracting its acceptance of cabinet mission plan, and another calling for 'direct action'. Working Committee called upon Muslims throughout India to observe 16 August as 'Direct Action Day'.
	Viceroy saw Nehru after League Resolution and asked him to give assurance to League. Nehru replied that he did not see what assurances he could give.
By end July	Elections completed for the 296 seats assigned in the constituent assembly to British-Indian provinces. Congress won all general seats except 9, and League won all Muslim seats except 5.
31 July	Jinnah replied to Viceroy's letter of 22 July that his Working Committee could not accept Viceroy's proposals.
6 August	Viceroy wrote to Nehru inviting him to make proposals for formation of interim government.

8 August	Viceroy replied to Jinnah's letter of 31 July saying that he had decided to invite Congress to form interim government.
	Congress Working Committee met at Wardha and decided to accept invitation to form interim government. Passed resolution making it clear that Congress accepted the 16 May statement in its entirety, but interpreted it so as to resolve inconsistencies contained in it. Congress hoped that League would join constituent assembly.
12 August	Viceroy issued communique announcing his invitation to President of Congress to form provisional government.
13 August	Nehru wrote to Jinnah suggesting personal discussion.
14 August	Sikh panthic board accepted statement of 16 May.
15 August	Jinnah replied to Nehru, followed by more correspondence and meeting. Nehru offered Jinnah 5 seats in interim government of 14. Deadlock.
16 August	'Direct Action Day' : public holiday in Bengal and Sind.
16-18 August	Great Calcutta killing.
17 August	Nehru explained to Viceroy that he would include in government six Congress nominees and three minority representatives and fill five Muslim seats with non-League Muslims — Viceroy averse to this.
18 August	Nehru met Viceroy on question of further approach to Jinnah.
19 August	Nehru wrote to Viceroy confirming his view on composition of government.
	Jinnah issued statement to press.

19-22 August	Discussions between Viceroy, Azad and Nehru.
22 August	Nehru wrote to Viceroy on question of coalition with League. Against 'appeasement' of League.
24 August	Press communique issued stating that King had accepted resignations of Governor-General's executive council and that Nehru, Patel, Prasad, Asaf Ali, Rajagopalachari, Sarat Chandra Bose, Matthai, Baldev Singh, Shafaat Ahmed Khan, Jagjivan Ram, Syed Ali Zaheer, and C.H. Bhabha, had been nominated in their place.
	Viceroy broadcast on formation of interim government.
	Jinnah after Viceroy's broadcast reiterated demand for division of India.
24/25 August	Wavell flew to Calcutta. Met Khwaja Nazimuddin.
27 August	Wavell met Gandhi and Nehru on his return from Calcutta. Advocated setting up of coalition governments both in Bengal and at the centre. Asked Congress to accept formula on grouping accepting mission's meaning. Could not summon constituent assembly until this was settled.
	Gandhi wrote to Viceroy. Viceroy wrote to Nehru asking him to place his formula before Congress Working Committee.
28 August	Nehru replied to Viceroy that Working Committee was surprised at sudden change in his approach. Congress position with regard to grouping clear. Unable to accept Viceroy's proposal.
2 September	Interim government took office without League.

7 September	Nehru broadcast on constituent assembly.
8 September	Jinnah gave interview to *Daily Mail* stating that Nehru had made no definite proposals to him.
10 September	Viceroy had discussions with Nehru and Rajagopalachari.
16 September	Viceroy saw Jinnah but no agreement reached.
25 September	Viceroy saw Jinnah : interim government discussed.
26 September	Viceroy saw Nehru and Gandhi.
2 October	Viceroy informed Jinnah that he had failed to secure any concession from Congress over nationalist Muslim issue. Asked League to come into government. Jinnah agreed to summon working committee. Jinnah then sent Viceroy note setting out nine points for elucidation.
4 October	Viceroy consulted Nehru on Jinnah's points and then replied to Jinnah.
	Nehru wrote to Viceroy stating that cabinet must be able to function together.
10-20 October	Communal disturbances in Noakhali.
12 October	Viceroy wrote to Jinnah.
13 October	Jinnah wrote to Wavell that League had decided to join interim government. He and Liaqat had interview with Viceroy.
14 October	Viceroy informed Nehru of his meeting with League leaders.
	Jinnah submitted five names for interim government.
15 October	Press communique issued on decision of League to join interim government.
23 October	Gandhi in statement on grouping clause said that no law-giver could give an authoritative interpretation of his own

	law. A duly constituted court of law must decide it.
25 October	Interim government reconstituted.
26 October	Muslim League members of interim government took office.
29 October	Gandhi arrived in Calcutta from Delhi.
30 October-7 November	Bihar outbreak. Viceroy, Nehru and Rajendra Prasad all visited the province.
6 November	Gandhi left Calcutta for Noakhali. Remained there until 2 March.
6-15 November	Communal outbreak at Garhmukteswar.
17 November	Jinnah wrote to Viceroy arguing that Congress had not accepted statement of 16 May and therefore it would be futile for him to summon his council. Urged Viceroy to postpone meeting of constituent assembly.
18/19 November	Viceroy saw Jinnah and Nehru about constituent assembly.
20 November	Viceroy issued invitations for meeting of constituent assembly. Jinnah called on League representatives not to participate.
24 November	Annual Session of Congress at Meerut demanded that League should either accept cabinet mission plan and come into constituent assembly or quit interim government.
26 November	Viceroy saw Nehru, Liaqat and Baldev Singh and invited them to London for discussions. Nehru refused invitation. Attlee sent personal invitation to Nehru, who then accepted. Attlee also sent personal invitation to Jinnah.
2 December	Wavell, Nehru, Baldev Singh, Jinnah and Liaqat arrived in London.
3-6 December	London Conference. No agreement reached.

6 December	Government put out statement clarifying cabinet mission plan.
7 December	Nehru and Baldev Singh returned to India. Jinnah and Liaqat stayed in England.
9 December	Constituent assembly met without League members, and adjourned until 20 January.
18 December	Attlee made his first approach to Mountbatten to succeed Wavell.
22 December	Congress Working Committee issued statement clarifying its attitude towards H.M.G.'s statement of 6 December.
Late December	V.P. Menon had lengthy discussion with Vallabhbhai Patel suggesting that power should be transferred to two Central Governments on basis of dominion status. Patel agreed and Menon sent outline of his plan to Secretary of State, but no action was taken.

1947

January	Jinnah returned to India : ill, took no part in affairs until early March.
5 January	A.I.C.C. met in Delhi and endorsed statement of Working Committee of 22 December : resolution passed 7 January.
20 January	Constituent Assembly met.
25 January	Liaqat Ali Khan issued statement putting various questions to Congress.
29 January	League Working Committee met in Karachi : called upon government to declare that plan of 16 May had failed, and demanded that constituent assembly should be dissolved.
1 February	Nehru had interview with Viceroy.
5 February	Viceroy received demand from Congress and minority members for resignation

	of League representatives from interim government.
6 February	Viceroy saw Liaqat.
7 February	Liaqat wrote to Viceroy about Congress demand for resignation of League members : stated that Congress had not accepted 16 May statement.
13 February	Nehru wrote to Viceroy and again demanded resignation of League members from interim government.
15 February	Vallabhbhai Patel stated that Congress would withdraw from interim government if League members remained.
20 February	Prime Minister made statement to Parliament announcing British intention of leaving India by June 1948. Mountbatten to succeed Wavell as Viceroy.
21 February	Wavell urged Nehru to get League into constituent assembly. He also saw Liaqat.
March	Food shortage; industrial unrest; strikes; communal rioting in Punjab.
March	League organized demonstrations against Congress Ministry in N.W.F.P. Large scale arrest of Leaguers.
2 March	Khizr Hyat Khan resigned as premier of Punjab. Khan of Mamdot (League) failed to form ministry.
	Gandhi left Noakhali for Bihar.
5 March	Sir Evan Jenkins, Governor of Punjab, took over administration of province under Section 93.
	Congress Working Committee met to consider statement of 20 February : invited League to discuss transfer of power : called for partition of Punjab and Bengal.

9 March	Nehru wrote to Wavell enclosing copies of Resolutions of Working Committee.
15 March	Liaqat's budget proposals called for a twenty-five per cent tax on business profits of more than Rs. 100,000.
22 March	Lord Mountbatten arrived in Delhi. Wrote to Gandhi and Jinnah inviting them to Delhi for discussions.
23 March	Wavell left Delhi.
24 March	Mountbatten sworn in as Viceroy.
	Mountbatten had interviews with members of interim government, especially Nehru and Liaqat over budget proposals — percentage of tax reduced.
25 March	Mountbatten saw Patel.
30 March	Gandhi left Bihar for Delhi.
31 March	Mountbatten saw Gandhi.
1 April	Gandhi in second interview with Mountbatten suggested that Viceroy should dismiss existing cabinet and invite Jinnah to form new one.
2 April	Mountbatten saw Gandhi again.
	Lord Pethick-Lawrence resigned as Secretary of State for India and was succeeded by Lord Listowel.
5 April	Mountbatten met Jinnah for first time.
8 April	Viceroy received letter from Liaqat asking for armed forces to be reorganized so that they could be more readily split between Pakistan and Hindustan. Mountbatten said there could be no splitting of Indian army before withdrawal of British.
April	Communal disturbances in Punjab and adjoining provinces, including Delhi. Agitation against Congress Ministry in N.W.F.P. Congress government in N.W.F.P. decided to release political

	prisoners, but they refused to accept their freedom unless ministry resigned.
8 April	Mountbatten raised with Jinnah question of appeal by both major parties for truce in communal disturbances.
9 April	British Residents in Indian states conferred in Delhi.
12 April	Gandhi wrote to Viceroy that his plan to hand over to Jinnah was not acceptable to Congress and that he was handing over all future negotiation to Working Committee.
14 April	Gandhi returned to Bihar.
15 April	Joint statement signed by Gandhi and Jinnah issued deploring violence and denouncing use of force for achievement of political ends.
15-16 April	Viceroy's plan put before Governors' Conference in New Delhi.
18 April	Mountbatten interviewed Sikh leaders who insisted that Punjab must be partitioned.
20 April	Nehru said Muslim League could have Pakistan on condition that they did not take away other parts of India which did not wish to join Pakistan.
24 April	Jinnah put out an appeal to reason in N.W.F.P.
28 April	Rajendra Prasad, President of constituent assembly, accepted principle of partition. Gandhi returned to Delhi.
28–30 April	Mountbatten visited the N.W.F.P.
2 May	Ismay and Abell flew to London with first draft of the Mountbatten plan (revised version of plan discussed with Governors in April).

4 May	Gandhi and Jinnah met while visiting Viceroy, their first meeting for three years.
6 May	Gandhi had three-hour meeting with Jinnah at Jinnah's house.
7 May	Mountbatten with V.P. Menon and Mièville, arrived in Simla.
	V.P. Menon asked to prepare paper on demission of power under present constitution.
8 May	Gandhi left Delhi for Calcutta.
	Nehru, with Krishna Menon, arrived in Simla : guests of Viceroy at Viceregal Lodge.
9 May	Vallabhbhai Patel made statement suggesting that power be transferred to Indian government on basis of dominion status.
10 May	Viceroy called conference attended by Nehru, Mièville and V.P. Menon to discuss Menon's plan.
	Mountbatten received from London plan taken by Ismay, as approved by British cabinet.
	It was announced that Viceroy would meet Jinnah, Liaqat, Nehru, Patel and Baldev Singh in Delhi on 17 May to present to them plan for transfer of power.
	Mountbatten showed plan to Nehru who rejected it.
11 May	Meeting with leaders postponed until 2 June.
	V.P. Menon prepared draft of his own plan.
14 May	Mountbatten returned to Delhi.
	Gandhi left Calcutta for Patna.
15 May	Mountbatten summoned to London for consultations.

15 May	Mountbatten saw Patel and Liaqat.
16 May	V.P. Menon drew up draft of eight 'Heads of Agreement' which was approved by Viceroy and shown to all leaders.
	Viceroy had consultations with leaders. New plan finalized. Nehru accepted it in writing; Jinnah verbally.
18 May	Mountbatten left Delhi for London, taking V.P. Menon and Erskine-Crum with him.
19 May	Mountbatten arrived in London.
19–30 May	Discussions between Mountbatten, Attlee, India and Burma committee, and opposition leaders. Nehru and Jinnah kept informed of progress of discussions.
22 May	Jinnah demanded an 800-mile corridor to link East and West Pakistan.
24 May	Gandhi left Bihar for Delhi.
25 May onwards	Gandhi at prayer meetings spoke in favour of a united India.
31 May	Mountbatten returned to India with final plan approved by British cabinet.
2 June	Meeting between Viceroy and Indian leaders. Viceroy saw Gandhi after main meeting.
	Congress Working Committee met and decided to accept plan : Kripalani wrote to Viceroy.
	Baldev Singh accepted plan on behalf of Sikhs.
2 June (midnight)	Viceroy saw Jinnah who gave verbal assurance about his acceptance of plan.
3 June	Second meeting between Mountbatten and Indian leaders, who agreed to plan. They were presented with paper on administrative consequences of partition.

	Members of states negotiating committee were told of plan.
	Plan announced over all-India radio by Viceroy : followed by Nehru, Jinnah and Baldev Singh. Plan also announced in House of Commons.
4 June	Mountbatten held Press Conference, at which he gave first formal indication that transfer of power would take place on 15 August, 1947 and not June 1948.
	Viceroy saw Gandhi just before his prayer meeting.
	Bhopal resigned as Chancellor of Chamber of Princes.
5 June	Mountbatten held third meeting with Indian leaders to discuss administrative consequences of partition.
After 3 June	Muslim League mass movements in Assam and N.W.F.P. abandoned.
8 June	At a meeting of interim government formula found for submitting policy decisions and high grade appointments direct to Viceroy to avoid dissension.
10 June	Plan ratified by council of Muslim League.
11 June	Joint Conference of Sikh organizations in Lahore welcomed division of Punjab.
13 June	Partition committee of interim government formed, with steering committee of two senior civil servants to co-ordinate work of expert committees charged with specific facets of partition.
14 June	A.I.C.C. meeting in Delhi ratified plan.
19-23 June	Mountbatten visited Kashmir.
20 June	Bengal Legislative Assembly opted for partition.
23 June	Mountbatten asked Jinnah for his decision on Governor-General question.

23 June	Punjab legislative assembly opted for partition.
26 June	Sind legislative assembly opted for Pakistan.
27 June	Partition Committee gave way to partition council of wider authority. Council decided that Sir Cyril Radcliffe should be invited to serve as Chairman of Punjab and Bengal Boundary Commissions.
30 June	Partition council agreed to procedure for division of armed forces. Auchinleck to remain as Supreme Commander after 15 August under joint defence council. Arbitral tribunal set up, Sir Patrick Spens President.
June	Baluchistan opted for Pakistan.
June	Violence in Punjab.
2 July	Mountbatten showed draft Indian Independence Bill to Indian leaders, and to Gandhi, for comment.
	Jinnah told Mountbatten that he himself wished to be Governor-General of Pakistan.
4 July	Indian Independence Bill introduced into House of Commons.
5 July	Liaqat asked Mountbatten to recommend Jinnah's name as Governor-General of Pakistan. He hoped that Mountbatten would remain as Governor-General of India.
	New states department inaugurated by Vallabhbhai Patel.
	Ismay and Campbell-Johnson left Delhi for London.
6-7 July	Referendum held in Sylhet, which decided to join East Bengal.
6-17 July	Referendum held in N.W.F.P. which decided to join Pakistan.

7 July	Ismay arrived in London and saw Attlee.
8 July	Attlee consulted opposition leaders over question of Mountbatten remaining as Governor-General of India. All agreed.
10 July	Debate on second reading of Indian Independence Bill in Commons-Small attendance.
By mid-July	All disputed areas had chosen and fresh elections were then held there for election of representatives to respective constituent assemblies.
14 July	Constituent Assembly began its Fourth Session attended by League members from non-Pakistan provinces.
16 July	Indian Independence Bill passed its third reading.
16–24 July	Bengal Boundary Commission in Session.
18 July	Indian Independence Act received royal assent.
19 July	Mountbatten announced establishment of two separate provisional governments, one for India and one for Pakistan.
21 July	Union Constitution Committee presented to Constituent Assembly draft constitution.
21-31 July	Punjab Boundary Commission in Session.
22 July	Ismay and Campbell-Johnson arrived in Delhi from London.
	Members of partition council announced a Punjab boundary force to be set up. Both governments pledged themselves to accept awards of Boundary Commission, and guaranteed protection of minorities.
25 July	Mountbatten addressed Chamber of Princes.

30 July	Mountbatten visited Calcutta.
End July	Gandhi paid brief visit to Kashmir and N.W.F.P.
1 August	Punjab boundary force set up.
4-6 August	Bengal Boundary Commission in Session to consider Sylhet.
5 August	Viceroy told Patel, Jinnah and Liaqat of information implicating Sikh leaders in sabotage plans.
6 August	Partition Council met for last time.
7 August	Jinnah flew to Karachi.
9 August	Gandhi arrived in Calcutta.
11 August	Constituent Assembly of Pakistan met and elected Jinnah President.
12 August	Bengal and Punjab awards complete. Sylhet award not yet ready.
13 August	Radcliffe award ready.
	Mountbatten flew to Karachi.
14 August	Mountbatten addressed Pakistan Constituent Assembly and then flew back to Delhi.
15 August	India and Pakistan became independent. Jinnah sworn in as Governor-General of Pakistan and Mountbatten as Governor-General of India. Pakistan cabinet headed by Liaqat; Indian cabinet by Nehru.
16 August	Mountbatten handed the Radcliffe Award to the leaders of both dominions in Delhi.
17 August	Radcliffe Award published.

INDEX

M

N

O

P

Q

R

S